THE IRONY OF STATE INTERVENTION

LARRY G. GERBER

THE IRONY OF
STATE
Intervention

American Industrial Relations Policy
in Comparative Perspective,
1914–1939

NORTHERN ILLINOIS UNIVERSITY PRESS / DEKALB

Library of Congress Cataloging-in-Publication Data

Gerber, Larry G., 1947–

  The irony of state intervention : American industrial relations policy in comparative perspective, 1914–1939 / Larry G. Gerber.

    p.   cm.

Includes bibliographical references and index.

ISBN-13: 978-0-87580-347-0 (clothbound : alk. paper)

ISBN-10: 0-87580-347-4 (clothbound : alk. paper)

1. Industrial relations—Government policy—United States. 2. Industrial relations—Government policy—Great Britain. I. Title.

HD8072.G43 2005

331'.097309041—dc22

2005009460

Contents

Acknowledgments

I have received various forms of support over the years that helped make completing this book possible. I would like to thank the National Endowment for the Humanities for a summer fellowship that helped me at a very early stage of my work, as well as Auburn University's College of Liberal Arts and Vice President for Research for providing financial assistance for research and writing.

Chapter 1 was published in an earlier form in the *Journal of American Studies,* volume 32 (1997) as "Shifting Perspectives on American Exceptionalism: Recent Literature on American Labor Relations and Labor Politics." I would like to thank Cambridge University Press for granting permission to publish this article in revised form. An earlier version of Chapter 4 appeared in the *Journal of Policy Studies,* volume 6 (1994) as "The National Industrial Act in Comparative Perspective: Organized Labor's Role in American and British Efforts at Industrial Planning." I would like to thank Pennsylvania State University Press for granting permission to publish this article in revised form.

This book has been much too long in the writing. Some of the people I wish to thank for reading early versions of some parts of the manuscript may even have forgotten they had done so or given up hope that I would ever finish this project. Long ago, Stephen Waring, Joe McCartin, and Howell Harris provided helpful comments and encouragement about my venture into comparative history. More recently, Auburn University colleagues Bill Trimble and Michael Melancon read a virtually complete draft of the manuscript and urged me to persist in completing the book. I would also like to acknowledge the help and encouragement I have received from Ellis Hawley, whose own work I have benefited from so much, and who has been so generous in his support. At Northern Illinois University Press, Martin Johnson initially offered useful suggestions for improving the manuscript, and Melody Herr has been very helpful in shepherding the book to completion.

Finally, I wish to give special thanks to my wife, Louise Katainen, who continually and lovingly urged me to see this project through to the end and did all she could to provide the support that would make it possible for me to do so.

THE IRONY OF STATE INTERVENTION

Introduction

No nation is more identified with the philosophy and practice of limited government than the United States. America not only proved a hospitable environment for the laissez-faire ideas of Adam Smith, but it also was slow to develop a powerful centralized state bureaucracy. Consequently, the United States is widely seen as having lagged behind other Western industrial democracies in establishing the state capacity necessary for the effective implementation of coherently formulated public policies. The failure to create a comprehensive social welfare system is the most frequently cited manifestation of the American state's alleged underdevelopment.[1]

In the field of industrial relations, however, the American state has long played an active and critically important role. Beginning in the late nineteenth and early twentieth centuries and culminating with the passage of the National Labor Relations Act (NLRA) in 1935, it played a highly intrusive role in the conduct of labor-management relations. The nature and degree of that state intervention would have been inconceivable during the same period in Britain, the one other major industrial democracy generally viewed as having a "weak state."[2] Throughout these years, most labor leaders, businessmen, and politicians in both countries normally expressed a preference, at least in theory, for minimizing the state's role in labor-management relations. Although neither state adopted a fully hands-off policy in practice, the British state helped to create a generally favorable environment for unions via indirect and nonintrusive means in what Otto Kahn-Freund described as a "collective laissez-faire" approach to industrial relations.[3] In contrast, the United States in the 1930s adopted legislation that gave the federal government extensive powers to ban certain "unfair labor practices" by management, to determine collective bargaining units, and to conduct union certification elections.

That same legislation would later serve as the basis for federal regulation of most aspects of unions' internal affairs.

Why, in spite of the strength of antistatism in the United States, did government involvement in labor relations become so intrusive? Why did the intervention made possible by New Deal labor legislation take the particular form it did? A comparison of developments in industrial relations policies in the United States with those in Britain from the Great War through the Great Depression shows how and why America's path diverged from Britain's, as well as why alternative and seriously considered paths were ultimately rejected in both countries.

The choice of Britain as a point of comparison is especially appropriate, not only because the United States and Britain shared a common heritage of antistatism, but also because in the nineteenth and early twentieth centuries Britain served as the source for many of America's legal and trade-union traditions. Americans most often looked to Britain as an instructive model, even if they drew differing lessons from the British experience. Britain's approach to industrial relations thus influenced people as diverse as Charles Schwab, the antiunion employer who headed United States Steel, and pro-union industrial relations expert John Commons, though they disagreed whether to emulate or to avoid British precedents. Even those Americans who admired British trade unionism often differed as to which aspects of that tradition provided the most useful guides to American workers. Many who respected British craft unionism at the same time doubted the wisdom of following its example of supporting an independent labor party. Yet whenever Americans considered their own nation's experience in a comparative framework, they were likely to think of Britain as the most appropriate point of reference.[4]

Comparison with Britain, where antistatism was also a powerful force, demonstrates that a uniquely American ideological or cultural context was not the primary factor shaping the development of the American system of industrial relations. Rather, the crucial factor was the structure of the American economy, which favored the early development of large-scale, bureaucratically organized corporations devoting significant resources to managerial hierarchies committed to wresting away control of the production process from shop-floor workers. In contrast to the smaller, less bureaucratically developed enterprises that dominated the British economy well into the twentieth century, and which had economic reasons for working with trade unions, larger-scale American corporations exhibited a degree of employer opposition to unionization that both stunted the development of the American labor movement and contributed to the interventionist role played by the state.

Employer hostility rooted in the particular structure of American business not only resulted in frequent antiunion state interventions before 1933 but also helps to explain the specific form of pro-labor state involvement in industrial relations that became an important part of the New Deal. New

Deal labor policy was not the product of a corporate conspiracy to co-opt the labor movement, but the history of employers' insistence on their "right to manage" and opposition to unions created a context for labor law reform that profoundly influenced the industrial relations regime that emerged after the New Deal. In turning to state power in an effort to counter the union avoidance tactics of American employers, reformers under the leadership of Senator Robert Wagner succeeded in creating a law that at least temporarily gave an impetus to increased unionization.

New Deal labor policy, however, did not transcend the historical and institutional context in which it developed. The weakness of organized labor at the beginning of the twenty-first century suggests that in spite of the intentions of its authors, New Deal labor legislation failed to establish a lasting basis for either a truly democratic form of industrial pluralism or a liberal version of corporatism. The problems facing the labor movement today stem not so much from continuing state involvement in industrial relations, but rather from the failure of that state involvement to overcome American employers' structurally rooted hostility to unionism.

During the two decades following World War II, when the developing cold war fostered a celebratory view of American exceptionalism, most contemporary industrial relations experts acclaimed the apparent triumph of what came to be known as "industrial pluralism."[5] This conception of labor-management relations was consistent with the broader pluralist interpretation of American society and politics that then dominated American social science. According to the pluralist model, the individual competition characteristic of America's nineteenth-century political economy had evolved into a form of group competition. Although the state played a more active role as a broker between interest groups, market forces, rather than state direction or control, continued to determine the final distribution of power and wealth. Postwar American pluralists tended to celebrate the political system they described, arguing that America's unique combination of sociopolitical stability and individual freedom resulted from the fact that American pluralism engendered cross-cutting loyalties to a variety of interest groups, rather than the single-minded sense of class consciousness that proved so divisive in other industrialized nations.[6] Industrial relations experts often wrote as if the emergence of a collective bargaining regime in which conservative, "job-conscious" unions negotiated agreements with socially responsible employers was the logical and virtually inevitable product of American conditions.

While praising the rise of industrial pluralism, students of American labor relations in the postwar era tended either to ignore or to downplay the possibility that other approaches to labor-management relations had ever represented real alternatives to the system that emerged after 1935. They also tended to ignore or to downplay the important role played by the state in what was widely heralded as a voluntaristic system. Scholars and other observers recognized that passage of the NLRA had been an important milestone because of the law's explicit statement that "encouraging the practice and procedure of collective bargaining" was henceforth "the policy of the United States."[7] Yet they usually failed to emphasize how far the NLRA actually departed from British-style "collective laissez-faire" by making the state the final arbiter in determining whether and how workers might be organized into unions. The British state did not completely abstain from encouraging collective bargaining, but the degree and breadth of intervention represented by the NLRA differed dramatically from any policy initiative that was seriously contemplated in Britain until decades later.

Although state involvement has persisted as a crucial factor in American labor relations into the twenty-first century, the NLRA's stated policy of encouraging unionization now seems like a dead letter. The collective bargaining model that appeared dominant in American industry in the post–World War II period no longer does so today. Even at its peak in the 1950s, unionization in the United States involved only about one-third of the American labor force and was less prevalent than in Britain or in most other Western European countries. From the perspective of the early twenty-first century, collective bargaining was at best rather short-lived as America's prevailing system of industrial relations; as early as the 1960s it was already on the decline in American industry. By the 1980s organized labor had come under severe attack, with the percentage of the labor force enrolled in unions declining so precipitously that observers were proclaiming the onset of the "post-union era."[8] The liberal pluralist model of labor relations that emerged in the wake of the passage of the NLRA in 1935 was thus neither inevitable nor very long-lasting in American history. Alternative institutional and ideological approaches to labor relations existed and even flourished in the United States both before and after 1935.

Comparing American developments to those taking place in Britain contributes to an understanding of the particular form of state intervention adopted in the United States in the 1930s. It is also necessary to examine the alternatives that received serious attention in the decades leading up to the passage of the NLRA. Throughout the first third of the twentieth century, some voices representing a management perspective continued to favor the preservation of the nineteenth-century system in which individual workers enjoyed the "liberty" to contract with individual employers over the terms of their labor with no direct state intervention. Well before the 1930s, however, most Americans involved in the conduct of industrial relations had come to accept the premise that some form of collective organization for workers was necessary in modern industrial society. What form that collective organization should take and what role the state should play in shaping the relationship between labor and management became controversial issues in the early decades of the twentieth century.

Recognizing that a purely individualistic approach to labor relations was increasingly anachronistic, many Americans nonetheless continued to favor collectivist models severely minimizing the role of the state. One such non-statist approach that had substantial appeal in the United States was the collective laissez-faire model that by the early twentieth century came to dominate Britain's approach to industrial relations. This model recognized the legitimacy of independent trade unions as the most appropriate and effective representatives of the interests of workers and gave unions certain legal immunities but stipulated that, in contrast to the regime ultimately established by the NLRA, the state refrain from becoming involved either in the internal affairs of unions or in any aspect of the collective bargaining process. Another nonstatist approach that appealed primarily to members of the business community was the establishment of company unions. Company unionism would prove far more significant in the United States than in Britain, where such organizations were rare. In the early 1930s, American employers' increasing reliance on management-initiated nonunion employee representation schemes would be a critical factor shaping New Deal labor legislation.

The particular form of state involvement in industrial relations embodied in the NLRA was not the only approach to state intervention that gained serious attention in the United States in these years. In both America and Britain, many influential economic actors were attracted to variants of what can be described as a "liberal corporatist" approach to restructuring the political economy. Such an approach seemed to hold out hope of replacing the uncertainties and instabilities of a competitive market-based system with order. Not only were corporatist proposals for a more active government role in the political economy widely discussed, but in certain instances some were implemented, at least partially. Very few participants in the formulation of industrial relations policy in this period actually used the term *corporatist* to describe their notions of state intervention in labor-management relations, especially after the term became tarnished by association with Benito Mussolini's increasingly repressive version of a fascist "Corporate State."[9] Yet, in a number of important respects, many of the proposals put forward on both sides of the Atlantic between 1914 and 1939 presaged the liberal forms of corporatism that emerged in Western Europe after 1945. These proposals and experiments are an important part of the story that follows. Understanding the continuing attraction of these ideas, as well as the reasons both America and Britain failed to develop into corporatist societies, sheds light on the paths each nation did actually follow.

Though generally not a term applied to liberal democracies before 1945, *corporatism* became a useful concept for describing the political economies that blossomed in much of postwar Europe. There is no agreement on a single definition, and corporatism comes in many varieties: authoritarian, liberal, societal, state, and bargained, to name a few. A key element in all definitions of corporatism, however, is the use by the state of private-sector functionally organized associations to formulate and/or implement economic policies that are not determined strictly by market forces. In contrast to a pluralist system, in which the state is largely a referee between organized workers and employers who still must compete in the marketplace, in a corporatist political economy organized interests cooperate with the state to produce outcomes consciously designed to serve the public interest.[10]

In the most extreme form of corporatism, what Colin Crouch labels "authoritarian corporatism," the functional organizations of workers and business interests integral to the system are literally creatures of the state.[11] Initiated by the state, they have no legitimacy of their own and play no independent role in policy making. Rather, as was the case under fascism, they exist to carry out the wishes of the state and to enforce discipline on their members. This form of corporatism never had any significant appeal in either the United States or Britain.

On the other hand, from the Great War through the Great Depression many Americans and Britons came to view more liberal forms of corporatism as attractive and viable possibilities for dealing with the economic problems confronting their nations. In the form now commonly referred to as "liberal corporatism," the functional associations that exercise a degree of governing authority arise from the autonomous activity of their members and only subsequently gain official recognition from the state. Because they are not simply creatures of the state, such organizations are able to exert influence over the formulation of policy, as well as to enforce policy on their members. Thus, for example, trade unions organized originally by workers themselves might in a liberal corporatist system come to play an officially sanctioned role in the formulation of a national incomes policy, but also be responsible for restraining rank-and-file pressures for wage levels exceeding those agreed upon in collaboration with state authorities. Similarly, employer organizations whose existence predated any formal relationship with the state might, in a liberal corporatist political economy, work with state officials to set price levels and then help to ensure the conformity of individual members.

Historian Ellis Hawley has been highly influential in arguing that a "corporatism of the liberal center" based on a belief in promoting economic planning and coordination through government assistance to and promotion of "non-competitive, role-ordered occupational or functional groupings" was a central feature of American economic development in the first half of the twentieth century. According to Hawley, at various times the state utilized a corporatist approach to try to foster economic prosperity and social peace by encouraging the development of "concerts of interests" within industries and between organizations representing business and labor as an alternative to both classical "laissez-faire liberalism" and the unilateral interventionism entailed in "welfare statism."[12]

This form of corporatism is not fully consistent with the model of corporatism that developed in post–World War II Europe, because it is not predicated on the government's use of its coercive powers to enforce decisions made collaboratively by organized interests in the private sector. Most non-

American social scientists writing in the 1970s and 1980s thus argued that corporatism, as they define the term, has been virtually nonexistent in the United States (and only slightly more significant in Britain).[13] Although the state plays an active role in encouraging cooperation among private-sector organizations, voluntary consent, not state compulsion, is the essence of the model described by Hawley. What he and other historians have also called "associationalism," however, exists on a collectivist continuum that stretches from a competitive model of pluralism to an authoritarian version of corporatism.[14] The form of political economy Hawley describes can thus be labeled "voluntary corporatism" to highlight the limited role envisioned for the state, as well as its reliance on collaboration among organized groups, rather than on the free play of market forces.

Presumably, liberal corporatism requires a system of "tripartism," a three-way collaboration between the state, unions, and employers. It is important to recognize that not all advocates of corporatism in the quarter century before World War II necessarily envisioned an equal role for all three players in the political economy. In fact, it was not uncommon in the interwar years for spokespersons from the American business community to call for a direct relationship between business and the state, leaving out organized labor. I use the term "conservative corporatism" to describe this vision of a bipartite partnership between organized business and the state. Of course, it was also possible for those favoring the interests of workers to call for a bipartite partnership between organized labor and the state that would have excluded employers, but this conception of "radical corporatism" had very little support in the United States; and it was hardly more significant in Britain.

In focusing on the role of the state in a comparative examination of the development of industrial relations in the United States and Britain, I borrow an analytical tool from political scientist Alan Cawson. In his work on corporatism, Cawson designates three different levels of economic policy making (including policies relating to industrial relations): the macro, the meso, and the micro.[15] The "macro-level" refers to policies affecting the political economy as a whole, such as monetary policy, fiscal policy, or incomes policy. In a corporatist system, state-labor-management interactions at the macro-level of the political economy typically involve the national government working with the "peak" organizations of employers and workers, that is, those organizations, such as the American Federation of Labor, the British Trades Union Congress, the United States Chamber of Commerce, or the Federation of British Industries, that bring together many different groups representing workers or employers. Most of the literature on corporatism in post-1945 Europe focuses on the macro-level of the political economy. The most often cited example of corporatist arrangements involves the establishment of a national incomes policy through negotiations between a central government and peak associations representing all workers' and all employers' organizations.

Cawson points out that important initiatives affecting industrial relations or the economy more broadly also take place at levels that do not encompass the entire nation. He refers to policies or practices involving a particular sector of the economy or a particular geographic region as operating
at the "meso-level" of the political economy. For instance, an arrangement
affecting the entire coal industry and involving collaboration between the
government, the coal mine operators' trade association, and the national
officers of the miners' union could be described as a form of "meso-level
corporatism." As will be demonstrated in the following pages, in both the
United States and Britain in the interwar period, proposals for meso-level
initiatives were more common than efforts to establish corporatist institutions at the macro-level.

Cawson also makes reference to the "micro-level" of the political economy. Initiatives or policies at this level affect an individual firm. He cites as
a fairly recent example of "micro-corporatism" in the American context the
federal government's bailout of Chrysler.[16] One of the crucial distinctions
between American and British systems of industrial relations in the first
third of the twentieth century is that the micro-level of industrial relations
was consistently more significant in the United States than in Britain.
Because the large-scale, bureaucratically organized business firm came to
dominate the American economy at a time when the typical British firm remained much smaller and without the management hierarchy characteristic of giant American corporations, British employers were much more
likely than their American counterparts to engage in multiemployer collective bargaining with unions. American employers preferred dealing with
their own workers directly, whether they were unionized or not, and were
more active than British employers in developing internal labor markets.
Consequently, while meso-level industrial relations were of greater importance in Britain, American employers and workers tended to focus on the
micro-level of the economy.

Distinguishing between the macro-, meso-, and micro-levels of industrial
relations is a key feature of the narrative presented here. New practices or
new ideas usually originated and developed at one level of organization before being generalized or particularized to a more or less inclusive level of
organization. At given moments in history, the pluralist or corporatist ideals
of competition or cooperation exerted more influence at one level of organization than at another. Representatives of labor, capital, or the state often
found it in their self-interest to appeal to corporatist values at one level of
organization, while rejecting them at another. Thus, a three-tiered analysis
of the evolution of industrial relations can yield insights that an undifferen-
tiated analytical framework might tend to obscure.

Much of this study examines the public policy debates in the United
States and Britain. Though I point out ideological similarities in American
and British thinking, I focus on the sharp differences in the actual form of
state action that developed in each nation in the first half of the twentieth

century. I stress how the two nations' differing economic structures ultimately produced different approaches to industrial relations. The strength of antistatism emerged as one of the key factors limiting the institutionalization of corporatism, especially at the macro-level of the political economy, in both the United States and Britain, but such antistatism did not prevent the United States from adopting the form of state intervention embedded in the NLRA. To understand this outcome, it is necessary to examine how the structure of business enterprise in the United States produced stronger and more effective employer hostility to unions in America than in Britain, and how that hostility prevented American unions from becoming as well established as British unions before the Great Depression and led to the greater degree of state intervention.

My narrative traces the evolution of public policy and labor-state-management relations between 1914 and 1939, but it is first necessary to provide a broad overview of developments before the start of the First World War. While I note the many parallels between the two nations, I explore the origins of what became a distinctively American approach to industrial relations. I then examine the critical impact of World War I, which in both countries brought about unprecedented state involvement in industrial relations, including experiments in corporatist arrangements, and a surge in union membership and strength. A retreat from state intervention and a quest to create new voluntaristic forms of industrial self-government are the central themes of the 1920s. Two separate but closely related questions form the basis for my examination of the Depression era. Why did the United States, but not Britain, make an attempt (through the National Recovery Administration) to create a comprehensive system of corporatism? Why did the Depression crisis ultimately provide the impetus for the creation of the interventionist NLRA framework for American industrial relations, which differed so substantially from the continuing British commitment to a relatively noninterventionist state policy? Although the detailed narrative ends with the 1930s, I include a brief epilogue on the increasing convergence of the American and British systems of industrial relations at the end of the twentieth century, as well as some final observations about the relevance of this study to contemporary American industrial relations.

CHAPTER ONE

The American and British Systems of Industrial Relations on the Eve of World War I

By the eve of World War I, the American and British labor movements and systems of industrial relations were beginning to follow divergent paths. The differences that were emerging were of recent origin, and it was still not clear in 1914 that these differences would prove long-lasting or would be more significant than the continuing similarities between the two nations' approaches to state-labor-management relations. Suspicion of state authority and a commitment to individualism have long been cited as characteristics of American society, but such attitudes were also widespread in Britain in the early twentieth century. Although workers in both nations were willing to accept certain limited forms of state action, in neither country before World War I was there extensive support among workers, or employers, for an active and ongoing role for the state in industrial relations. Especially in the United States, many employers still rejected the need to engage in any form of collective bargaining with their employees. While American and British workers generally favored a flexible philosophy of voluntarism that called for autonomous trade unions functioning in a pluralist system of collective laissez-faire, British unions by 1914 had been considerably more successful in institutionalizing this framework into law.

In the late nineteenth century, there was what one scholar has described as an identifiable "Anglo-American pattern" of labor organization with workers belonging to craft unions and focusing primarily on marketplace issues while participating in politics "through 'catch-all' rather than class-specific parties."[1] The American labor movement was not monolithically antipolitical and nonideological, nor were most British workers eager to embrace socialism or to support the creation of an independent labor party. Traditional claims about American labor exceptionalism not only understate the militancy and class consciousness of American workers at the turn of the century but also overstate the radicalism—in terms of both politics and labor-management relations—of British workers before World War I.[2]

Although it is important not to exaggerate the differences between the American and British labor movements and systems of industrial relations prior to 1914, on the eve of the First World War significant distinctions were beginning to become apparent. Specifically, what would prove to be an enduring gap was developing in the levels of success enjoyed by American and British unions in organizing workers and gaining acceptance of collective bargaining. British employers and unions were also beginning to make increasing use of meso-level district or nationwide agreements covering entire industries, whereas in the United States, virtually all discussions of industrial relations focused at the micro-level of the political economy, that is, the individual employer or individual place of work. In addition, the decision by the leadership of the American Federation of Labor (AFL) not to follow the example of the British Trades Union Congress (TUC) by supporting the creation of an independent labor party would, in coming years, prove critical in distinguishing the American from the British labor movement.

Initial Similarities

In the mid-1880s the American and British labor movements had a great deal in common. Workers, especially skilled craftsmen, on both sides of the Atlantic responded similarly to the transformation of wage labor that was occurring in the late nineteenth century, as they sought to defend their control of the shop floor through collective action. The total labor force in the United States was close to 40 percent larger than that of Britain, but because Britain was more fully industrialized, the number of persons employed outside of agriculture was actually quite similar in the two countries. Consequently, union members constituted a significantly larger percentage of the entire labor force in Britain than in America in the 1880s. If one considers only nonagricultural labor, though, union density at the time the Knights of Labor was at its peak in 1886 may well have been slightly greater in the United States. Union membership and density figures for the period before 1890 are by no means definitive, but estimates of union membership in the United States in 1886 range from approximately 900,000 (750,000 belonging to the Knights of Labor and 150,000 belonging to the craft unions that created the American Federation of Labor) to about 1,200,000. In Britain total union membership at the end of 1888 was 750,000.[3] Labor militancy and labor involvement in politics, especially at the state and local levels, were at least as widespread in America as in Britain. The United States in this period may well even have been the most strike-prone nation in the world.[4]

A number of scholars see the collapse of the Knights of Labor after 1886 as the critical watershed in the development of a more constricted American labor movement. Yet, as late as 1904, well after the Knights had disappeared and a decade and a half after Britain had experienced a wave of organizing victories for the "new unionism" among semiskilled and unskilled workers, the overall density of union organization among nonagricultural workers was only marginally lower in America (11%) than in Britain (12%). Moreover, in certain major industries the percentage of unionized workers was actually higher in the United States. In 1904 the percentage of American wage earners belonging to unions was 32 in construction, 31 in nonrail transport, and 25 in railways. The comparable figures for Britain were 25 percent, 13 percent, and 11 percent.[5] Important differences had begun to develop in the role of collective bargaining in the two nations, but following a rapid expansion in union membership around the turn of the century, the American labor movement in 1904 appeared in many ways to have once again matched its British counterpart in the success of its organizing efforts. Moreover, while the AFL that emerged as the dominant labor organization in the United States after 1886 may have rejected the broader political strategy and republican vision of the Knights of Labor, it played an active, though largely nonpartisan, role in politics that did not contrast markedly with the role played by trade unions in British politics before 1906.[6]

On both sides of the Atlantic, union leaders such as Samuel Gompers in the United States and Keir Hardie in Britain had as their primary political objective gaining freedom from government restraints in their efforts to organize workers and pressure employers to engage in collective bargaining. In Britain, as early as 1824–1825 Parliament took the first important steps to legitimize the position of British trade unions by repealing the Combination Acts that had made unions illegal. Even more significant, Parliament in 1871 gave trade unions protection from common law prosecutions as illegal conspiracies in restraint of trade. Such protection was strengthened by additional legislation in 1875 specifically legalizing a number of union actions, including peaceful picketing. Still, after 1890 British judges began to create new grounds for interfering with union activities, culminating in the Taff Vale decision of 1901, in which the House of Lords ruled that a union, though lacking a corporate existence, could still be held liable for civil damages. Getting Parliament to establish the absolute immunity of unions from tort liability then became the principal focus of the TUC's political strategy.[7]

British workers in the early twentieth century were by no means united in support of a class-based political party with a socialist agenda. Ross McKibbin contends that Werner Sombart's much-discussed question about the failure of American labor to adopt a Marxist perspective could just as appropriately be applied to British labor before 1914.[8] An independent

British Labour Party with representation in Parliament did not come into existence until 1906, and in the years prior to the First World War this party neither won the support of anything close to a majority of workers nor adopted an explicitly socialist platform. Most British workers continued to vote Liberal, and as late as 1910 the Labour Party, whose explicit purpose was to elect workers to Parliament rather than to socialize the British economy, was able to capture only 7 percent of the total vote in national elections. Without its collaborative relationship with the Liberals, by virtue of which Labour candidates were able to run without Liberal opposition for selected seats in the House of Commons, the Labour Party in 1910 would never have succeeded in electing 42 MPs (out of a total of 670).[9]

In spite of the British Labour Party's limited electoral appeal, Britain's parliamentary system and the precarious position of the Liberal Party in the years before the First World War enabled the small Labour minority in Parliament to exercise a degree of influence well beyond its numbers. That influence, though, was largely exercised in behalf of trade union goals that differed little in their essentials from the goals pursued by unions in the United States in the same period. The TUC took the critical step of moving toward independent political action because of its dissatisfaction with the Liberal Party's failure to select workingmen as candidates for Parliament and because of growing concern about adverse court decisions that undermined the protections established by the favorable legislation of the 1870s. The Taff Vale decision of 1901 "proved to be the turning point" for organized labor's move toward independent politics.[10]

The subsequent willingness of the Liberal majority in Parliament to respond to Labour's pressure by nullifying the effects of Taff Vale only reinforced the resolve of union leaders to continue on their new course. The Liberal government also responded to Labour concerns by passing the Trade Union Act of 1913. This law largely negated a 1909 judicial ruling by the House of Lords (the Osborne judgment) that prohibited unions from using their funds for political purposes, more specifically, for supporting the Labour Party. The law allowed unions to spend funds on political objects, so long as the majority of the membership approved and individual members retained the right to "contract out" of having part of their dues used for political purposes.[11] Yet, as historian Henry Pelling has observed, the Labour Party grew not because of "any widespread enthusiasm for state intervention," but because of "the desire of the union officials to escape that encroachment of state authority which they detected in the Taff Vale judgment."[12]

Collective laissez-faire remained the dominant philosophy of most British workers before World War I.[13] In many respects, the Labour Party and the British trade union movement remained more committed to a voluntarist philosophy than were the new Liberals of the early twentieth century. When Herbert Asquith's Liberal government first raised the prospect of instituting national health and unemployment insurance, the labor movement evidenced little enthusiasm for such an expanded role for the state. Only after the government in 1911 proposed an embryonic form of liberal corporatism in which the unions were assured a role in the administration of the new insurance system did Labour and the TUC begin to look more favorably on Britain's fledgling welfare state.[14]

With regard to collective bargaining and the determination of wages and working conditions, British unions accepted only very limited forms of state involvement. While strongly opposing compulsory arbitration, organized labor in Britain did back the Conciliation Act of 1896, which provided machinery for voluntary mediation and thereby implicitly recognized the legitimacy of trade unions. Union leaders also supported the Trade Boards Act of 1909, which allowed for setting minimum wages in those "sweated trades" that lacked any effective union organization, and the Eight Hours Act of 1909, which established a maximum workday for miners. The TUC was initially not enthusiastic about the Trade Boards legislation, fearing that the minimum wages it established might become de facto maximum rates. Although the language of the act was gender-neutral, it was widely understood that the law would apply principally to women workers.[15]

In the United States, the leadership of the AFL resisted calls for creating an independent labor party in national politics. In contrast to Britain, however, before World War I the United States had a sizable political party with an avowedly socialist ideology. The American Socialist Party of Eugene Debs captured nearly as large a percentage of the total vote in the 1912 presidential election (6%) as the nonideological British Labour Party won in the last prewar election (7%).[16] In neither Britain nor America did a majority of workers (or even of trade unionists) adopt an explicitly socialist outlook in this period, but the number of American unions willing to proclaim their support for socialism was comparable to the number of British unions voicing a similar commitment. A Socialist candidate for president of the AFL in 1912 received one-third of the vote at the annual convention.[17]

Like their British counterparts in the prewar years, even the antisocialist leaders of the AFL sought to gain more direct representation in government by electing trade unionists to office, and by 1912 seventeen union members won seats in Congress.[18] American unions at the local, state, and federal levels were also vigorously involved in election campaigning and in seeking government action that would benefit organized labor. As was the case with British unions, the main impetus for political action was the desire to counter adverse court rulings, especially the increasingly common use of injunctions in labor disputes following the adoption of the Sherman Antitrust Act in 1890. When the AFL in 1906 adopted a "Bill of Grievances" calling upon the federal government to enact a variety of pro-labor measures, an anti-injunction law was at the top of the list. Other proposals included eight-hour workday legislation, immigration restriction, and a bill to provide for the safety of seamen. William Green, a member of the United Mine Workers and future president of the AFL, who served in the Ohio State

Senate before the First World War, was typical of many American unionists in this period in his support for state workmen's compensation, minimum wage, and health insurance laws.[19]

American labor's voluntarist ideology, like that of the British TUC, was thus quite flexible, but a pluralist conception of free collective bargaining remained the central tenet of each movement's ideology. American unions were as firmly opposed to state dictation of the terms of employment through any form of compulsory arbitration or legislative fiat as were their British counterparts, but as was the case in Britain, American labor leaders were willing to accept a limited role for the state as a mediator in industrial conflicts, primarily because such intervention appeared to give added legitimacy to unions. Before the creation of a separate Department of Labor in 1913, Congress passed no general legislation comparable to Britain's Conciliation Act. However, between 1878 and 1915, thirty-two states passed legislation providing for voluntary mediation, in most cases with labor support. In addition, although most labor leaders (and employers) in the United States focused on the micro-level of industrial relations, just as Britain adopted special legislation (the Eight Hours Act) to deal with the coal industry because of its peculiar importance to the public, so too did Congress pass the Erdman and Newlands acts to allow for federal mediation in the critically important railroad industry. The railway unions favored the Erdman Act, which also contained a provision outlawing yellow-dog contracts, but the AFL leadership opposed the law because of wording that implied that unions could be held legally responsible for the actions of individual members.[20]

Although collective bargaining in both countries normally took place without any direct government involvement (American labor injunctions restricting union activities being an important though episodic exception), discussions did begin to take place in both Britain and America in this period about the possibility of one form of government involvement in the development of industry-wide agreements that might be considered a harbinger of a liberal form of corporatism. Reflecting the more advanced state of centralized collective bargaining in Britain, the British began as early as the 1890s to consider the possibility of giving legal force to industry-wide voluntary agreements arrived at by organized labor and organized employers. In 1912 Labour Party leader Ramsay MacDonald incorporated this idea into a bill he introduced in Parliament.[21] MacDonald's proposal served as an inspiration for Julius Cohen, one of the architects of the protocol between organized workers and employers in the American clothing industry, to make a similar recommendation to the United States Industrial Relations Commission in 1914.[22]

In Britain, there was one government-sponsored effort to create an institution that could operate across the whole spectrum of the economy, but this experiment in dealing with macro-level industrial relations proved to be a nonstarter. In the midst of the labor turmoil of 1911 and at the urging of the Board of Trade, the Liberal government in Britain created an Industrial Council consisting of thirteen well-known industrialists and thirteen trade union leaders and chaired by George Askwith, the government's civil servant with primary responsibility for mediating labor disputes. The council was charged with serving both as a medium of conciliation in trade disputes affecting the well-being of the country and as "an effective instrument of central co-operation between Capital and Labour, which could also relate collective bargaining and the wage structure to the needs of the economy."[23] The new body proved a total failure as a conciliator. Its lone "accomplishment" in terms of its second charge was to come out in support of the idea that the government consider making collective bargaining agreements legally enforceable throughout an entire trade or industry, so long as the union and employers' association involved jointly made such a request and the Board of Trade found the agreement acceptable.[24]

In the United States, ad hoc government-sponsored national industrial commissions were created on two separate occasions between 1898 and 1912 to examine the problems creating industrial strife.[25] Notwithstanding the creation of the Department of Commerce and Labor in 1903 (which was opposed by organized labor because of its exclusively business orientation), prior to World War I the federal government made no effort to establish any official standing body to foster cooperation between labor and capital.[26] For a brief period of time, however, a voluntary private organization, the National Civic Federation, did attempt to carry out many of the same tasks assigned to Britain's Industrial Council.[27] In sum, in neither country before World War I was there much support for any form of ongoing state involvement in industrial relations, including any version of government-sanctioned corporatism.

Emerging Differences

Although it would be misleading to posit a simplistic contrast between a supposedly class-conscious, socialist-oriented, and politically militant British working class and a presumably passive, apolitical, and nonideological American working class, two crucial differences were beginning to distinguish the American from the British labor movement on the eve of the First World War. First, although the American Socialist Party attracted as many supporters as the British Labour Party prior to World War I, the formal establishment of the Labour Party in Britain in 1906 and the AFL's adamant rejection of independent labor politics marked the beginning of a critical divide between the two labor movements. Socialists were prominent in individual unions in the United States, but the lack of cooperation between the leadership of the Socialist Party and the leadership of the nation's preeminent labor organization proved crucial in denying socialism an institutional base upon which to build.[28]

Second, the ten years from 1904 to 1914 witnessed a growing gap between the United States and Britain in levels of union organization and the extent of collective bargaining. Whereas in the past the later-to-industrialize United States had lagged behind Britain in union density only to catch up with spurts of union growth, the difference that arose between 1904 and 1914 proved to be long-lasting. Union membership as a proportion of the nonagricultural labor force doubled in Britain in this period, reaching 25 percent, while in the United States union density actually declined slightly in these ten years, falling to approximately 10 percent.[29] The developing gap in union density was matched by a similar contrast in the extent to which collective bargaining gained legitimacy as the principal model for industrial relations. Not only were far more workers in Britain covered by collective bargaining agreements, but these agreements increasingly occurred with the more or less willing cooperation of organized employers. In addition, the British state itself after 1910 increasingly began to deal with unions representing public employees, thereby further legitimizing trade unionism. By 1914 over 40 percent of all local government and education employees—nearly one-quarter of a million people—belonged to unions; whereas in the United States only 3 percent of public service employees belonged to unions.[30]

The peak organizations of workers and employers in both America and Britain were still relatively weak before World War I and could not claim to be entirely representative of their respective constituencies. Consequently, no significant macro-level industrial relations institutions existed. Meso-level institutional arrangements were much more fully developed in Britain, where national collective bargaining agreements had become the norm in the cotton weaving, cotton spinning, engineering, shipbuilding, building, and footwear industries. In most other sectors of the economy, collective bargaining in Britain most often took place by district, rather than within the boundaries of a single firm.[31] Although a burst of experimentation with centralized systems of collective bargaining occurred in the United States around the turn of the century, by 1914 the only significant national agreements in force were in the printing, pottery, and glass industries. District-level collective bargaining was also much less common in the United States before the First World War, occurring mainly in the coal, clothing, and construction industries. Collective bargaining, when it did occur, normally took place with individual employers.[32]

What factors account for the divergence between the American and British labor movements and systems of industrial relations that began to emerge by the eve of World War I? To what extent did the AFL's decision to oppose the creation of a labor party and its failure to match the British labor movement's success after 1904 in organizing workers stem from the same causes? Although proponents of American labor exceptionalism have often claimed that America's long-standing values of individualism and antistatism provide a large part of the answer, such values were hardly distinctively American in the prewar period.

A variety of factors that are not strictly ideological or cultural offer potentially more useful explanations of the growing divergence between the two labor movements. These include the distinctive character of the American state, the particular organizational makeup of the American labor movement, differences in the structure and organization of industry, and the critical role played by both public policy and employer actions in limiting the options available to American workers. Observers going back as far as Werner Sombart and Selig Perlman have cited such factors as the American system of winner-take-all elections, the early granting of suffrage to the white male working class, and the decentralized system of American federalism as obstacles to the development of a national labor party. Yet these factors, by themselves, cannot explain the divergent approaches to politics taken by unions in the United States and Britain after the turn of the century.[33]

Some historians emphasize the role of the judiciary within the American state as the crucial factor determining the political strategy adopted by American workers in the watershed decades of the 1880s and 1890s, arguing that the power and insularity of a hostile judiciary ultimately turned American workers away from politics and toward a narrowly constricted form of business unionism.[34] Whereas in Britain Parliament successfully enacted legislation to reverse judicial interpretations of the law that were hostile to unions, in the United States legislative efforts before 1914 to rein in the power of judges proved futile. Ironically, the passage of the Sherman Antitrust Act in 1890, whose ostensible purpose was to place limits on the growth of big business, gave to American judges further legal justification for enjoining a variety of labor union practices, including sympathy strikes and secondary boycotts, as unlawful restraints of trade. American unions were thereby subject to more intrusive and hostile forms of state intervention than were British labor organizations.

Unions were not illegal in prewar America, but they enjoyed none of the legal immunities possessed by unions in Britain. Thus, in the Danbury Hatters case of 1908, the Supreme Court ruled not only that unions were subject to the antitrust laws but also that they could be sued for civil damages. While the British Parliament was able effectively to reverse a similar judicial decree, when the United States Congress sought to provide unions with some protection from legal action under the Sherman law by including a provision to that effect in the Clayton Act of 1914, subsequent judicial interpretation virtually nullified the law's benefits to labor.[35]

In contrast to the supremacy of Parliament in Britain, the independent judiciary in the United States was virtually impervious to popular pressures for labor reform exerted by workers through the electoral system. Although British judges had attempted to interpret the law in ways that were inimical to the interests of organized labor, parliamentary supremacy made it possible for the British trade union movement to utilize political means to achieve the triumph of an "abstentionist" approach to labor law that was premised on the assumption that unions should be free from state interference in their efforts to organize workers and to bargain collectively with employers.[36] British law neither explicitly encouraged unionization nor provided for direct government involvement in the private-sector collective bargaining process, but organized labor in Britain during the late nineteenth century—and especially after 1906—was able through its engagement in politics to shape the law to create a favorable environment in which unions were free to organize.

The greater independence of the American judiciary allowed it to act more effectively than Britain's judiciary to hamper labor's efforts to organize or use state power for the benefit of workers. The continuing frustration of seeing pro-labor state legislation nullified by the courts and, even worse, suffering from increasing judicial intervention in labor disputes in the form of antiunion injunctions in the 1880s and 1890s, did contribute to American labor leaders such as Samuel Gompers adopting an antistatist ideology that regarded state intervention in industrial relations as undesirable and that rejected as impractical and a waste of scarce resources efforts to use state power to implement a broad class-based approach to reform.

Yet it is important not to overstate the differences that had emerged between the British and American labor movements by the first years of the twentieth century or to ignore other factors that were even more important than judicial power in shaping the American system of industrial relations and labor politics. Unions at the local and state levels in the late nineteenth and early twentieth centuries did not respond to judicial hostility by repudiating politics and state action altogether. As late as 1901 the AFL was pursuing a political strategy of gaining legal protections for workers and unions that was not very different from the strategy of union leaders in Britain and Germany.[37] Labor's commitment to voluntarism after the 1890s was not unqualified, and there was a strong parallel between the AFL's fear of state intervention in labor-management relations and the continuing appeal of the philosophy of collective laissez-faire for the British labor movement in the early years of the twentieth century.[38] It is thus necessary to turn to other possible explanations for what happened in the decade before the First World War.

Another factor that has been cited by historians to explain the developing contrast in political strategies adopted by the AFL and the TUC is the difference in the constituent elements that made up each labor federation. Following the collapse of the Knights of Labor, the American labor movement came to be dominated by "exclusive" or "closed" craft unions that by their very nature were less likely than "open" or "inclusive" industrial unions to pursue a broad-based political strategy. Gary Marks claims that the "AFL was unique among Western union federations in its composition. No other union federation in the Western world was so dominated by closed craft unions."[39]

"Closed" or "exclusive" unions are organized along craft lines and see their power as based on restricting the supply of labor in a given job territory. They have a narrowly defined approach to recruiting, and their relatively small membership is spread thinly across the country. Consequently, they see political activity as being of only "marginal" value to their efforts to regulate working conditions. In contrast, "open" or "inclusive" unions seek to enroll all workers in a particular industry and depend on the force of large numbers of members in geographically concentrated areas. Because of the virtual impossibility of controlling their labor market without outside pressure and support, inclusive unions are much more likely than exclusive unions to turn to politics to accomplish their objectives.[40]

Craft unions on both sides of the Atlantic generally lacked a commitment to independent politics. Conversely, inclusive unions in both America and Britain shared a common interest in political action. Such unions were the principal source of support within the labor movements of both countries for independent labor action in politics, and, in particular, for the development of union-based socialist parties. Although open unions continued to be a minority in the labor movements of both nations at the turn of the century, they attracted more members in Britain and subsequently played a key role in the British labor movement's ultimate affiliation with the new Labour Party.[41]

The question remains why inclusive, broader-based unions were more successful in prewar Britain than in the United States. The Knights of Labor in the 1880s had experienced some success in organizing workers regardless of skill, but the collapse of the Knights helped discredit subsequent efforts to organize the increasing number of unskilled and semiskilled workers in the American economy. Craft unions still played the central role in the British TUC prior to World War I, and large numbers of Irish immigrants were coming into the labor market. Organized labor in Britain, however, did not have to confront the problem of dealing with such overwhelming numbers of unskilled and racially and ethnically diverse workers as did organized labor in the United States. To a certain extent, this made it easier for the British labor movement to be more flexible in devising ways to incorporate the less rapidly expanding force of unskilled workers into "labourers'" or "general" unions.[42] These unions served as convenient alternatives to unions strictly organized on either a craft or an industrial basis. Ironically, the United States, which may have had the highest proportion of unskilled factory workers of any industrial nation, was also the nation in which the established craft-dominated unions seemed least able or least willing to organize the unskilled.

The inability of the American labor movement to be as successful as Britain's labor movement in fostering the development of inclusive unions was only one aspect of the larger failure of American unions to keep up with the overall level of unionization achieved by organized labor in Britain in the decade before World War I. The key question, then, is why American unions fared so poorly in comparison to their British counterparts after 1904 in their efforts to establish collective bargaining as the dominant model for industrial relations. Differences in ideological orientation or political structures do not provide a convincing answer. Racial and ethnic divisions within the American working class are only a part of the solution to this puzzle.

The most compelling explanation stems from the contrasting economic and technological contexts in which labor-management relations developed in the two nations in the early twentieth century. The timing of industrialization, which enabled American manufacturers to be less dependent on skilled craftsmen with already-established union traditions, together with the substantially larger size and more fully developed managerial structure of American firms, created conditions that ultimately made union organizing more difficult and led American employers to adopt a considerably more hostile position toward unions.

More technologically advanced, capital-intensive, American firms were able to make greater use of unskilled or semiskilled workers in the production process and thus became less dependent on unionized skilled craft labor than were their British counterparts. For example, unskilled workers made up about 50 percent of the labor force in the Pittsburgh steel industry prior to World War I; whereas the comparable figure for Sheffield was only 30 percent.[43] Both Jeffrey Haydu and William Lazonick convincingly argue that in contrast to first-to-industrialize Britain, where craft-based unions had established a solid foothold in most industries while production was on a small scale and required the intensive use of skilled labor, in the United States many later-developing industries were able, from their beginnings, to adopt labor-saving mass-production technologies before unions had become well entrenched. Unskilled or semiskilled workers were more difficult for American unions to organize, not only because racial and ethnic conflicts were a particular problem in this segment of America's diverse labor force, but also because they worked in settings where unionized craft workers had not already established strategic positions of power. The consequent difficulty unions faced in enrolling members is illustrated by a comparison of the American and British metalworking industries. In 1900 only 11 percent of Americans working in machine shops belonged to the International Association of Machinists (IAM), while over four times that percentage of employees in Britain's engineering industry belonged to the Amalgamated Society of Engineers (ASE).[44]

Most British manufacturing employers operated on such a small scale that even though they may have wished to extend their control over all aspects of the shop floor, they lacked the managerial resources to do so on their own. On the eve of World War I, firms with fewer than one hundred workers accounted for 97 percent of all manufacturing in Britain.[45] Many employers, therefore, were willing to continue to rely on craft unions to exercise a good deal of autonomy in the organization of work, especially since British industrialists remained more dependent on labor-intensive forms of technology than did their American counterparts. Moreover, many British employers came to see advantages to multiemployer collective bargaining as a means of limiting destructive competition over wages and controlling rank-and-file militancy on the shop floor. Written agreements with national unions had the potential of reducing unauthorized work stoppages and gaining union assent to a greater degree of management control of the production process.[46]

In spite of the differences in industrial organization between the United States and Britain that were already becoming apparent before 1900, there were some industries in the United States that did attempt to adopt the kind of industry-wide collective bargaining that was becoming broadly institutionalized at the time in Britain. As noted earlier, the American printing, pottery, and glass industries had well-established national collective bargaining systems by the eve of World War I. The experience of the critical machine-trades industry was, however, more typical, in that it demonstrated the ultimate rejection of such an approach by most American employers, who became ever more insistent on establishing their untrammeled "right to manage."

In 1900 the nation's machine shop owners tried what proved to be a short-lived experiment with industry-wide collective bargaining when the National Metal Trades Association (NMTA) signed an agreement with the IAM, but the so-called Murray Hill Agreement quickly collapsed. American employers, in contrast to British machine shop owners, soon realized that they could more effectively limit craft restrictions on production techniques by eliminating unions than by cooperating with them. Haydu concludes that given "the weakness of the IAM, employers found it a less valuable ally in the management of industrial change as well as a less formidable opponent to unilateral employer control than was the ASE in Britain."[47] Moreover, American employers in most industries, including metalworking, tended to be less concerned about taking wages out of competition as they came to adopt what Peter Swenson refers to as a "segmentalist" approach to industrial relations that entailed "a decentralized firm-level strategy of providing higher wages and benefits than other firms" while at the same time resisting workers' efforts to unionize.[48]

In a few more competitive, less technologically developed industries such as printing and coal mining, which remained similar in structure to the typical British industry, American employers did follow the British model of centralized collective bargaining. Conversely, in Britain, in cases such as chemicals where an industry's organization and development occurred relatively late, so that modern technology and a significant degree of market concentration were established before unions had been able to gain a foothold among production workers, British employers seemed perfectly capable of adopting an "American" approach to both labor relations and technological modernization.[49]

The more capital-intensive nature of American industry and the more highly bureaucratized organization of American business firms, characteristics that became even more pronounced after the great wave of mergers around the turn of the century, also resulted in a higher percentage of the nonagricultural labor force in the United States being employed in non-production-line jobs. Britain had a higher percentage of its entire working population involved in the tertiary (service) sector than did the United States (40% as compared to 35%). However, when one excludes the large number of Americans (33% of the population) working in the primary sector (agriculture), 56 percent of the remaining nonagricultural labor force was employed in the tertiary sector. In Britain the figure was 47 percent. In fact, the United States was the only nation in the world before the First World War to have more workers employed in the tertiary than in the secondary (production) sector of the economy.[50] Throughout the industrialized world in this period, white-collar and service workers, especially those employed in the private sector, were far less likely than production workers to belong to unions, so that this distinctive feature of the prewar American economy also contributed to the lower density of union membership in the United States.

American firms' greater reliance on advanced technology and their more extensive use of management hierarchies—factors that help explain American employers' greater hostility to unions and reluctance to engage in multiemployer collective bargaining—were directly related to the fact that American firms were typically much larger than British companies. Britain was more thoroughly industrialized than America, with nearly twice as large a percentage of its labor force in 1900 engaged in manufacturing, mining, and building. Nevertheless, in contrast to the American economy, in which large, vertically integrated firms functioned as oligopolies in many industries, Britain's economy in the years before the First World War was still characterized primarily by competition among relatively small, often family-owned, companies that had limited managerial resources to devote to the control of labor and hence were more willing to engage in multiemployer collective bargaining with unions.[51]

In 1901, when United States Steel was organized as America's first billion-dollar corporation, the largest enterprise in Britain was capitalized at less than $60 million. Although both nations experienced merger movements at the turn of the century, the total value of mergers in Britain's peak year of activity was only $110 million, while the value of mergers in the United States' peak year was over $2 billion.[52] American entrepreneurs in the latter part of the nineteenth century pioneered in creating huge, vertically integrated, multiunit business firms whose aim, according to Alfred Chandler, was to take "the place of market mechanisms in coordinating the activities of the economy and allocating its resources." Increasingly, these firms sought to avoid any interference, including that of unions, with their control of all inputs into the production process. By the early years of the twentieth century, giant corporations exercising the "visible hand of management" played a key role in the American political economy.[53]

A combination of factors accounted for the differences in size and scope of American and British business firms. One factor was the larger scale of the American domestic market, which, though more geographically expansive than Britain's, was less socially and regionally differentiated. This factor, as well as the lack of well-established marketing networks in the United States as compared to Britain, provided greater incentives for American businesspeople to pursue a strategy of both horizontal and vertical integration that resulted in the building of companies of unprecedented size.[54] Differences in the structure of capital markets also contributed to the rise of larger firms in the United States. Britain's better-developed banking system meant that existing firms, regardless of their size, usually had little difficulty raising needed capital, especially because demands for capital were constrained by the more labor-intensive approach to manufacturing of British firms. In the United States, the banking system was less developed, so that firms had greater difficulty raising capital through normal banking channels. As a result, large firms that could gain access to capital through the services of financiers such as J. P. Morgan gained a significant competitive advantage and were able in many cases to drive smaller rivals out of business or to restrict their entry into rapidly growing industries.[55]

Public policy, especially regarding tariffs and antitrust, also played an important role in the greater prevalence of large-scale firms in the United States. In both tariff and antitrust policy, the American state played a significantly more interventionist role than did the British state. Whereas in the period before 1913 the United States maintained a protective tariff, Britain remained the world's foremost supporter of free trade. Britain's greater commitment to free trade further accentuated the more competitive nature of its economy and made the growth of large-scale monopolistic enterprises less likely.[56]

Americans and Britons shared a concern about the dangers of concentrated power and a common law tradition prohibiting conspiracies leading to "unreasonable" restraints of trade. Only in the United States, however, did antimonopoly sentiment play a crucial role in national politics and lead to the adoption of legislation seeking to control the use of restrictive trade agreements. Ironically, the passage of the Sherman Antitrust Act in 1890 ultimately reinforced the trend toward integration and mergers in the United States, since the federal government soon found that it could more readily invoke the law to prevent cartel agreements among many firms than to break up individual enterprises, no matter how large. In contrast, the reluctance of the British to sanction state intervention in the marketplace, even in the negative form of an antitrust policy, and their greater willingness to tolerate collusive private agreements among firms, so long as those agreements did not produce "unreasonable" harm to the public interest, resulted in an acceptance of cartel arrangements that reduced the incentives for outright consolidation and made more likely the advent of multiemployer collective bargaining with unions.[57]

Hostility to unions among American employers was not restricted to large-scale firms, but the antiunion stance that also became common among small-scale employers in the United States should be understood in the context of the climate created by America's dominant business enterprises. In his case study of Philadelphia metal-trades employers, Howell Harris has demonstrated that open-shop policies came to predominate among smaller-scale manufacturers after 1904 in large part because the antiunion policies of the city's one large metal-trade firm and of local, state, and federal governments created an environment that legitimized hostility to unions.[58]

The contrasting attitudes of American and British employers toward unions not only goes a long way toward explaining the lower density of unionization in the United States but also is pertinent to the earlier discussion concerning the failure of the American labor movement to support the development of a labor party. Lloyd Ulman has argued that in societies with strong labor parties, employers might well be more inclined to recognize unions and engage in collective bargaining in order to defuse worker support for more radical measures that might be implemented through state action.[59] The growing disparity in rates of unionization between the United States and Britain did develop during the decade prior to World War I, in which the British Labour Party came into being and began to exercise some influence in Parliament. However, as noted above, in 1914 the Labour Party did not yet seem to pose that much more of a threat to British employers than did the American Socialist Party to American capitalists, and, as will be discussed in the following chapter, the greatest challenge to British capitalism during the war years that lay immediately ahead came not from the Labour Party, but rather from radical elements within the trade union movement.[60] Thus, to understand the contrast between American and British employer attitudes toward unions in this period, it is more useful to focus on the economic and technological context in which management choices were framed, rather than on employers' perception of the possible threat posed by labor's political initiatives.

Traditional analyses of American labor exceptionalism too often have tended to ignore the crucial role played by management in shaping the nation's industrial relations system.[61] The most distinctive feature of the American system as it developed by the early twentieth century was the strength of employer opposition to unions that was a product of American economic conditions. The hostility of American employers was already a factor in the collapse of the Knights of Labor in the 1880s.[62] That hostility became even more critical after the turn of the century in constraining the development of unions, as those in control of increasingly large corporate enterprises used their vast resources to counter efforts by their workers to organize in an effort to retain some control over the production process.[63]

Conclusion

What conclusions, then, can be drawn from this discussion of American labor exceptionalism on the eve of World War I? First, to understand the differences between the American and British systems of industrial relations that were emerging by 1914, it is necessary to focus at least as much on the attitudes and actions of employers as on the views and predispositions of workers. In analyzing the contrasting positions of American and British employers, such factors as the structure of business enterprise and the level of technological development carry greater explanatory power than general assumptions about differences in either national character or ideological traditions.

Second, state actors also played a role in the creation of each nation's system of industrial relations. In contrast to the British state, which had by 1914 at least implicitly legitimized the role of unions within a pluralist system of collective laissez-faire, the American state continued through more directly interventionist policies to support the perpetuation of an environment that was less hospitable to the growth of unions and labor politics. The structure of the American state made it easier for antiunion judges in the United States, as compared to Britain, to act unilaterally to constrict organized labor's freedom of action. Yet, even if the difference in state structures between the United States and Britain contributed to the growing divergence in the two nations' systems of industrial relations, the difference in state structures by itself is hardly a sufficient cause of that divergence. Had American employers been less hostile to unions, the constraining actions of American judges might not have been decisive. Judicial hostility, in other words, became significant because it reinforced the already-existing antiunion policies of American employers, who, in the words of Sanford Jacoby, "faced a different set of incentives and had more substantial resources to resist unionization than was true of employers elsewhere."[64]

Third, even though obvious contrasts had developed by 1914 between the American and British approaches to the problems of labor-management and labor-state relations, the differences that existed in 1914 were of relatively recent vintage. The two nations continued to share an abiding faith in individualism and a deep-seated suspicion of state power, even though American employers were willing to resort to the courts for assistance in strike situations. Corporatist conceptions of industrial relations had little appeal on either side of the Atlantic before World War I.

In the United States more than in Britain, many employers and judges continued to oppose collective bargaining and state regulation of working conditions, on the grounds that workers ought to be free to reach individual agreements with their employers about the conditions of their employment. Such a view was increasingly anachronistic in a political economy characterized by immense concentrations of capital. It was also rather hypocritical coming from individuals who were willing to call upon the power of the courts to restrain the actions of organized labor. However, the principal alternative conception of industrial relations that had emerged in both nations by 1914 did not challenge the underlying antistatism of nineteenth-century laissez-faire individualism. Rather, the labor movements in both the United States and Britain advanced a conception of "collectivist laissez-faire," according to which organized workers would be empowered to safeguard their own interests by bargaining collectively with organized capital.[65]

The bread-and-butter unionism advocated by most leaders of the AFL and the TUC in the prewar period represented an essentially pluralistic version of collectivism predicated on competition between organized groups over narrowly defined objectives relating to wages and working conditions. Individual workers could no longer deal with small-scale entrepreneurs on a highly personal basis, but labor relations could be conducted within a system of collectivist laissez-faire in which organized labor and organized capital could negotiate agreements without significant state intervention. Labor leaders such as Samuel Gompers recognized an inevitable conflict of interest between workers and employers, but they assumed that bilateral bargaining within the context of mutually acceptable ground rules could allow workers steadily to improve their lot within the existing system of competitive capitalism. Only in the case of women and children, whom many advocates of collectivist laissez-faire considered incapable of self-organization and thus in need of special protection, did direct state involvement seem justified.[66]

A pervasive antistatism thus helped to shape the way most people in both countries viewed the problem of industrial relations. This antistatism made both America and Britain unlikely prospects for any form of ongoing state involvement in this field, let alone for the development of corporatist institutions involving the establishment of formal tripartite relations between labor, management, and the state. Ironically, while there was virtually no support among either workers or employers in either the United States or Britain for continuous state intervention in micro-level industrial relations, proposals for state enforcement of meso-level industry-wide collective bargaining agreements did at least begin to surface in both countries prior to World War I. In comparison to the increasing role, especially in Britain, of meso-level trade associations and labor unions, the peak associations of workers and employers had not yet become significant institutions on either side of the Atlantic. It would not be until the demands of war mobilization made both Britons and Americans more receptive to a larger role for the state and more aware of the importance of viewing the problems of industrial relations in the broader context of the performance of the economy as a whole that macro-corporatist ideas would begin to gain a serious hearing on both sides of the Atlantic.

CHAPTER TWO

The Impact of World War I

Experimenting with Corporatism

In both the United States and Britain, World War I had a dramatic impact on the relationship between workers, employers, and the state. The enormous task of mobilizing national resources to conduct a global war to "make the world safe for democracy" and the home front a "land fit for heroes" raised critical questions about the role of both the state and workers in the conduct of industry. The development of tight labor markets and the requirements of national mobilization resulted not only in unprecedented government intervention in the field of industrial relations and state-sponsored efforts at centralized economic planning but also in a rapid acceleration of prewar trends toward the collective organization of labor and capital. The state would largely withdraw from its activist role once peace returned. Yet the war had a lasting effect on the organization of industry and would leave an enduring legacy of corporatist ideas and actual experience with state intervention in the economy that would, especially in the United States, once again be called upon in the crisis of the Great Depression

While the governments of the United States and Britain enlarged the scope of their activities in virtually all aspects of life, neither government had in place the personnel or administrative structures to carry out the massive mobilization effort on its own. Lacking the tradition of centralized state authority characteristic of the other major belligerents, and being dependent on the virtual monopoly of industrial expertise possessed by those operating in the private sector, both the American and British governments had to pursue the economic objectives of war mobilization by adopting a rudimentary form of corporatism in which they devolved state power onto already-existing private-sector organizations.

Contemporaries often described the system of incipient corporatism that resulted as "self-government in industry."[1]

In implementing this approach to industrial mobilization, American and British government policies gave added legitimacy to organizations representing workers and employers. Between 1914 and 1920 union membership increased by 92 percent in America and by 101 percent in Britain.[2] In the United States, the peak organization of unionized workers, the American Federation of Labor (AFL), achieved new recognition from the federal government; whereas in Britain meso-level workers' organizations such as the Amalgamated Society of Engineers (ASE) made the greatest gains in authority. At the same time, industrial mergers, which had dropped off substantially in both countries after 1902, once again picked up dramatically. In the United States, the capitalization of mergers averaged only about $200 million per year between 1912 and 1914, but between 1917 and 1919, the figure was nearly $600 million per year.[3] In addition, meso- and macro-level employer organizations also gained new significance. In both the United States and Britain, important new macro-level employers' organizations came into existence during the war. In both countries, unions, in particular, had to pay a price for state action legitimizing their role in the political economy. As participants in the state's war mobilization, trade union officials often had to defer to a state-defined "national interest," even when such a course of action inhibited their ability to advance the particular interests of rank-and-file union members.

Although the American and British governments relied primarily on voluntary cooperation and on the establishment of more formalized relationships with private-sector organizations of workers and employers to mobilize industry for war, the threat of government coercion became an essential element of the new relationship between the state, employers, and workers. With the wartime expansion of the state's role in the area of industrial relations, certain crucial questions arose: Would the creation of corporatist structures for mobilizing the economy serve only the overarching interests of the state, or would the growth of state power benefit either capital or labor at the expense of the opposing side in industry? Would the innovations in public policy and private-sector relationships introduced during the war emergency have permanent effects on the American and British systems of industrial relations?

The development of new mechanisms for ordering the relationship between workers, employers, and the state occurred at all three levels of the political economy. Especially in Britain, the onset of war quickly brought about an unprecedented degree of state intervention at the level of the shop floor. Developments at the micro-level of the political economy remained the greatest concern for the majority of British and American workers and employers, and the most intense wartime struggles over the organization of industrial relations took place at the level of the individual firm. In the case of the United States, the most important institutional legacy of the war era proved to be the development of shop committees. However, in both countries, the state made significant efforts at industry-wide economic planning during the war, and both governments also explored new means of coordinating the overall performance of the economy through the establishment of macro-level institutions. During the turbulent transition to peace, important elements of the leadership of each nation's labor movement began to press for a new role for organized labor at the meso- and macro-levels of the political economy.

On both sides of the Atlantic, an ambiguously defined and hotly contested concept of "industrial democracy" came to play a significant role in discussions of how best to organize industrial relations. People from all sectors of society concluded that the war experience demonstrated that the continuation of a conflict-based system of industrial relations was likely to produce anarchic consequences that would be intolerable in the future. In the immediate postwar period, both countries witnessed a resurgence of conservatism and the introduction of government policies that undermined the power that organized labor had gained during the war years. Nevertheless, the war era still left a reservoir of corporatist ideas that would influence future developments in both the United States and Britain.

Organizing for War

Britain's experience in the early years of World War I served in many ways as a harbinger of subsequent developments in the United States. By 1915, the Liberal government of Herbert Asquith recognized the impossibility of continuing to conduct "business as usual" and the need for the state to assume some responsibility for managing Britain's war economy. Although the approach later adopted by Woodrow Wilson's administration to the problems of organizing the American economy for war was not identical to the course set earlier by Britain's government, the parallels between the British and American approaches to state intervention, and particularly to the role envisioned for organized labor in each government's scheme of industrial mobilization, are striking.

In creating a wartime Ministry of Munitions, Britain's Liberal government sought to give a single state agency authority over virtually all aspects of armaments production. By war's end, the ministry, with over 65,000 people on its payroll, had become Britain's largest employer of labor.[4] In assuming direction over all "controlled establishments" involved in the production of munitions, the ministry exercised authority over the allocation of workers and contracts, as well as over the setting of prices.

Much of the ministry's work was carried out not by dictates from the state, but rather through an elaborate system of committees operating at the meso- and micro-levels of the economy on which organized employers and organized labor were represented. Those responsible for coordinating the overall mobilization effort from the ministry's central office were neither official representatives of existing private-sector organizations nor ca-reer civil servants or politicians. David Lloyd George, the first head of the new ministry, proudly proclaimed that "the Ministry of Munitions was from first to last a business-man organisation" and that the "most dis-tinctive feature" of the new government agency was the appointment he "made of successful business men to the chief executive posts."[5] His choice of men to staff the ministry was based on what he saw as individ-ual merit, and not on whether the person selected represented the busi-ness interests with which the ministry would have to deal. Many of the leading figures in the ministry charged with responsibility for maximiz-ing armaments production did not have backgrounds in the munitions industry. Yet, by deciding to rely almost exclusively on men with busi-ness experience, Lloyd George excluded individuals from the ranks of la-bor from playing an important role in overseeing the overall conduct of the mobilization effort. Those with roots in the labor movement were re-stricted to service on the various committees established by the ministry to deal specifically with labor issues.

During the war, Parliament also approved the creation of another new ministry, the Ministry of Labour, which, unlike the Ministry of Munitions, was to be permanent, and which was established by Lloyd George as a means of winning Labour Party backing for his leadership of a new coali-tion government.[6] Although the creation of a Ministry of Labour symbol-ized the growing power of Britain's labor movement in British politics, the Labour Ministry played only a minor role in the war mobilization. Even on questions relating to industrial relations, the Ministry of Munitions exer-cised much greater authority during the war.

Shortly after the United States entered World War I, President Wilson ap-pointed the War Industries Board (WIB) to supervise America's war mobi-lization. In contrast to Britain's Ministry of Munitions, the American WIB had less direct responsibility for armaments production and never itself mushroomed into a very large bureaucracy. At no time did the WIB have more than 1,500 employees.[7] Still, the WIB did become involved in estab-lishing production priorities for the economy and in some forms of price fixing. Like Britain's mobilization agency, the WIB relied almost exclu-sively on the services of businessmen as it sought to provide some degree of macro-level planning for the war economy. Whereas the Ministry of Munitions was at least headed by a government minister, the WIB was headed first by Cleveland manufacturer Frank Scott and then by Wall Street financier Bernard Baruch.[8] The American mobilization agency did have one union man on its executive committee. Nevertheless, as was the case in Britain, the labor spokesperson, Hugh Frayne, was called upon principally in matters relating directly to labor. Frayne served on the WIB's Price-Fixing Committee, but Grosvenor Clarkson, the semi-official historian of the WIB, admits that Frayne was put on the WIB not "to rep-resent labor, but to manage it."[9]

Labor's views were better represented in two separate wartime agencies, the National War Labor Board and the National War Labor Policies Board, which President Wilson established to deal specifically with labor issues. Whereas in Britain the new Ministry of Labour played only a minimal role in the war mobilization, Secretary of Labor William B. Wilson, a union man who had headed the Department of Labor since it had first been organized in 1913, played a leading part in the Wilson administration's handling of labor questions during the war.[10] In neither the United States nor Britain did representatives of organized labor either actively seek or obtain much influence over the government's efforts to engage in broad macro-level economic planning, except in matters relating to the supply of labor and conditions of work.

Contacts took place between the government and officials from the principal labor union federations in each country, though union officials were typically more involved in implementing than in formulating government policy. Especially in Britain these macro-level contacts were less significant than those that occurred between the state and individual unions. While government consultation with leaders of Britain's Trades Union Congress (TUC) on matters affecting workers had begun in earnest almost a decade before the outbreak of the First World War, Britain's wartime government generally found it expedient to deal directly with key individual unions such as the ASE or with interunion industry-wide organizations such as the Federation of Engineering and Shipbuilding Trades. The war thus encouraged meso-level amalgamations and federations between unions more than the expansion of the TUC's powers.[11]

In the United States, the growing status of the AFL just before World War I was reflected in Woodrow Wilson's willingness to go along with the recommendations of AFL president Samuel Gompers in choosing the labor representatives to the Commission on Industrial Relations established in 1913 by an act of Congress.[12] In 1916, when Wilson created an Advisory Commission to the Cabinet-level Council of National Defense to begin preparations for a possible war mobilization of industry, he named Gompers as the single spokesperson for labor on the seven-member body. The AFL thus gained a significant degree of legitimacy by virtue of the Wilson administration's recognition of the labor federation as the principal representative of American workers.

The differing positions adopted by the American Socialist Party and the British Labour Party on their respective nation's involvement in the war also had a significant impact on the fortunes of each nation's peak organization for workers. In Britain, the Labour Party not only supported the war effort but after 1915 became part of the coalition government headed by the Liberals. The growing strength of the Labour Party meant that it—not the TUC—"emerged as the principal source of such wartime coordination as the labour movement achieved" during the war.[13] In the United States, the leaders of the American Socialist Party became the most outspoken critics of

American participation in the war, with party leader Eugene Debs going to jail for his opposition to the draft. Consequently, in contrast to Britain, where the prowar Labour Party could serve the government as an alternative to the TUC as an institutional voice representing working-class interests, the largely antiwar American Socialist Party offered the Wilson administration no such alternative. The Gompers-led AFL, on the other hand, became involved in supporting the war mobilization effort even before American entry into the war.[14]

Contacts between the government of each country and peak organizations representing employers also developed on both sides of the Atlantic during the war. In America, the United States Chamber of Commerce, which had been founded in 1912, assumed a leadership role in economic preparedness activities as early as 1915 and then quickly grew in stature as it developed especially close ties with the WIB.[15] The chamber was not the only organization that sought to represent a cross section of important elements of the business community, since both the older National Association of Manufacturers (NAM) and the National Industrial Conference Board, organized in 1916, also sought to speak for American manufacturing. Although the NAM, which came into existence in 1895, had helped sponsor the formation of the Chamber of Commerce, serious differences between the two organizations had quickly developed.[16] In Britain, some members of the government actually helped to encourage the formation in 1916 of a new organization, the Federation of British Industries (FBI), to serve as the first important peak organization for British manufacturing and employer associations, though as was the case with the United States Chamber of Commerce, the FBI did not speak with a single voice for a united business community.[17]

Each government's main purpose in developing these contacts was its desire to have peak organizations representing business assist in the formation of industry-wide trade associations where such organizations did not already exist. The lack of comprehensive economic data, the relative weakness of the only recently established peak organizations of employers and workers and their inability to represent their constituencies in an authoritative manner, and the absence of a tradition of powerful centralized state institutions meant that government efforts to mobilize the economy for war still focused primarily on industry-wide or regional planning, or on micro-level issues involving individual firms, rather than on the creation of powerful macro-level planning institutions.[18] Lloyd George himself recalled that in organizing the Ministry of Munitions he "stressed the importance of local responsibility and of systematic decentralization."[19]

Government officials in both the United States and Britain justified the development of state-sponsored district and industry-wide corporatist institutions by pointing to the need for both labor and capital to cooperate with the state in defense of the national interest. Organized labor, however, was generally less well represented than organized employers in the meso-level institutions established by the state to manage war production. In Britain, the Ministry of Munitions sponsored the creation of nearly fifty local area committees "to assist in munitions production and allocate contracts, so as to make the best use of the engineering resources" in each district.[20] Although Labor Advisory Boards with union representatives participated in carrying out policies affecting working conditions, in only a handful of cases was labor also represented on the Boards of Management that assumed all other management functions in the mobilization effort.[21] Similarly for those industries not directly under the control of the Ministry of Munitions, such as cotton, wool, and shipping, for which the government set up industry-wide committees to coordinate wartime economic activity, organized labor played a much less prominent role than organized employers. This was less true in the coal industry, where the country's single largest union, the Miners' Federation of Great Britain, was a powerful force.[22] Unions thus became incorporated into the government mobilization program largely because of the state's need to have them assist in the implementation of policies that organized labor had played little role in drafting. In contrast, the trade associations that cooperated in the war mobilization were involved more fully in both the formulation and implementation of policy.

The situation was similar in America. In its dealings with individual industries, the WIB relied almost exclusively on industry trade associations acting as War Service Committees of the Chamber of Commerce of the United States. The WIB was itself organized primarily along the lines of particular commodities, and each commodity section head was drawn in almost all cases from the ranks of the relevant industry trade association. Labor was excluded completely under this arrangement. Although regional and metropolitan organization was less important in America's mobilization scheme than in Britain's, here, too, new state initiatives involved creating committees composed of representatives of local business interests. In deciding on such "management" issues as the allocation of government contracts, neither state officials nor employers thought that labor was entitled to play any significant role; nor did union leaders press for such a role. They shared TUC president Harry Gosling's view: "We workmen do not ask that we should be admitted to any share in what is essentially the employer's business."[23]

Workers themselves were more concerned with issues growing directly out of their experience at their particular place of employment. While the leaders of both the British and American labor movements did not foreswear a desire to have their governments recognize organized labor's right to play a role in the new meso- and macro-level institutions being created by the state to oversee the war economy, their greatest concern was how the increased legitimacy of government recognition could be translated into expanding membership rolls for individual unions and improved wages and working conditions.

In Britain, conflict over workshop organization and the emergence of a vocal movement for workers' control of the production process quickly came to the fore after Britain entered the war. By March 1915, the British government began to take unprecedented steps to involve the state in efforts to change traditional shop-floor practices in the munitions industries. At that time, Chancellor of the Exchequer Lloyd George entered into formal negotiations with over thirty unions, the most important of which was the ASE, to win their support for suspending trade union practices that had the effect of limiting production in crucial war industries. Most important, Lloyd George sought union acceptance of wartime dilution, that is, the use of unskilled or semiskilled workers in jobs formerly reserved for trained craftsmen holding union cards. In exchange, the government promised to limit war profits and to ensure that once hostilities ended the unions would be able to restore any restrictive practices that they had abandoned to aid the war effort. In the negotiations leading to the agreement, Walter Runciman, president of the Board of Trade, proposed that a portion of the excess profits be distributed among the workers, but neither the engineering firms nor the ASE favored such a policy. British unions generally were skeptical of profit-sharing schemes, because they tied the workforce too closely to an individual employer. Lloyd George also succeeded in getting the union leadership to agree that in labor disputes involving war-related work, workers would refrain from work stoppages and, instead, accept some form of arbitration. The so-called Treasury Agreement between Lloyd George and the unions was soon given the force of law with the passage in June 1915 of the Munitions of War Act.[24]

Dilution, of course, was not simply a product of the First World War. Throughout the industrialized world, a deskilling process that undermined the distinctions between skilled and semiskilled labor had long been at work, as employers sought to extend their control over the production process in order to increase both efficiency and profits.[25] Dilution was a particularly contentious issue in Britain for two reasons. First, in contrast to the United States, where managerial control of the production process was much more fully developed, British industry still relied more heavily on skilled craftsmen who exercised considerable control over what took place on the shop floor. Efforts to rationalize production, therefore, more directly challenged existing practices. Second, while skilled craftsmen in Britain had fought many battles with employers before 1914 to preserve their traditional prerogatives, what quickly distinguished the process of dilution during the war years was the active role played by the state.

In many respects, the British government's intervention in wartime industrial relations was "one-sided," in that the concessions made by labor were more significant than the concessions made by capital.[26] State controls allowed substantial wartime profits while placing greater restraints on wages. The state also attempted to restrict the flow of scarce labor into nonessential industries by requiring that munitions workers who sought a change of employment obtain "leaving certificates" from their current employers. Even though dilution and the ending of other restrictive trade union practices were to be considered only temporary measures, government policy created a precedent for strengthening employers' managerial control over the workplace that contributed to the increasing use of scientific management techniques after the war.[27]

It is misleading, though, to view the state's intervention in micro-level industrial relations strictly as a result of the employers' success in capturing state authority for their own purposes.[28] Lloyd George and other government officials were motivated, first and foremost, by their desire to ensure maximum war production. The Munitions of War Act, therefore, was intended to bring both workers and employers "within the sphere of Government regulation of the factors of production."[29] The Ministry of Munitions entrusted local-level enforcement of the labor provisions of the Munitions of War Act to tripartite tribunals chaired by agents of the state. Traditional collective bargaining relationships were thus supplanted by a tripartite system of corporatist industrial relations in which the interests of the state were theoretically paramount. At the outset of the war, employers were as fearful as union leaders of the possible consequences of government-mandated corporatism, since they shared with labor a concern that state intervention might, in the end, prove more beneficial to the opposing side in industry.[30]

The state may have acted to advance its own conception of the national interest, and not simply as the instrument of capital, but the burden of the state's efforts to maximize production still fell more heavily on workers, since capital's more strategic position in the political economy made employers less easily subject to government controls. Important sections of the British working class responded to the war mobilization by supporting a militant shop stewards' movement that engaged in unauthorized work stoppages and advocated a new approach to workshop organization. The shop stewards' movement operated independent of the existing trade union structures. While protesting the seeming inequities in the sacrifices demanded of workers and employers, the shop stewards actively resisted government efforts to impose dilution. In demanding workers' control of the production process, the movement crossed traditional trade union boundaries by establishing workshop organizations open to all workers regardless of craft. Even though the shop stewards' movement was relatively short-lived and was based mainly in Britain's engineering industry, it attracted a great deal of attention from contemporaries and has become a subject of heated debate among historians, who disagree about the reasons for the movement's emergence and about its ultimate goals and significance.[31]

In explaining the origins of the shop stewards' insurgency, James Hinton, the movement's leading historian, places particular importance on the issue of dilution. According to Hinton, the conflict over dilution caused skilled craftsmen in the engineering industry to consider the issue of workers' control in a new light. As a result, "the subversive potential that had always been locked within the craft tradition was . . . released," thereby unleashing, if only temporarily, the tradition's "revolutionary possibilities."[32] The movement for workers' control may have originated among skilled engineers, but it served as a vehicle for the organization of unskilled and semi-skilled workers who had not been fully integrated into existing unions and who would benefit from the development of shop-floor organizations."[33]

Other historians have downplayed the importance of dilution, contending that wage issues were generally the most important factors causing labor unrest and that the shop stewards' movement, rather than being in any way revolutionary, was largely a product of the essentially conservative desire of skilled craftsmen to maintain their privileged position. There is little question that workers, especially craftsmen, reacted to the fact that war-induced inflation put constant pressure on their purchasing power at the same time that the shortage of labor caused a significant decline in wage differentials between skilled and unskilled workers. Inadequate and crowded housing conditions in most industrial areas also fueled worker discontent.[34] However, in Britain more than in any other belligerent nation, government-mandated dilution became a particularly contentious issue, so that the precise form of wartime labor militancy was much influenced by the government's unprecedented intervention at the workshop level.[35]

The shop stewards' movement entailed more than a simple defense of the narrow interests of a privileged segment of the British labor force. In proposing the development of workshop organizations open to all workers as a means of establishing workers' control over shop-floor practices, the leadership of the shop stewards' movement expressed rank-and-file discontent with the willingness of national union officials to accept "the statization of trade unions" under seemingly unfavorable terms whereby unions would be more responsible for disciplining their members than would be employer associations.[36] It is wrong, though, to draw too rigid a dividing line between trade union officials and rank-and-file workers, since unauthorized job actions at times had the tacit approval of local union leaders and because most workers were undoubtedly sympathetic to the patriotic efforts of union leaders to assist the state's mobilization for war. Nevertheless, by actively cooperating with the government in the war mobilization effort in order to help win the war and to gain greater legitimacy for organized labor, the national leaders of the ASE and other British unions became constrained in their ability to support militant job actions that would have interfered with war production. Although the Clydeside shop stewards initially called for a system of "joint management" of the process of dilution, in which workers' committees, employers, and the state would each play a role, the movement soon rejected the specific form of corporatist industrial relations adopted by the government, contending that it was imbalanced in favor of the interests of employers.[37]

The shop stewards' movement also rejected a pluralistic model of industrial relations in which collective bargaining took place within the context of an implicit acceptance by workers of the employers' basic right to manage. One of the leading figures in the shop stewards' movement, William Gallacher, proclaimed that the movement's "ultimate aim" was to create "one powerful organization that [would] place the workers in complete control of the industry."[38]

The wartime insurgency was largely inspired by three somewhat different conceptions of workers' control—industrial unionism, revolutionary syndicalism, and guild socialism—all of which reflected a suspicion of state authority. All three doctrines had been developed before the war, but had little appeal to workers before Britain's wartime mobilization. In spite of important differences between these three doctrines, one of which, the industrial unionism of Daniel De Leon, was American in origin, all three shared the common goal of creating a non-bureaucratic system of socialized industry based on actual workers' control at the level of the shop floor, rather than state ownership and operation. In this sense, all three approaches to workers' control were grounded in a deep-seated antistatism.[39]

Even after 1914 the highly sectarian political groups explicitly advocating these ideologies never attracted large memberships. Although radical socialists played a prominent role in the shop stewards' movement, historians who contend that Britain was by no means confronted with a revolutionary situation during the war are surely correct in their assessment. The shop stewards' movement represented only a minority of British workers, and few of the movement's supporters were truly revolutionary.[40] Wartime conditions, however, made it possible for a radical conception of workers' control focusing on shop-floor issues to have an important impact on British labor.[41]

As an intermediate step on the way to complete control, industrial unionists such as Gallacher, syndicalists such as Tom Mann, and guild socialists such as G. D. H. Cole all advocated the introduction of the "Collective Contract." This proposal involved the signing of an agreement between officially recognized representatives of a works committee and company officers calling for the production of a specified output for a designated contract price, but giving the works committee full discretion over the way in which production would be carried out and over the way in which the money paid for the final product would be distributed among the workers in the plant.[42]

In seeking to establish as much worker autonomy as possible, the radical leaders of the shop stewards' movement rejected the notion that the collectivism of the future ought to be based on a cooperative partnership between labor and capital. As Gallacher and John Paton argued:

> A share in control does not imply that the workers should enter into partnership or any sort of alliance with the employer, or incur joint responsibility with him, or be identified with him in any way. All forms of co-partnership—collective or individual—are based on the theory that the interests of the exploiter and exploited are identical, whereas they are, in fact, mutually antagonistic and irreconcilable.[43]

Although the idea of outright workers' control at the shop-floor level gained a following among certain segments of the British labor movement during the war, the less radical concept of joint labor-management cooperation in establishing mutually agreeable workshop practices had a considerably broader appeal. The Lloyd George government itself contributed to the legitimization of the idea of joint control by virtue of the work of the Whitley Committee. The establishment in 1916 of this subcommittee of the Cabinet Committee on Reconstruction was in good part a response to the growth of the shop stewards' movement and the increasing demands for workers' control. The committee's charge was to make recommendations on ways of achieving an improvement in industrial relations after the war, but the committee's proposals were made public well before the end of hostilities. J. H. Whitley, a Liberal member of Parliament who later became Speaker of the House of Commons, headed the committee, which also included four representatives of large-scale industry, four trade unionists, and four economists and social work activists. The Whitley Committee issued a series of five highly publicized reports in 1917 and 1918.[44]

The committee argued that effective joint labor-management institutions could be created to produce "industrial harmony and efficiency." In what was clearly an attempt to respond to issues raised by the shop stewards' movement, the Whitley Committee put particular emphasis on the importance of works committees, referring to them as a cornerstone "of the industrial structure which we have recommended." While acknowledging that issues such as wages and hours were normally best settled by district or national agreements (a point still not widely accepted in the United States), the Whitley Committee asserted that many questions were "peculiar to the individual workshop or factory" and thus ought to be dealt with by works councils.[45]

The committee was especially concerned with countering suggestions that joint works councils were in any way intended as an alternative to trade union organization, stating that "the setting up of works committees without the cooperation of the trade-unions" would "stand in the way of the improved industrial relationships" the Whitley scheme was designed to foster. Works councils, the committee contended, would be valuable precisely because they would help make possible the "complete and coherent organization of the trade on both sides" of industry, which the committee described as its ultimate goal.[46] Although all-grades factory committees arose as independent organizations during the war, many were later reincorporated into the existing union structure and thereby ultimately did more to revitalize unions than to displace them.[47]

Similarly, in the United States the secretary of the National War Labor Board (NWLB), W. Jett Lauck, noted that the war stimulated workers' demands "for a greater measure of control" in industry and the development of new approaches to workshop organization.[48] While the state played a key role in these developments, there were significant differences between the American and British approaches to state intervention in micro-level industrial relations during the war. Both governments adopted policies that helped to legitimize unions and contributed to an expansion of union membership. Such wartime policies were particularly important in the United States because they marked a greater departure from prewar practices. However, state support for unions remained considerably more equivocal in the United States than in Britain and would not survive the end of the war mobilization.[49]

Even before America entered World War I, Woodrow Wilson had established a more pro-labor record than any previous president.[50] It was not, however, until the creation of the NWLB that the government explicitly affirmed "the right of workers to organize in trade-unions, and to bargain collectively through chosen representatives." The NWLB also proclaimed the principle that this right "not be denied, abridged, or interfered with by the employers in any manner whatsoever."[51] Wilson himself observed that the war mobilization demonstrated the need to establish "a new relation between capital and labor" in order to achieve "the genuine democratization of industry based upon a full recognition" of the right of workers, "in whatever rank, to participate in some organic way in every decision which directly affects their welfare."[52]

In general, though, the American state played a less direct role than the British state in trying to compel changes in traditional shop-floor practices. Most important, the Wilson administration did very little in the area of dilution, partly because American involvement in the war was of such limited duration, but also because American plants already made fuller use of modern technology and unskilled or semiskilled workers than did British factories. Whereas the Ministry of Munitions in Britain established tripartite tribunals to enforce new government regulations concerning shop-floor practices, no such bodies were established in the United States.[53]

On the other hand, the American NWLB did play a crucial role in fostering the creation of shop committees or works councils elected by all workers regardless of craft. The more extensive intervention by the American state in this area was a consequence of the greater weakness of organized labor in the United States and the stronger resistance of American employers to dealing with independent unions. Ironically, whereas in Britain the initiative for the establishment of shop committees cutting across traditional craft-union boundaries clearly came from a radical shop stewards' movement that was challenging the authority of the state, employers, and established unions, in the United States the impetus for creating such new workshop organizations came largely from a government agency that was responding to the lack of a collective voice among workers, but which was unwilling to compel employers to engage in a union-based form of collective bargaining. In Britain the strength of union organization prior to 1914 not only allowed the government to rely on existing unions to assist in an orderly war mobilization but also enabled those unions later to absorb most of the independent factory committees established during the war. In the United States, in contrast, the commitment of employers to the maintenance of open shops meant that so long as the Wilson administration was unwilling to enforce compulsory unionization, an alternative to traditional unionism was necessary if workers were to enjoy some form of collective representation.

Even as the NWLB sought to uphold the right of workers to join unions, it was influenced by the recently published recommendations of the Whitley Committee in turning to all-grades works councils as an immediate means of allowing workers to have some voice at the shop-floor level in the war mobilization. During 1918, the NWLB itself conducted elections for shop committees in many war plants where employers continued to resist formal union recognition. In Britain the establishment of workshop committees during the war ultimately contributed to a strengthening of the country's unions. In the United States, on the other hand, the creation of works committees, which was largely a product of the war, tended to have the opposite effect, since these committees constituted a precursor of the company unionism that emerged in the postwar period.[54]

Although the NWLB did not favor works councils as a means of preventing the development of independent unions, most employers saw the new form of workshop organization precisely in that light. So-called employee representation plans, or company unions, took various forms, including the Leitch plan, which entailed the establishment of a cumbersome system of worker representation modeled on the United States Constitution, and the more influential Rockefeller plan, which called for less formal joint labor-management committees to facilitate communication between workers and management. Most, though not all, employee representation plans excluded official union involvement and left no question that the ultimate "management of the properties, and the direction of the working forces, shall be vested exclusively in the company."[55] Company unions had been virtually nonexistent in American industry before the turn of the century, and as late as 1917 only twelve companies reported having such plans in operation. Two years later, the number of companies with employee representation plans had increased more than tenfold.[56] In Britain, employer-sponsored works committees were extremely rare, and the few examples that did exist during the war years had been established by Quaker employers who were also willing to recognize trade unions.[57] This developing contrast between the prevalence of company unions in America and Britain would prove to be a key factor in the subsequent divergence in the state's role in industrial relations in the two nations.

While many, if not most, employer-initiated employee representation schemes may have been intended as antiunion devices, Clarence Hicks, one of the pioneers in the company union movement, correctly claimed that such plans helped to fill the void left by the AFL's traditional reluctance to organize across craft lines or among the unskilled and semiskilled.[58] In this sense, the American company union movement and the radical British shop stewards' movement were both, in part, responses to shortcomings in the craft-union tradition. The British radicals who advocated the idea of workshop organization envisioned such organization within the context of a strong and independent union movement and had, as their ultimate goal, complete workers' control of industry. On the other hand, most American employers who envisioned the incorporation of organized—though nonunionized—labor into a new system of industrial relations wished to see management's control over the production process strengthened, not weakened. Even so, historian Joseph McCartin has demonstrated that NWLB-sponsored elections of shop committees during the war often had "unanticipated results," including the victory of unionists who encouraged militancy among their fellow workers.[59]

In addition, some employers did have less cynical reasons for supporting the establishment of shop committees. As a result of America's war experience, a number of the leading industrial relations experts associated with the scientific management movement began to extol workshop organization, in combination with effective, well-disciplined unions, as a means of getting workers to cooperate with the introduction of more rational production methods.[60] In Britain, where employer-initiated shop committees were considerably less common than in America, the few vocal proponents of this form of organization were not antiunion conservatives, but rather liberal-minded Quaker employers such as Seebohm Rowntree, who would pioneer a progressive, union-friendly form of personnel management.[61] Ironically, in America, as in Britain, some of the most progressive leaders of the workers' control movement acknowledged the potential benefits of scientific management while at the same time insisting that workers be allowed to play a major role in shaping and controlling the implementation of any changes in shop-floor practices.

In some instances, workers themselves initiated the organization of shop committees. As in Britain, war-inspired demands for workers' control went hand in hand with efforts by skilled craftsmen to establish new mechanisms for asserting their authority over the production process. During the war years a surge of strike activity focusing on issues of workers' control occurred that was unprecedented in American history.[62] At least some of the skilled craftsmen who led the movement for workers' control saw shop committees as a promising tool for challenging not only the authority of autocratic management but also the narrow sectionalism and timidity of the AFL's mostly craft-based union leaders. In contrast to Britain, though, what one historian has labeled "progressive factory politics" in America did not have to operate wholly independent of local union offices. Whereas in Britain traditional unionists dominated virtually all levels of a well-established union hierarchy, in the United States, where workers were still struggling to create stable union structures at all levels of the political economy, radical activists by 1917 had gained control of many local Metal Trades Councils and International Association of Machinists lodges.[63]

Workshop organization could thus serve to advance the cause of militant labor activists, as well as the interests of the state and of employers. Historian Steve Fraser has correctly observed that "workers' control" and "industrial democracy" were "two enormously evocative and equally imprecise formulations" that aptly expressed "the era's sense of possibility and uncertainty and its attempt to domesticate the energies released as the old order disintegrated."[64] Even many employers who sought to avoid dealing with independent unions recognized the need to respond to a growing sense of dissatisfaction with an industrial relations system predicated on the seemingly obsolete concepts of individualism and laissez-faire competition. On both the right and the left, the war thus stimulated efforts to develop alternatives to a pluralistic, conflict-based approach to labor-management relations. Incipient versions of corporatism were among the alternatives that emerged. Although state intervention in industrial relations reached unprecedented proportions during World War I, it remained to be seen whether the state's new role would continue once peace was restored abroad.

Transition to Peace

While the Wilson administration did virtually no advance planning for the transition to a peacetime economy, Lloyd George's government established a Ministry of Reconstruction more than a year before the Armistice.[65] As noted previously, the much-heralded Whitley Committee had responsibility for devising means of fostering harmonious industrial relations in postwar Britain. The committee's recommendations were the centerpiece of the government's initial proposals for bringing about a more rational organization of British industry. In important respects, the Whitley Council scheme was based on certain corporatist assumptions that by 1918 had become accepted, at least at the level of rhetoric, as virtual truisms in most public discussions of industrial relations. At the same time, ambivalence about the use of the state's coercive powers continued to characterize the committee's approach.[66]

The committee's recommendations were not limited to the establishment of micro-level works councils discussed earlier. The government panel proposed the creation on an industry-by-industry basis of a comprehensive, three-tiered system of national, district, and works councils. The panel's recommendations for joint labor-management committees implicitly acknowledged that the state's extensive intervention in industrial relations during the war was to be significantly reduced in peacetime. The national, district, and works councils the committee envisaged becoming a permanent part of the British political economy were to be bipartite, not tripartite, in structure. Representatives of the state would no longer be responsible for establishing specific rules to guide the conduct of shop-floor practices, nor would they normally be involved administratively in the resolution of disputes.

The state would play a significant role in encouraging the formation of joint labor-management workshop organizations in what might be described as a system of voluntary corporatism.

Supporters of the Whitley Councils system envisioned it as a way for workers and employers to work out agreements on wages and working conditions, to adjust grievances, and to discuss all other matters of mutual concern. Those involved in reconstruction planning thus saw the councils as a necessary means of achieving the government's main postwar objectives: the twin goals of industrial peace and increased output. In contrast to the war mobilization, in which the state created corporatist institutions to carry out fairly specific policies that had largely been framed by state actors, the Whitley Council scheme would allow the state to establish only the broadest of goals.

In arguing that "adequate organisation on the part of both employers and workpeople" was an "essential condition of securing a permanent improvement" in industrial relations, the Whitley Committee made it clear that the system of joint councils it was recommending was to be based on the complete cooperation of existing organizations of workers and employers and that Whitley Councils "should be composed *only* of representatives of Trade Unions and Employers' Associations [emphasis added]" already in existence.[67]

The Whitley Committee thus tacitly conceded the state's institutional weakness and reaffirmed the principles of voluntarism that had long guided Britain's approach to industrial relations. When Minister of Labour G. H. Roberts circulated the Whitley Reports to employers' associations and trade unions in 1917, he argued that, if properly implemented, the Whitley scheme would prove "how greatly the task of the State can be alleviated by a self-governing body capable of taking charge of the interests" of an entire industry. State intervention, in the words of the Whitley Committee, "should vary inversely with the degree of organisation in industries." Only in industries in which unions and employers' associations were insufficiently developed might it be necessary for the state to become directly involved in resolving issues of controversy normally settled by collective bargaining.[68]

Precedent for direct government involvement in the setting of wages in certain unorganized industries actually predated the war. The Trade Boards Act of 1909, introduced into Parliament by Winston Churchill, enabled the government to establish Trade Boards having the power to fix legal minimum wage rates for industries in which "sweating" was a serious problem. At the time the Whitley Reports came out, four Trade Boards existed. Representatives of the workers and employers of the industries in question sat on each board, but "public" representatives appointed by the government held the balance of power. The Whitley Committee recommended that the Trade Boards approach be extended to all unorganized industries and that the Trade Boards thus created be utilized, at least temporarily, "as a means of supplying a regular machinery for negotiation and decision" on a wide variety of questions, not just wage rates.[69]

Trade Boards, according to J. H. Whitley, were to serve primarily "as a stepping-stone to higher things, namely, responsible self-government within the industries themselves."[70] Once an industry with a Trade Board achieved an effective organization of both its workers and employers, the Trade Board could give way to a Whitley Council free of direct government involvement. Most members of Parliament shared this view of the purpose of Trade Boards and supported legislation in 1918 that adopted the Whitley Committee's recommendation on this particular issue. Conservative MP Waldorf Astor, for example, praised the Trade Boards bill because it was based on "the principle of self-government by the industry concerned," rather than the idea that industry should "be interfered with or governed by any bureaucracy or by Parliament."[71]

The Whitley Committee saw no need for the passage of legislation to give force to its main recommendations, since the joint industrial councils it proposed did not require the use of government coercion or sanctions. The committee did hark back to the proposals for legalizing trade agreements that had often been discussed before the war by noting that it might become "desirable at some later stage for the State to give the sanction of law to agreements made by the Councils," but only if "the initiative in this direction" came from "the Councils themselves."[72] Such sanctions would have been intended to prevent a small but recalcitrant minority in an industry from frustrating the effective implementation of an agreement arrived at by the voluntary efforts of a majority of both workers and employers.[73]

Some members of the business community were enthusiastic about the possibilities inherent in the development of new ties between industry and the state. Dudley Docker was perhaps the most enthusiastic business exponent of a full-blown corporatism. The Birmingham industrialist was a leading figure in the British merger movement at the turn of the century and then became the individual most responsible for the founding of the FBI. Not only did he favor the kind of meso- and micro-level organization outlined in the Whitley Committee reports, but he also envisioned the peak organizations of employers and workers becoming directly involved in shaping the government's efforts at "framing" macro-level "industrial legislation." Docker was especially intent on seeing state-sanctioned cartels (and tariff protection) established to help British industry compete successfully for foreign markets in the postwar period. He also favored the creation of a trade or export bank under government auspices but "largely supported by manufacturers with their own money, in order that they may have their share of control."[74]

In addition, Docker was one of a number of important businessmen who supported the establishment of a ministry of commerce or industry to serve as a direct representative of the interests of employers in the councils of government. Although Lloyd George had conceded to labor's wishes by creating the separate, but relatively powerless, Ministry of Labour, his government remained leery of permanently giving over to organized interests too much direct control over the formulation of economic policy. In responding to the proposal for a new ministry of commerce, the Machinery of Government reconstruction subcommittee headed by Viscount Haldane expressed the serious misgivings many government officials had about the development of corporatist mechanisms that might be dominated by private interests:

> What is aimed at is that the control and regulation which becomes necessary should be exercised virtually, not by a Ministry which would be specialised, competent, and expert, and able to safeguard the interests of the community as a whole; but by the influence of dominant corporate bodies representing either employers or workmen, upon a ministry which, it is asserted, ought to represent 'Industry' and could be made to express the views of 'Industry' (or of the particular industry concerned), as against those of the rest of the community.

Haldane concluded that if "the supreme function of Government, and of every Minister, is to assert the common interest of the community as a whole," then it was necessary to reject "the proposal for a Ministry" that would represent only "the interests of those engaged in industry, whether employers or employed."[75]

Docker and the FBI were by no means representative of the entire business community. The majority of businessmen remained at best ambivalent—and in many cases were altogether hostile—about the kind of corporatist society Docker envisioned. They continued to be fearful of the possible consequences of more direct state involvement in the economy and also were less enthusiastic about the potential benefits of closer collaboration with the leadership of organized labor.[76]

Although the recommendations of the Whitley Committee won a good deal of acclaim in the British press, as well as the support of the FBI and of many prominent business and labor leaders, in practice, effective implementation of the Whitley scheme proved extremely difficult, since few employers or trade union officials were yet ready to act on the assumption that capital and labor in each industry shared a common interest.[77] At the ideological level, corporatism had developed a powerful appeal, but with the return to a peacetime economy, the institutionalization of corporatist ideals proved far more difficult. In three of Britain's most important industries— coal, railways, and transport—no Whitley Councils were even established.

Yet another approach to the meso-level restructuring of industry that sought to move away from a competitive, conflict-based model gained support from important elements of the labor movement. As World War I came to an end, the powerful unions in the coal, railway, and transport industries, which together made up the Triple Alliance, pressed for the implementation of an explicitly socialist version of collectivism entailing nationalization of their respective industries. With the publication in 1918 of its widely heralded manifesto, "Labour and the New Social Order," the Labour

Party also went on record for the first time as favoring nationalization of major industries.[78] Leading sectors of the British labor movement thus sought to use state power in a way that would radically change the basis for industrial relations. However, just as the business community was divided and ambivalent about the possible uses of state power to create a corporatist system of industrial organization, so too was the British labor movement not of one mind about the benefits to be gained from a state takeover of industry.

In the months immediately following the Armistice, the coal industry became the focus of the growing movement for nationalization, since British miners appeared to be in the best position for gaining government approval for nationalization of their industry. One student of British industrial relations considers the miners' proposal for nationalizing the coal industry "the most important document produced by the British workers in their struggle for workers' control."[79] Miners' Federation Secretary Frank Hodges described the union's proposal as a means of achieving "self-government" in the coal industry. The plan called for a nationalized industry to be operated under a system of joint control between the workers and the government, with national and district councils, composed equally of union and government representatives, exercising managerial authority. In addition, men chosen by miners on the spot, and technical experts selected by the district council, were to sit on pit councils.[80]

Historian Robert Currie argues that the miners' support for nationalization stemmed almost solely from their belief in the likely "cash rewards" of public ownership. In Currie's view, the real aim of the miners was higher wages, not actual workers' control of the industry, so that they were proposing a meso-level restructuring of the industry only because of their concern for traditional micro-level collective bargaining issues. The miners' demand for nationalization was, it is true, inextricably linked to their insistence on the establishment of a national wage standard. Nonetheless, their specific proposal for restructuring the coal industry would have influenced all aspects of industrial relations, not just the determination of wages. It clearly reflected their growing realization that in an increasingly collectivized economy, issues of industry-wide structure were inseparable from concerns about conditions in individual pits. In fact, G. D. H. Cole, Britain's leading guild socialist, helped the miners develop their plan for nationalization, believing that it might serve as a pragmatic first step in a broader campaign to implement the ideals of guild socialism.[81]

The Lloyd George government responded to the workers' proposal and to the threat of a nationwide coal strike in early 1919 by calling on Parliament to create a special commission to make recommendations about the future of the British coal industry. The Sankey Commission, as it came to be known, was headed by Sir John Sankey, a judge of the King's Bench. The remaining positions on the commission were divided equally between supporters of the miners and supporters of the mine owners. Among the labor sympathizers on the commission were socialist economists Sidney Webb and R. H. Tawney. While the miners were unable to persuade a majority of the Sankey Commission to support the union's original scheme of workers' control, they were able to win Justice Sankey's support for a watered-down form of nationalization that would have allotted to the miners one-third of the seats on the governing board of a nationalized coal industry. The remaining seats would have been equally divided between representatives of the consumers of coal and representatives of the technical and commercial experts of the industry. The commission members sympathetic to the operators refused to consider any socialist version of corporatism, but they did support the creation of a three-tiered system of national, district, and pit councils similar to the Whitley scheme.[82] The Sankey plan of nationalization clearly went beyond the type of joint control of industry envisioned in the Whitley Committee's recommendations. Yet both bodies implicitly rejected individualist and laissez-faire assumptions and proposed new institutional mechanisms that were intended to make cooperation and harmony, rather than competition and conflict, the guiding principles of Britain's political economy.

In the United States at the end of World War I, a proposal closely paralleling the Sankey Commission's recommended system of tripartite control, but applying to railroads rather than coal, also gained a good deal of attention. Because of a near collapse in service, the government had taken over the railroads during the last year of the war. As was the case with the British coal industry, the American railroad system was in poor shape economically, with many weak companies acting as a burden on the entire industry, so that full and immediate decontrol seemed unattractive to almost all concerned. In 1919 the railway unions stood united in support of a plan of permanent nationalization developed by their counsel, Glenn Plumb. The Plumb Plan called for the creation of a public corporation whose board of directors would have had one-third of its members appointed by the president of the United States, one-third chosen by the technical and administrative staff of the railroads, and one-third selected by the employees. Any excess profits earned by the railroads were to be divided equally between the employees, including the managerial staff, and the government.[83]

Plumb explained to the House Committee on Interstate Commerce that he had devised his plan in order to put an end to the "industrial warfare" resulting from a system in which capital, labor, and the consuming public each had to be "on guard to protect its own [interest] without regard to the interests of others."

> The continuance of such a system can be based only upon a government which can provide the might to enforce the demands of that interest which at the time controls the government. A democratic government instead of controlling such an industrial situation is controlled by one or the other of these warring fundamental interests and so can no longer function as true democracy in government.

The establishment of his proposed tripartite system of joint control in the railroad industry, Plumb claimed, would result in a collaborative effort by all those involved in the industry to serve the public interest. The entire function of labor organization would be transformed, since men under the new system would join labor unions, not just to gain higher wages at the expense of the employer's profits but in order to be part of "the machinery" necessary for achieving "industrial democracy."[84]

Such language clearly reflected corporatist assumptions about the possibility of creating a new industrial system based on the principles of cooperation and functional integration. Although the supporters of the Plumb Plan usually defended the plan in corporatist terms, they were not always consistent in this regard, nor were they as self-consciously radical in their conception of nationalization as were the guild socialists and industrial unionists who occupied important positions of leadership in the British labor movement. Plumb himself at times justified his plan by emphasizing the way in which it would prevent labor and capital from uniting at the expense of consumers, since the latter group would also be represented on the proposed railroad corporation's board of directors in order to guard against excessive rates and excessive labor costs. In using this rationale for his plan, Plumb was expressing a pluralist conception of industrial organization that contradicted his frequent claims about the possibility of establishing a true harmony of interests based on a shared devotion to the ideal of service.

While an ideological commitment to the idea of workers' control was important in the development of the British miners' proposal for nationalization, such a commitment was less of a factor in the traditionally conservative railway unions' support for the Plumb Plan. A. B. Garretson, president of the Order of Railway Conductors and spokesman for all the operating brotherhoods, said virtually nothing about the workers' control aspects of the Plumb Plan in his testimony before the Senate Interstate Commerce Committee. Rather, he praised the plan as "the first legitimate profit-sharing scheme that has been presented in a public utility in this country," claiming that it provided for "an equitable division of the profit from an enterprise between all who were parties to it."[85] It would thus be more true of American than of British labor that its seeming radicalism in supporting nationalization reflected not so much a "class-conscious" commitment to the ideals of socialism and workers' control as a "wage-conscious" outlook.[86]

In spite of these qualifications, the campaign for the Plumb Plan was but one manifestation of a growing interest in corporatist ideas in America, and especially in the prospect of creating new meso-level institutions that would enable more rational planning for American industry. In 1919, the convention of the United Mine Workers of America adopted a resolution calling for a similar program of nationalization for the coal industry, and in the following year, against the opposition of Samuel Gompers, the AFL convention voted in support of government ownership of the railroads.[87] Sidney and Beatrice Webb, the prime movers behind Fabian socialism in Britain, cited the Plumb Plan as

a constructive approach to the problem of creating a new institutional framework to make the conduct of industry more efficient. The railroad unions'
willingness to accept scientific management as an integral part of their plan
must have been particularly appealing to the Webbs.[88]

Even critics of the Plumb Plan, such as former Interstate Commerce
Commissioner George Anderson, acknowledged that no proposal for the reorganization of the nation's railroad system could have "any reasonable
prospect of success" unless it recognized "the fundamental need of a radically changed status of labor" and a new system of organization that would
facilitate cooperation, rather than "economic warfare," between labor and
management. Thus, Anderson declared that "the men who contribute faith-
ful, efficient and long-continued service in the transportation industry" had
as much right to be represented in the management of the railroads and "to
be held responsible for the wise exercise of managerial powers as are the
contributors of capital." Anderson himself supported establishing a tripartite system of control within a framework of joint private and public ownership of the railroads, with workers, stockholders, and the government having equal representation on the railroads' board of directors.[89]

Anderson's views closely parallel the approach outlined in Britain's
Whitley reports. Although the British Labour Party's socialist manifesto,
"Labour and the New Social Order," was an inspiration to many left-wing
progressives in the United States, the more moderate corporatism of the
Whitley Councils scheme was undoubtedly more attractive to most
Americans concerned with restructuring industry.[90] The Whitley Councils
scheme was widely discussed in the United States. The NWLB was directly
influenced by the Whitley Committee's call for workshop organizations,
and at the Reconstruction Congress sponsored by the United States
Chamber of Commerce in December 1918, John D. Rockefeller, Jr., voiced
support for "the formation of joint works' committees, of joint district
councils, and annual joint conferences of all the parties in interest in a single industrial corporation," as well as for joint conferences "to include all
plants in the same industry, all industries in a community, in a nation, and
in the various nations." Articles about the Whitley plan also appeared right
after the war in such periodicals as *The Nation, The New Republic, Survey, The
Dial*, and *The Atlantic Monthly*. The Washington-based Bureau of Industrial
Research published a book in 1919 containing all the Whitley Reports, as
well as certain related documents.[91] In June of the same year, Wilson adviser
Joe Tumulty recommended that the president support the development of a
policy "similar to the Whitley programme."[92]

The practice of establishing joint councils was much more advanced in
Britain, but in the years immediately before the war, efforts had been made
in the American garment industry to establish joint works and district committees that were similar to the councils advocated by the Whitley
Committee. Although the system developed in the American needle trades
put more emphasis on dispute settlement than did the Whitley Councils

scheme and, consequently, utilized full-time, salaried, impartial experts to chair the joint conferences that were set up, it too was predicated on a "positive-sum vision of collective bargaining" in which rationalized production techniques were to go hand in hand with more stable wages and profits.[93] Sidney Hillman, the head of the Amalgamated Clothing Workers (ACW) and leading force behind the development of the industry's joint councils system, was an admirer of Whitleyism. In 1919 the impartial chair of the New York conference explicitly called for the creation of a "National Joint Council . . . along lines similar to the Whitley Councils in England." Subsequently, an informal, though short-lived, national council was established in the clothing industry.[94]

Still, American employers were generally less predisposed to cooperative efforts with organized labor than were their British counterparts. At war's end, several influential members of the business community were eager to build on the war mobilization experience by having the state continue after the Armistice to give official sanction to industry-wide agreements, but their vision of a new corporatism was essentially bipartite, rather than tripartite, since they excluded representatives of labor from their plans for industry-government cooperation. Whereas the lure of tariff protection proved to be the greatest attraction for British manufacturers—such as Dudley Docker—who sought more formal contacts between organized business interests and the government, in the United States the prospect of antitrust law revision served a similar function in winning business converts to the idea of closer ties between business and the state.

The establishment of the Industrial Board of the Department of Commerce in February 1919 represented the most important attempt in the immediate postwar period to create an ongoing institutional basis for at least a limited form of American corporatism. Chaired by former WIB official George Peek and staffed primarily by other business leaders with WIB experience, the Industrial Board sought during its brief existence to reach open agreements with trade associations on appropriate prices that all government purchasing agencies would pay for basic commodities. The scheme was publicly justified as a temporary measure to ease the nation's economy through the transition from a war to a peacetime footing, but the proposal reflected the broader desire of much of the business community, including the NAM and the Chamber of Commerce, to eliminate antitrust law prohibitions on industry-wide price agreements. Although price agreements were obviously of importance to American workers, the sole "representative" of labor on the Industrial Board was the United States commissioner of immigration, Anthony Caminetti, who had been selected by Secretary of Labor Wilson. The Industrial Board quickly collapsed because of opposition from Walker Hines, head of the Railroad Administration, and Secretary of the Treasury Carter Glass, who believed that the board's willingness to accept inflated prices in a proposed agreement with the steel industry demonstrated the need to preserve the integrity of the antitrust laws.[95]

In the months immediately following the end of the war, American business leaders thus went a little further down the road to creating an institutional basis for a business-dominated form of corporatism than did their British counterparts, but in both countries state actors were ultimately responsible for frustrating the most ambitious plans of the business corporatists. Although British unions were clearly in a better position to become involved in any corporatist restructuring of industry, in both nations organized labor's role in the postwar order remained at best problematic.

On both sides of the Atlantic, labor militancy and industrial conflict reached a climax in the immediate postwar period. The United States in 1919 experienced more extensive strike activity than in any other year in the nation's history, with over 20 percent of all employed workers involved at one time or another in work stoppages. Strike activity in Great Britain in 1919 did not occur at such unprecedented levels, but the number of working days lost was more than three times greater than in 1913 or in a typical year in the decade to follow.[96]

In response to this postwar crisis in industrial relations, Woodrow Wilson and David Lloyd George each called national industrial conferences to which representatives of management, labor, and the public were invited to try to develop a consensus as to the best means of achieving more harmonious labor relations. The conferences entailed the most ambitious attempts yet in both the United States and Britain to create state-sponsored macro-level institutions that could provide a means for the peak organizations of employers and workers to cooperate in influencing government policy. However, the failure of both conferences to produce lasting results also marked the beginning of a significant decline in the power of organized labor and in the willingness of both governments to sponsor further institutional innovation.

When the National Industrial Conference of Great Britain first convened in late February 1919, nationwide strikes in the coal and railway industries seemed imminent. Although Lloyd George may well have used the conference as part of a strategy of delay to undercut support for the Triple Alliance, many of those involved in reconstruction planning were hopeful that this gathering of representatives of organized labor and organized capital would be able to pave the way for a new, more cooperative, approach to industrial relations. The conference was characterized by apparent harmony and agreement on certain basic principles, but its ultimate failure to bring about any concrete changes in the nation's system of industrial relations stemmed not only from the government's unwillingness to follow through wholeheartedly on the conference's recommendations but also from the still-prevalent feeling among both employers and workers that industrial relations problems were best dealt with at the micro- or meso-level of the economy, rather than by a macro-level institution.[97]

It was, nevertheless, a reflection of the enhanced legitimacy of collective organization that the government invited the TUC and the FBI to select the nearly one thousand individuals who would actually attend the conference. The labor and employer delegations chose representatives to serve on a joint committee that was created to make specific recommendations to the conference. This committee subsequently issued a report reiterating the widely held belief that comprehensive worker and employer organization was desirable and that the concept of joint councils put forth by the Whitley Committee would contribute to better relations between labor and management. The select committee, moreover, went a step further. It recommended the establishment of a permanent National Industrial Council (NIC), whose members would be elected by the existing employee and employer organizations. The NIC was to be officially recognized by the government as the representative voice of industry and was to be consulted on all issues of relevance to industry as a whole. Such an organization would, in essence, serve as the culmination of the Whitley Council scheme that was then in an early stage of development. So widespread was the popular appeal of Whitleyism at this time that even Allan Smith, the head of the Engineering Employers' Federation, who served as chair of the employers' group on the joint committee, felt compelled publicly to support the Whitley Councils approach, even though he opposed such cooperation in private and became instrumental in founding another organization, the National Confederation of Employers' Organisations, which took a more antilabor position than the FBI.[98]

In the United States in October of 1919, President Wilson summoned representatives of labor, capital, and the public to meet in a National Industrial Conference that convened just as the country was experiencing its first nationwide steel strike. The AFL and the nation's railway brotherhoods chose the labor delegation, which was headed by Samuel Gompers. Since no single employer organization could speak authoritatively on behalf of capital, Wilson asked several employer organizations, including the National Industrial Conference Board and the United States Chamber of Commerce, but not the more overtly antiunion NAM, to send representatives to the conference. Among the individuals Wilson selected to represent the "public" were former WIB chairman Bernard Baruch, John D. Rockefeller, Jr., and Elbert Gary of United States Steel.[99] At the outset, the delegates agreed that a majority within each of the three groups would have to approve any resolution before it could be adopted by the conference.[100] Group identities were thus recognized as crucial, with each group being given a veto over the conference's proceedings. The requirement of a majority vote within each group also stemmed from the fact that American employers were even less unified and less effectively organized on a national basis than their British counterparts. Still, the method of convening both the British and American industrial conferences of 1919 reflected a clear recognition of the principle of functional representation and the importance of group organization.

In contrast to the relative harmony of the conference that had taken place several months earlier in London, the delegates to the Washington conference proved unable even to reach agreement over general principles. Whereas British employers accepted the legitimacy of independent unions and therefore were able to move on to agreeing, at least in theory, with organized labor about the desirability of establishing joint meso- and macro-level institutions, the unwillingness of most American employers to deal with unions at the micro-level of the political economy meant that the American National Industrial Conference could make no progress on meso- or macro-level issues.

All three groups at the conference expressed support for the general principle of worker organization, with the public and labor groups jointly offering a resolution affirming "the right of wage earners to organize in trade and labor unions, to bargain collectively," and "to be represented by representatives of their own choosing."[101] John D. Rockefeller, Jr., defended this resolution with a general line of argument that had become quite familiar during the war:

> Representation is a principle which is fundamentally just and vital to the successful conduct of industry. This is the principle upon which the democratic government of our country is founded. On the battle fields of France this nation poured out its blood freely in order that democracy might be maintained at home and that its beneficent institutions might become available in other lands as well. Surely it is not consistent for us as Americans to demand democracy in government and practice autocracy in industry.[102]

The employer group, however, refused to accept an unqualified endorsement of collective bargaining. The employers argued that shop organization was preferable to the industry-wide scale of organization associated with trade unionism and that shop councils would be more effective in reestablishing the sense of intimacy between labor and management that had once characterized industry. The employers claimed that it would be counterproductive to have workers choose as their bargaining agents individuals who were not fellow employees and who, therefore, might actually be representing "outside influences" that threatened to undermine "harmonious relations" within the shop. In criticizing the employers' proposals, Samuel Gompers actually made specific reference to what he viewed as "the mistake" that was made in England with regard to the wartime development of "the shop steward method of organization." Of course, even in Britain, much of the established trade union leadership was also hostile to the shop stewards' movement.[103]

The hypocrisy of the employers' position was revealed by their eagerness to reap the benefits of industry-wide organization for themselves, as evidenced by the strong support in the business community for antitrust law revision. Ironically, the leaders of the American labor movement, who had before and even during the war concentrated largely on shop-floor and micro-level collective bargaining issues, had at least begun to recognize the importance of dealing with the problems of workers at the meso-level of the economy. Thus, the conservative craft-oriented leadership of the AFL had felt compelled to support the nationwide strike of steelworkers in 1919, and in a proposal resembling the British Whitley Councils plan, the AFL-dominated labor delegation called for each of the nation's industries to create a "national conference board" on which "the organized workers and associated employers" would be equally represented.[104]

Because the three delegations at the conference were unable to reach agreement on the fundamental issue of collective bargaining, the conference ended in deadlock. The collapse of the first National Industrial Conference led Woodrow Wilson to issue a call for another conference to be organized on a different basis. This time, Wilson invited seventeen individuals who theoretically represented the public, rather than any particular group, to seek agreement on a set of recommendations to improve labor-management relations in the United States. The two key figures in this second conference were William B. Wilson, then secretary of labor, and Herbert Hoover, also a former member of Woodrow Wilson's war administration. Other participants included two former attorneys general, Thomas Gregory and George Wickersham, and prominent businessmen Owen Young of General Electric and Julius Rosenwald of Sears Roebuck. Wilson chose not to include any unionists on the list of participants.

The second National Industrial Conference began its deliberations in December 1919 and issued its final report the following March. In addition to recommending the creation of the National Industrial Board and a system of regional adjustment conferences to assist in the voluntary arbitration of labor disputes, the report also came out strongly in favor of the principle of employee representation in the form of workshop organization. In contrast to the position taken by the employer group at the first National Industrial Conference, the participants in the second conference made clear their belief that the relation between unions and shop committees ought to be "a complementary, and not a mutually exclusive one." Any effort by employers to utilize employee representation as a means "to undermine the unions," they declared, would prove an obstacle to any hopes of creating "a lasting agency of industrial peace." The conference report also expressed approval for attempts to extend "the principles of employee representation beyond the individual plant" and described the "voluntary joint councils" already established in the clothing and printing industries as "fruitful experiments in industrial organization."[105]

The recommendations of the second conference had little impact. Congress basically ignored the conference's report, and many of the nation's leading employers began the twenties by embarking upon a campaign to guarantee the open shop throughout American industry. The Plumb Plan also won little support in Congress, which returned the railroads to private ownership through the Transportation (Esch-Cummins) Act of 1920. The law, which passed despite the objections of the railway unions, established the Railway Labor Board to assist in the settling of labor disputes in the industry, but this board was appointed by the president, rather than chosen by the railway unions and employer organizations. The board was empowered to render judgments about wages and working conditions, and even though such decisions did not have the force of law, they had the potential of undermining the position of the unions.[106] The advent of a sharp recession in 1921, moreover, undermined the entire position of organized labor in America. In retrospect, it is clear that in 1919 the union movement was about to enter a period of decline.

In Britain, too, expectations of a new era in industrial relations were soon dashed. In contrast to the United States, industry-wide collective bargaining (without state involvement) had become solidly established in many sectors of the British economy, but efforts to form Whitley Councils proved disappointing. Even in those industries that succeeded in organizing on a nationwide basis, few works-level councils were created. The NIC proposed by the industrial conference of 1919 never really got off the ground either, since neither the Lloyd George government nor most of the leading employer associations and individual unions in the country were prepared to give real power to such a body. Lloyd George also ignored the Sankey Commission's recommendations for nationalizing the coal mines. In the end, Lloyd George's government-sponsored conferences, committees, and commissions had served as delaying tactics to defuse labor militancy in the immediate postwar period. As in the United States, the onset of deflation and unemployment after the war also weakened the position of trade unions. Although British law and public policy would continue to provide a more hospitable environment for collective bargaining than did American law and public policy, in both countries the state by 1920 had become less sympathetic to the interests of organized labor than it had been during the war.

Labor's economic position in each country was ambiguous as the twenties began. Even if workers in both countries may not have benefited as much from the government's war mobilization as did many employers, there can be little question that at war's end workers in both countries were better off than they had been prior to the war and that unions were also stronger than they had been. Politically, the tripling of the British electorate resulting from the 1918 adoption of the Representation of the People Act greatly strengthened workers' power and helped make possible the rise of the Labour Party to a prominent position in British politics.[107] The British labor movement remained far more successful than its American counterpart in organizing workers, but in both nations union density in 1920 was higher than at any previous time in history, with 45 percent of British and 17 percent of American workers belonging to unions.[108] Although not all workers benefited equally from the economic impact of the war years, real wages for nonagricultural labor, as a whole, were higher in both countries in 1920 than ever before.[109] Each labor movement, though, suffered important defeats in conflicts with management in the immediate postwar period, so that by the beginning of the 1920s, labor's bargaining power was clearly beginning to erode.

Conclusion

What, then, was the First World War's legacy for industrial relations in the United States and Britain? Was all the rhetoric about "industrial democracy" and "industrial self-government" under the aegis of the state essentially meaningless? Certainly, the war left no permanent legacy of corporatist institutions, especially at the macro-level of the political economy. Even at the meso-level of the economy, aside from a number of relatively ineffectual Whitley Councils in Britain and the equally ineffective Railway Labor Board in the United States, no significant state-sponsored corporatist institutions with responsibility for either formulating or implementing government economic policies, in general, or industrial relations policies, in particular, survived into the twenties.

Yet, in both the United States and Britain, the industry-level and peak organizations of workers and employers were stronger in 1920 than they had been in 1914. Almost as many manufacturing trade associations were organized in the United States between 1910 and 1919 as had been organized previously in the country's entire history. In Britain, also, the rise of trade associations was so rapid during the war years as to prompt a special study by the Ministry of Reconstruction on the impact of these organizations.[110] The recently organized peak organizations for business also greatly expanded in both countries during the war. The number of organizational members (as opposed to individual or associate members) of the United States Chamber of Commerce approximately doubled between 1915 and 1919; total membership in Britain's FBI more than quadrupled between 1917 and 1920. In neither country, though, could a single peak organization force a common position on all employers. In the United States, the Chamber of Commerce, the NAM, and the National Industrial Conference Board each helped coordinate business opinion, but none exercised any control over its members. In Britain, the employer federations that had initially joined the FBI had withdrawn by 1920 to establish their own separate organization, the National Confederation of Employers' Organisations.[111] Although the peak organizations of workers did not wield great power in either country, they had gained greater institutional legitimacy and recognition because of their involvement in the war mobilization. Informal ties between the state and the functional organizations of workers and employers would continue beyond the war. Still, neither the American nor the British government was prepared to hand over to these organizations the power to formulate state policy or to rely on them as the principal means for carrying out policies determined by responsible government officials.

Yet it would be wrong to view the developments of the war years as only a temporary aberration in the evolution of industrial relations or to dismiss as inconsequential the widespread public appeal to corporatist ideals that developed on both sides of the Atlantic between 1914 and 1919. Ideology and institutions exist in dynamic tension. The experiences of both America and Britain during the war era further undermined the traditions of laissez-faire individualism that were already under attack before the war, creating a powerful alternative vision of a political economy organized on the basis of cooperation and some form of planning and functional integration. Thus, such diverse groups as the British supporters of guild socialism, the advocates of Whitley Councils, and the American businessmen who backed company unionism all rejected, though in different ways and for different reasons, the controlled conflict model that was at the heart of a pluralist conception of the political economy. The retreat from direct state involvement in the political economy on both sides of the Atlantic after the war reflected the continuing wariness Americans and Britons felt about the state's use of its coercive powers to restructure labor-management relations, but it did not mean that such an approach had completely lost its attraction for individuals from virtually all sectors of society.

Ironically, it was often the supporters of a more strictly pluralist conception of political economy who now called upon the state to play a more directly interventionist role in industrial relations. Particularly in the United States, where the disparity in power between organized labor and organized capital was clearly greater than in Britain, and where the concerns of consumers were politically influential, some people who might properly be described as pluralists concluded that the state might have to serve as a "third party" in negotiations between labor and management to safeguard the interests of the "public."[112] Proposals for compulsory arbitration or for tripartite boards with government representation were thus more common in America than in Britain, in spite of the fact that on most other issues, especially those involving social welfare, Americans were generally more antistatist than Britons.

It is also important to recognize that neither the context nor the effects of the state's postwar retreat from direct involvement in industrial relations were identical in the two nations. In Britain employers generally accepted the need to engage in collective bargaining with unions, which by 1920 represented nearly 50 percent of the workforce. Union strength would decline in the years ahead, but few union sympathizers believed that continuing direct state intervention was necessary to keep unions an integral part of the British political economy. In the United States, on the other hand, even with the tremendous growth of the war period, unions still represented only about one in five nonagricultural workers. Most employers were intent at war's end on reaffirming the open shop as the norm in American industrial relations, though some industry leaders saw the advantage of exploring new employer-sponsored forms of nonunion employee representation. The leaders of organized labor in America may have hoped that an end to the state's involvement in industrial relations would still allow for the continuing expansion of unions in a system of collective laissez-faire, but such hopes would prove to be unrealistic. When confronted with the crisis of the Great Depression, both the advocates of unionism and business proponents of industry cooperation would look back to the war experience for precedents for reviving a more interventionist role for the state in the economy.

CHAPTER THREE

The Twenties

The Retreat from Wartime Corporatist Experiments and the Quest for New Forms of Voluntary Organization

During the 1920s, no state-sponsored innovations in industrial relations occurred in either the United States or Britain to compare in importance with those that had taken place during World War I or that would soon take place in New Deal America. Yet it would be a mistake to assume that the postwar decade simply marked a return to the prewar status quo in labor-management relations on either side of the Atlantic. Corporatist-influenced ideas regarding functional integration, as well as other new approaches to collective organization, now had considerably greater currency than before the war. The war's legacy could be seen not only in public discussions but also in the actual practice of labor-management relations. Especially in the United States, the postwar decade served as an important bridge between the fledgling corporatism of World War I and the innovations in industrial relations policy associated with the New Deal. Although the American and British systems of industrial relations continued to differ in important ways, there were also significant parallels during the 1920s between developments taking place in the two nations.

One obvious parallel was the declining strength of organized labor. Union membership fell substantially in both countries following peaks attained in 1920. Collective bargaining remained more widespread in Britain than in the United States, but British unions suffered proportionately even greater losses during the 1920s, with membership dropping 42 percent in comparison to a 34 percent falloff for American unions. By the end of the 1920s, union density in both nations had fallen back almost to pre–World War I levels.[1]

The fall in union membership resulted from similar causes in America and Britain. Although the American and British governments both pulled back from their extensive wartime involvements in labor-management relations and economic planning, important state actions in both countries in the years after the war helped to create the less favorable climate for unions that persisted throughout the twenties.[2] Even before the inauguration of Warren Harding marked America's "return to normalcy" in 1921, the Wilson administration in 1919 and 1920 had demonstrated by its handling of the two National Industrial Conferences and the issue of restoring the railroads to private ownership that the war's end meant the government's abandonment of the pro-labor policies of the National War Labor Board and War Labor Policies Board. Similarly, in Britain, once Lloyd George had triumphed in the elections of December 1918, he began to take a less supportive attitude toward the role of organized labor. Before his coalition cabinet gave way to a Conservative government in 1922, he had helped to block nationalization of the coal mines and succeeded in diminishing the power of the Triple Alliance of mine, railroad, and transport workers. Thus, before conservative Republican and Tory governments returned to power, Democratic and Liberal administrations had already begun to undermine the power of organized labor in each country.

In responding to major labor crises later in the decade, Republican and Conservative governments acted in ways that further weakened each nation's labor movement. In the United States, federal government intervention in the railway shopmen's strike of 1922 in the form of a sweeping antiunion injunction was a significant factor in ending a period of militancy among American unions. In Britain, the Baldwin government's putting down of the General Strike of 1926 had a similar impact, although even after its crushing of the General Strike, the British state continued to maintain policies that were more favorable to unions. Thus, the Conservative-backed Trade Disputes Act of 1927 was designed primarily to undermine union financial support for the Labour Party, rather than to bring about changes in the collective bargaining regime that characterized much of British industry. The British state also remained more willing than the American state to recognize the collective bargaining rights of its own employees. In the United States in 1930 only 8 percent of government workers were unionized, which represented about 7 percent of all union members. In Britain, by contrast, over 50 percent of government employees were unionized, representing 12 percent of all unionists in the country. Although union members remained a very small percentage of all government employees in the United States, the public sector was one of the rare areas of union growth during the 1920s, with membership rising from 161,400 in 1920 to 264,100 in 1930. Public sector union membership in Britain during this period remained almost constant at approximately 590,000, which contrasted to the serious decline taking place in most other sectors of the economy.[3]

In addition to state action, other factors contributed significantly to the steep drop in union membership that occurred in both nations after 1920. The onset of serious postwar depressions caused unemployment to jump from 2 to 12 percent in the United States between 1919 and 1921 and from 2 to 15 percent in Britain during the same period. The collapse of the job market clearly undermined labor's bargaining position with employers and had lasting effects even after the job market improved.[4] Changes in the structure of the labor market also factored into the decline of unions. In both nations the proportion of jobs in sectors of the economy in which unions historically had the greatest strength fell during the 1920s. In the United States, employment in manufacturing, mining, and transportation dropped by 10 percent between 1920 and 1930, while rising over 30 percent in government and services, sectors that were largely unorganized. In Britain, the number of jobs in the distribution sector, which had little union presence, grew by over 15 percent, while the heavily organized coal mining industry saw a job loss of approximately 13 percent.[5] Moreover, in the United States a concerted effort by employers to roll back the gains of unions and to restore the open shop contributed to the decline of union membership.

No successful efforts occurred in this period in either the United States or Britain to revive the comprehensive wartime experiments in tripartite corporatism that had been quickly jettisoned in the transition to peace. Still, in neither country did the postwar decade witness a complete restoration of prewar patterns of thought and practice in the field of industrial relations. The war's continuing legacy could be seen in a variety of initiatives in both countries during the postwar decade to establish new forms of functional representation and new approaches to industrial relations that were not predicated on direct state involvement. Writing in 1920, Arthur Gleason expectantly claimed that "England is slowly building new organs of government . . . outside of Parliament" so that "the economic life of the nation will largely function through trade unions, industrial councils, and shop committees."[6] Similarly, just prior to the end of World War I, American Federation of Labor (AFL) leader Matthew Woll predicted that the postwar period in America would not see a return to prewar practices, but rather would be marked by a "prolonged struggle" between the principles of state control and "associational" control.[7] Neither the United States nor Britain were likely candidates for the kind of statist corporatism that would soon appear in Italy and Germany, but in both nations leading figures in government, business, and labor acknowledged the need for new forms of collective organization and more effective coordination between groups and across sectors of the economy, as well as the possibility that the state might be able to play at least an indirect role in encouraging such developments.

During the 1920s, Britain's corporate structure began more closely to resemble that of the United States, as mergers led to greater concentration in industry and larger firm size. Exactly comparable figures for the percentage of workers employed in plants with five hundred or more wage earners are not available, but there are data for the 1930s showing that approximately one-third of the total manufacturing labor force in each country worked in such plants, with the American percentage somewhat exceeding the British. In addition, the largest one hundred manufacturing firms in Britain, which before the war controlled a much smaller proportion of national output than did America's one hundred largest firms (16% compared to 22%), by 1930 had come to equal the relative share achieved by their American counterparts (26%). However, the typical American manufacturing plant remained more technologically advanced and less dependent on skilled labor. One indication of this important difference is that the horse-power-per-worker ratio in American manufacturing as a whole was double that of British industry.[8] Thus even with the growth in firm size and industrial concentration, British economists and businessmen continued to argue that further efforts at rationalizing industry were necessary to keep up with American and German competition.[9]

The continuation of a more labor-intensive form of manufacturing, together with the inheritance of the past, which included an underdeveloped tradition of managerial control of the shop floor and the widespread acceptance of the legitimacy of unions, created a context in which newly formed British corporate giants were more likely to work with organized labor than were large-scale American firms. There were, of course, important exceptions. In some mass-production industries such as automobiles, labor-management relations occurred in an environment that was largely union-free.[10] In addition, the continuing legacy of past practice meant that issues relating to industrial relations were still far more likely to be dealt with at the meso-level of the economy in Britain than in the United States, where the individual firm remained the primary locus for labor-management interactions.

Macro-level Initiatives

In neither country did macro-level institutions play an important role in the political economy, but there were at least some prominent business, labor, and government leaders who envisioned the possibility of achieving enhanced economic efficiency and more harmonious labor-management relations through macro-level initiatives involving the peak organizations of employers and workers. These organizations remained relatively weak in both Britain and the United States, but at least in Britain they grew in significance during the postwar decade. The collapse of the Triple Alliance of miners, railwaymen, and transport workers during the failed coal strike of 1921 convinced British unions to entrust greater authority to the recently created Trades Union Congress (TUC) General Council, which then played a crucial role in the General Strike of 1926. Similarly, although most British business firms looked to meso-level associations to bargain collectively with labor, the National Confederation of Employers' Organisations (NCEO), which split off from the Federation of British Industries (FBI) in 1920, emerged as the principal peak organization of employers addressing labor issues in this period. By the end of the twenties, the NCEO represented associations employing approximately 60 percent of all British workers.[11]

Ironically, Britain's failed General Strike of 1926 created the context for the most noteworthy initiative at macro-level employer-union cooperation of the postwar decade, the so-called Mond-Turner talks. The TUC General Council called the General Strike in support of coal miners' efforts to resist wage reductions and job losses resulting in part from the government's decision to end subsidies for the coal industry. The nine-day General Strike was an unprecedented instance of class conflict and clearly the most dramatic event of the decade affecting labor relations. Because the strike transformed an industrial dispute into what appeared to be a threat to the state itself, Baldwin's Conservative government took steps to ensure the strike would not succeed. Nevertheless, historians generally agree with Alan Fox's conclusion that "the most significant aspect of the episode was the way it revealed the continued predominance on both sides of those forces and traditions that were anxious to contain rather than bid up class conflict. From this point of view, it illustrates continuity rather than marking a turning-point."[12] Even after their victory in the General Strike, British coal operators made little effort to abandon collective bargaining with the miners' union and even put more stock in national and district agreements to undermine pit-level militancy.[13] The state's intervention to end the strike was clearly exceptional and in no way represented a repudiation of the collective bargaining model that remained basic to British industrial relations.

In 1927, at the very time that Stanley Baldwin was moving ahead with legislation to outlaw future general strikes and to limit union contributions to the Labour Party, his minister of labour, Sir Arthur Steel-Maitland, worked behind the scenes to encourage Sir William Weir of the NCEO and Ernest Bevin of the TUC to arrange for bilateral talks between the leaders of organized labor and industry to determine how unions and employers could cooperate to improve labor-management relations and raise wages through increases in productivity. Although the NCEO, as well as the FBI, initially declined to participate, Sir Alfred Mond, Conservative MP and head of Imperial Chemical Industries, organized a group of prominent business leaders (including Lord Weir) drawn from many of Britain's largest and most modern corporations to meet with TUC president Ben Turner and other union officials. A series of meetings occurred in 1928, leading to a joint interim report that took as its starting point a recognition of the value of trade unions, and which included resolutions opposing dismissals or punishments of workers for legitimate union activities, favoring the creation of a national industrial council, and supporting efforts to rationalize industry. The NCEO and FBI failed to endorse the report but the following year witnessed the first tentative meetings between all three peak organizations of labor and industry, at which the issues of rationalization and unemployment were considered.[14]

Although nothing concrete came out of these discussions involving the peak organizations of workers and employers, they are, nevertheless, significant for a number of reasons. First, it is hard to imagine that such talks could have occurred prior to the war, or even before the General Strike. Not only did union leaders such as Bevin and Walter Citrine now see a pressing need to reaffirm organized labor's legitimacy and willingness to act in a responsible manner, but so too did industry leaders such as Weir and Mond appreciate the desirability of restoring a sense of stability to industrial relations following the upheaval of 1926.

Second, the context in which the discussions took place was shaped by two economic factors that helped to make Britain a more likely setting than America for such an effort. The American economy was based on high levels of productivity and modern production techniques, while in the twenties concerns were often expressed that British industry was inefficient and had fallen behind its American and German competition. Consequently, calls for rationalization of industry and increased worker productivity had a greater sense of urgency. Mond, and at least some other supporters of rationalization, argued that the cooperation of already-well-established trade unions would be essential to modernize British industry, and in Bevin, Citrine, and other leaders of the TUC they found union officials who were willing to explore the possibility of union participation in such efforts.[15] Although pressures to rationalize production were less urgent and less widespread in the generally more efficient American economy, they did arise in certain "sick" industries, especially coal, textiles, and railways, and elicited a similar response from union leaders. While the leadership of the AFL in this period also tried to portray itself as a potential partner for management in further improving industry's efficiency, employers in the United States generally saw little need to engage America's weak unions in their efforts to achieve even more efficient methods of production, so that no macro-level initiatives comparable to the Mond-Turner talks occurred.[16]

Third, in contrast to the situation in the United States, British manufacturers generally exercised less influence over government economic policy than did the country's internationally minded financial interests and, therefore, had an incentive to look to organized labor as a political ally. Whereas union officials in the United States rarely concerned themselves with financial issues and government monetary policy, in Britain industrialists such as Mond found common cause with TUC leaders in challenging the restrictive monetary policy favored by the Treasury and City of London at the expense of British manufacturing. The Mond-Turner joint report thus included resolutions dealing with both rationalization (to be coupled with higher real wages) and the need for a flexible monetary policy.[17]

Fourth, none of the principals involved in these meetings envisioned the state becoming directly involved in new initiatives to improve labor-management relations.[18] In this sense, even in conception, the Mond-Turner talks did not represent a fully corporatist approach to organizing the British political economy. Yet these tentative discussions, which took place with at least the indirect encouragement of the state, advanced well beyond a strictly pluralist model of industrial relations by bringing together industry and labor leaders who sought to deal collaboratively with labor-management problems at the macro-level of the economy. Significantly, the talks produced a call for the permanent establishment of a national industrial council with representatives from the TUC, NCEO, and FBI, a proposal that harked back to legislation almost adopted by Parliament in 1924.[19]

The same year the Mond-Turner group was calling for such a permanent bipartite body, the Liberal Party was going on record as favoring the creation of a more explicitly corporatist tripartite council of industry, which would have included representatives of the public and which would have had the authority to grant legal sanction to decisions of industry-wide Whitley Councils.[20] The same Liberal Party document advocating a council of industry also echoed an earlier proposal by four prominent Conservatives to establish an "Economic General Staff . . . to advise and to assist the Government of the day in dealing with the complicated issues which arise in connection with industry."[21] Britons of virtually all political leanings remained leery of direct state involvement in the day-to-day conduct of industrial relations, but both Liberals and Conservatives cited Herbert Hoover's activities as secretary of commerce as a model for government efforts to encourage economic efficiency through the collection and dissemination of statistics.[22]

Finally, British firms may have been more likely than their American counterparts to see multiemployer collective bargaining as in their own interest, but most were still not willing to see their particular industry associations cede power over industrial relations to the NCEO or to any other macro-level organization. There was also opposition within the trade union movement to the centralization of authority, though the TUC in the late twenties was better able to speak for labor than the NCEO was for employers. The primary focus of labor-management interactions in Britain thus remained at the meso-level of the economy.[23]

In the United States, the peak organizations of workers and employers were no more powerful than in Britain, and they may well have become less influential as the decade progressed. Following the death of Samuel Gompers in 1924, the AFL's limited effectiveness as a central authority for organized labor all but disappeared when the weak William Green became president.[24] Although the National Association of Manufacturers (NAM) grew substantially in membership immediately after the war, largely as a result of its active role in trying to roll back the gains of organized labor, once the tide of union expansion had been reversed, membership in NAM fell—

by nearly 40 percent between 1921 and 1926. The Chamber of Commerce remained the most broadly representative organization for American business, developing a close relationship with Herbert Hoover's Commerce Department, but its main focus was not on issues relating to labor. The other major peak organization for employers, the National Industrial Conference Board, became primarily a research institution. In contrast to the situation in Britain, where the peak organizations of employers explicitly recognized the useful role of trade unions and saw the TUC as at least a potential partner, the leadership of NAM took a firm position in behalf of the open shop, or what it referred to as the "American Plan," and rejected the AFL as the legitimate voice of workers. The Chamber of Commerce took a less active role, but also went on record as favoring the open shop.[25]

Although no macro-level initiatives in the United States went as far as even the limited contacts between organized employers and organized labor that occurred in Britain during the 1920s, the leadership of the AFL, through the Portland Manifesto of 1923 and another resolution adopted by the AFL convention in 1925, expressed its interest in the establishment of an "industrial congress" or "industrial parliament" with representatives who could legitimately claim to "speak for all organic groupings" in the economy.[26] Samuel Gompers, like British Fabian socialist George Bernard Shaw, even looked with some favor on Italian fascism's early efforts at creating such a corporatist economy.[27] Gompers, Matthew Woll, and other AFL leaders who supported the creation of some form of national industrial council, however, shared the concerns of their British counterparts that the state not be directly involved either in compelling the peak organizations of workers and employers to participate or in using its power prematurely to "bring into being at a single stroke full-fledged industrial government," favoring, instead, such institutional development through natural "evolutionary" processes.[28] Nevertheless, the AFL resolution of 1925, which was drafted after consultation with Secretary of Commerce Herbert Hoover and received support from Ralph Easley of the National Civic Federation, called upon the cabinet secretary to use his good offices to summon a conference of leaders of industry, labor, and agriculture to lay the groundwork for future collaborative efforts.[29] In 1928 AFL official John Frey revived the idea of calling upon Hoover to bring together labor and management leaders to solve industry problems, though he envisioned such a conference taking place in private and without direct government participation.[30]

The AFL was not the only voice calling for the establishment of some form of permanent quasi-corporatist national industrial council in the 1920s. Immediately following the second National Industrial Conference of 1920, Republican senator William Kenyon introduced a bill that would have established a national labor board, with representatives of capital, labor, and the public to enforce a common code of labor relations throughout industry.[31] In 1928, following consultations with the leadership of the AFL, the American Bar Association formally backed federal legislation that would have created a national industrial council with representatives of employers' associations, organized labor, farmers' organizations, the bar, and the secretaries of commerce and labor, to engage in continuous study of the conditions in industry that were likely to cause strikes.[32] Neither of these legislative initiatives produced concrete results, but they are evidence of the continuing interest in new approaches to macro-level industrial relations that had been used during the war and that would once again, after the onset of the Great Depression, become the basis for New Deal policy initiatives.

Meso-level Initiatives

While the weakness of the peak organizations of workers and employers severely limited the possibility for implementing macro-level changes in industrial relations, in both the United States and Britain the meso-level of the economy seemed to be a more promising arena for corporatist-influenced experimentation. In both countries, some concrete steps were taken along these lines during the twenties. Herbert Hoover's efforts as secretary of commerce to promote an "associative state" built upon the development of voluntary industry-wide organizations has received a great deal of attention from historians.[33] Hoover was by no means unique in his conception of a new political economy based on "industrial self-government." Rather, his vision should be seen as reflecting a broad intellectual movement in the Anglo-American world that sought to find a middle ground between the statist corporatism then emerging in some nations in Europe and the antistatist conflict-based model of competition that characterized much of prewar American thinking about the political economy.

Organizational fragmentation, though, also posed a problem for effective industry-wide initiatives. Workers in both the United States and Britain were organized primarily by craft rather than by industry. In spite of the accession of William Green of the United Mine Workers (UMW) to the presidency of the AFL, the American labor movement remained firmly wedded to craft unionism. The TUC adopted resolutions indicating its support for the development of industrial unionism but did little to act on them.[34] Although power within the existing unions tended to shift in this period from the shop floor to full-time union officials, national unions often could not act authoritatively for all their members. Even in Britain, where national labor agreements had become common by the 1920s, the institutional basis for a comprehensive form of effective industrial self-government was not fully developed.[35] The number of national trade associations in the United States nearly tripled during the decade, but American industries continued to be dominated either by a handful of corporate giants or by such intense competition among very large numbers of producers that trade associations, lacking the ability to resort to state power, found it very difficult to enforce agreements.[36] On both sides of the Atlantic, most business, labor, and political leaders who favored meso-level experimentation remained reluctant to support the kind of direct state involvement that might have helped to overcome the existing obstacles to meaningful industry-wide collaboration between workers and employers.

Hoover viewed industrial self-government primarily as a means by which employers could cooperate with one another to eliminate cutthroat competition and rationalize production. In comparison to most British proponents of industry-wide organization, Hoover was less concerned with institutionalizing the role of national unions in the effort to improve efficiency and productivity. Nevertheless, he often sought union support for his efforts and found a favorable reception from the leaders of organized labor. The leadership of the AFL, like that of the TUC, reacted to the deteriorating bargaining position of workers in the 1920s by trying to moderate its earlier opposition to scientific management and by portraying unions as necessary partners in any industry efforts to improve efficiency.[37] The AFL Executive Committee, echoing the views of Hoover, on several occasions endorsed what it called "the self-determination of industry," by which it meant that organized workers, organized employers, as well as the technical experts in a particular industry, would collaborate to ensure order and efficiency while preserving a significant degree of autonomy.[38] The AFL leadership continued to oppose "the domination of industry by political bodies," but Matthew Woll proclaimed that organized labor "favors control by bodies truly representative of industry and it realizes that such bodies can be organized only under the supervision of government."[39] Some advocates of the institutionalization of industry-wide labor-management collaboration, such as industrial relations experts W. Jett Lauck and James Myers, acknowledged the need to have the state appoint representatives to these bodies to legitimize any actions they might take.[40]

An experiment in meso-level corporatism that applied across virtually all sectors of the American economy would have to await the coming of the New Deal, but in at least three troubled industries, serious efforts were made during the 1920s to involve organized labor and organized employers in collaborative schemes to establish labor peace and improve economic performance. In each case the industry was atypical, because unions had well-established positions before the decade began, and competitive pressures within the industry were so great that employers looked to state involvement or union assistance to help stabilize conditions.

Even before the war, progressive thinkers such as Felix Frankfurter had viewed the clothing industry as a potential model of industrial self-government. Sidney Hillman's industrial union, the Amalgamated Clothing Workers (ACW), had emerged as the main force for bringing stability and order to the industry through its ability to introduce industry-wide labor standards. The postwar depression at the beginning of the 1920s caused Frankfurter to advocate public involvement in an industry-wide council, so that the state would then be in a position to justify its enforcement of uniform standards on all employers.[41] Such direct state intervention did not occur, and the

ACW subsequently lost members during the 1920s as the industry continued to experience hard times. Even without state intervention Hillman was
able to work with industry employers to pioneer collectively bargained unemployment insurance and employment stabilization agreements.
Historian Steve Fraser sees Hillman's "new unionism" in this period, with its
acceptance of the principles of scientific management and industry-wide organization, as a "dress rehearsal for the New Deal."[42]

The American coal industry in the postwar decade, like its British counterpart, was plagued by intense price competition, overproduction, and a
loss of jobs. As in Britain, it included the nation's most important industrial union, John L. Lewis's United Mine Workers. As a result of these two
factors, the coal industry became the subject of a number of corporatist-
inspired initiatives in this period. Responding to a major coal strike in 1922,
Senator Kenyon, who had previously called for the establishment of a national industrial council, proposed legislation creating a tripartite labor
board to oversee labor-management relations in the industry and to guarantee the enforcement of an industrial code for workers that included the
right to organize and bargain collectively. Congress failed to act on
Kenyon's bill, but it did create a United States Coal Commission, composed
strictly of public representatives, to study the problems of the coal industry.
The commission rejected direct government intervention as a means of
solving the industry's problems and produced a platitudinous report that
had virtually no effect. The ineffectiveness of the commission, though, did
not mean an end to government encouragement of voluntary action by the
UMW and the coal operators to stabilize conditions in the industry.[43]

Hoover made the coal industry an important test case for his vision of an
associative state. A significant number of coal operators continued to look
to the UMW as the most likely means of bringing some order to the industry by removing wages from competition.[44] Lewis appeared to be a promising partner for management because he was willing to support efforts to increase productivity, even at the expense of jobs, if wage levels were
maintained.[45] The industry, however, was deeply divided between union
and nonunion employers, and a total collapse of the collective bargaining
regime and a major disruption in coal production appeared imminent in
late 1923. Hoover, as secretary of commerce, played a pivotal, though
largely behind-the-scenes, role in bringing the operators and the UMW together in 1924 to sign the Jacksonville Agreement. Initially hailed as a triumph of voluntary labor-management cooperation, the agreement soon became a dead letter as nonunion operators refused to accept its wage
standards and Hoover failed to intervene to put pressure on those firms that
were undercutting their competitors. The fate of the Jacksonville Agreement
thus foreshadowed problems that would become widespread throughout
the economy after 1929.[46]

Even before the collapse of the Jacksonville Agreement, Lewis had concluded that direct state intervention in the coal industry would probably be

necessary not only to protect miners' wages and to safeguard steady work but also to foster greater efficiency through the rationalization of production. He recognized that such an effort would require exempting the industry from the antitrust laws. Union weakness and the chaotic conditions in the coal industry had convinced Lewis that a corporatist, rather than a strictly voluntarist, approach was necessary to address labor's concerns.[47] By 1928, with the UMW's membership and influence rapidly diminishing, Lewis supported a new legislative initiative by Republican senator James Watson to establish a powerful federal coal commission that would regulate prices, wages, and profits and also would protect the right of miners to unionize. Introduced shortly before the presidential election and without the backing of either Calvin Coolidge or Herbert Hoover, Watson's proposal never made it through Congress, but the idea would soon be revived once Franklin Roosevelt became president.[48]

In the railway industry, some form of ongoing federal intervention in labor-management relations antedated the war. That intervention had been further institutionalized, albeit over organized labor's objections, with congressional passage of the Transportation Act of 1920. The act created a tripartite Railway Labor Board (RLB) with power to set wages and conditions of employment. Although W. Jett Lauck praised the RLB shortly after its creation for promulgating an industrial code that asserted the right of workers to organize and bargain collectively through representatives of their own choosing and condemned the use of labor spies by management, the so-called public members of the RLB soon proved hostile to labor's economic interests. RLB-approved cuts in wage rates subsequently led to the railway shopmen's strike of 1922, the largest and most significant instance of labor strife of the decade, involving 400,000 workers. In a throwback to the Pullman strike of the 1890s, the federal government then helped to crush the strike through the infamous Wilkerson injunction. The injunction was a far more drastic attack on the rights of unions than would be the British government's intervention in the General Strike of 1926, in that it prohibited not only peaceful picketing but also all efforts by the railway union leaders to encourage workers to strike.[49]

The failed strike of 1922 greatly undermined the power not only of the railway shopcrafts unions but also of organized labor as a whole. It also led to widespread dissatisfaction with the RLB and calls from union leaders and politicians of both parties for new legislation to create a more stable basis for labor-management relations on the nation's railways. This agitation ultimately led to the passage of the Railway Labor Act of 1926, the most important piece of federal labor legislation adopted during the 1920s. One of the law's principal authors, labor lawyer Donald Richberg, referred to the act as "fundamentally the most enlightened labor legislation ever enacted," because he saw it as an example of "employers and employees engaged in a deliberate effort to democratize industry—to try the process of 'self-government.'"[50]

Acting as the agent of the Railway Labor Executives Association, Richberg had initially drafted what came to be known as the Howell-Barkley Bill. The proposed legislation introduced in Congress in 1924 would have replaced the decision-making RLB with a bipartite labor-management board of mediation, required the establishment of national boards of adjustment to deal with disputes arising out of current contracts, and granted formal recognition to the existing operating and nonoperating unions. Such a proposal would have significantly undermined the railroads' efforts to develop company unions. To counter the appeal of such legislation, President Coolidge and Secretary Hoover worked both publicly and privately to encourage the carriers to sit down with representatives of the unions to draft a bill that would have industry-wide support and the blessing of the administration.

The Railway Labor Act that was finally passed in 1926 was a product of compromise between the unions and the carriers. It provided for a presidentially appointed national Board of Mediation, with representatives of the workers and employers but not the public, which had none of the unilateral decision-making powers of the RLB; a government-mandated cooling-off period in the event of a labor dispute threatening the national interest; and the establishment of boards of adjustment that could be system-wide rather than national in jurisdiction. The law also proclaimed the right of workers to organize and bargain collectively. While Richberg, for one, saw the law as a model to be emulated by labor and management in other sectors of the economy wishing to create "industrial republics" by joint agreement, few historians would now agree with his highly laudatory contemporary assessment of the law. Still there is substantial debate among historians about the law's significance and meaning.

Howell Harris has argued that the Railway Labor Act entailed a form of government intervention that was entirely alien to British labor law. Instead of attempting "to establish and protect an arena for collective action and voluntarist, adversarial labour relations free from judicial meddling," the American law caused unions to become "enmeshed in a complex and unsatisfactory *federal* procedure governing contract negotiation." Ruth O'Brien goes even further, claiming that the law established the ideological foundation for the New Deal's later institutionalization of a dominant federal role in the conduct of labor relations based on a theory of "responsible unionism" focusing on the rights of individual workers to representation rather than the rights of unions as collective organizations. O'Brien concludes that the circumstances of the law's adoption demonstrate the "Republican origins of New Deal labor policy."[51]

There is some merit to these claims. Both before and after the passage of the act, the American state tended to be more directly involved in labor-management relations than was the British state. In part, this was because there was stronger sentiment in America for "consumers" to have their interests protected in labor-management agreements. A government-mandated cooling-off period, as called for in the law, would have been almost inconceivable at this time in Britain, even in the wake of the General Strike. It is also true that the Railway Labor Act to a certain extent helped pave the way for later New Deal state intervention in industrial relations.

Yet it is important to recognize that in important ways the legislation represented a retreat from the level of direct state involvement that had characterized the Transportation Act of 1920. This was the major reason the railway unions supported the passage of the Railway Labor Act. The unions' highest priority was to dismantle the RLB, whose decisions, though nonbinding, had greatly hampered their efforts to resist wage cuts. The reliance on a new mediation agency and boards of adjustment without public representatives, in their view, meant a return to a more purely voluntary system of collective bargaining. To achieve the elimination of the RLB, the railway unions were willing to give up their demand that the law explicitly recognize the existing national unions as the legitimate representatives of the industry's operating and nonoperating workers and to drop their insistence on requiring national—as opposed to system—boards of adjustment to handle grievances.

There were also critical differences between the approach embodied in the Railway Labor Act and the substantially greater interventionism of later New Deal labor legislation. In stark contrast to subsequent New Deal labor policy, the law was permissive with regard to the development of company unions and established no clear guidelines as to how workers should choose their own representatives. Thus, rather than focusing on the extent to which the Railway Labor Act entailed a significant degree of state intervention in labor-management relations, it would be more accurate to view it as a rejection of a dominant role for the state. While rejecting a strictly corporatist approach to industrial relations, the law did reflect the appeal that a voluntaristic form of corporatism had for individuals like Richberg, who envisioned state action helping labor and capital achieve a more collaborative relationship.

In addition, because of its critical importance to the entire economy, the railway industry in both the United States and Britain remained a rather special case, subject to greater government oversight and regulation than any other industry. Thus Britain, too, through the Railways Act of 1921, provided for a level of state involvement that was exceptional. Unlike the American Railway Act, the British law did explicitly acknowledge the role of existing unions in the Whitley-like system of local and national committees it authorized. The British legislation, moreover, established a National Wages Board (NWB) that included consumer representatives, though one of these was actually designated by the TUC. The NWB was comparable in its powers to the RLB, but whereas the antiunion bias of the Republican-appointed members of the RLB had led to the disaster of the 1922 strike, the greater acceptance of unions in Britain meant that during the 1920s the public members of the NWB helped to preserve union gains against pressures by management to reverse them. In fact, the National Union of

Railwaymen had given up its demand for labor representatives on the boards of directors of the newly reorganized railway companies that emerged as a result of the 1921 law in exchange for the carriers' agreement to support the permanent continuation of the wartime-initiated NWB.[52] The apparent success of the NWB in helping to maintain labor peace for the railroads led the Liberal Party, later in the decade, to call for the creation of a similar body for the troubled coal industry.[53]

While there were no really practical efforts in the United States during the 1920s to institutionalize meso-level forms of labor-management cooperation beyond a few struggling industries, in Britain the joint industrial council scheme advanced by the Whitley Committee continued to hold out the possibility for a more far-ranging approach that might apply across the entire economy. However, after the initial surge in the formation of joint councils in many industries immediately following World War I, only one new body was established after 1921, and many of the councils that had been formed before that time subsequently ceased functioning. In many industries where national collective bargaining provided the basis for labor-management relations, neither the unions nor the employers saw any advantage in adopting the Whitley approach. In industries in which employers were disorganized and unions weak, there was inadequate support for trying to move toward a more centralized approach to industrial relations. Although the Whitley scheme had never been given legislative sanction, the Lloyd George government had at first effectively used its good offices to encourage the voluntary development of joint councils. Once the postwar labor crisis came to an end, though, active government support for the scheme, both under Lloyd George and then under the Conservatives, faded.[54]

Nevertheless, throughout the 1920s many supporters of the Whitley scheme sought to give greater effect to the approach through the direct use of state power. At one point, legislation that would have made the joint industrial councils more corporatist in form was nearly adopted by Parliament. Not long after the Whitley Councils had been initiated, an FBI committee observed in 1920 that "the success of these Councils must depend on the loyal acceptance of their decisions by both sides," noting that some councils "are already applying for legislation to give legal validity to their decisions." The FBI committee concluded: "It is obvious that the general adoption of this course would greatly increase the effectiveness of the scheme."[55] In the same year, a conference with representatives from forty-five existing joint industrial councils adopted a resolution calling for state enforcement of joint agreements.[56]

When the Labour Party formed its first, though short-lived, government in 1924, legislation was introduced by Liberal MP and former employer-member of the printing industry's joint industrial council Frank Murrell that would have allowed a Whitley Council to seek approval from the minister of labour for state enforcement of its decisions. The TUC had gone on record in 1922 opposing giving legal force to Whitley Council decisions, fearing that such power would turn into a form of "compulsory arbitration." A few radical Labour MPs spoke against the bill in the parliamentary debate, arguing that the proposal represented a means of trying to avoid the emergence of a socialist order. Nevertheless, the bill passed a second reading in the House of Commons with only sixteen dissenting votes and likely might have become law had the Labour government not fallen soon thereafter.[57]

The idea did not die in 1924. The TUC annual congress in 1926 adopted a resolution in favor of "giving to National Agreements voluntarily entered into and approved by Joint Industrial Councils" the same status as wage standards established by Trade Boards, "with the object of ensuring the observance of fair conditions of labour by all engaged in the industry whenever requested by the parties to the agreement." The General Council clarified the meaning of the resolution by restating its concern that no legal obligations be imposed on workers or their unions, but agreeing to help draft a bill that would pertain strictly to employers living up to agreements concerning wages and hours.[58] In its major policy statement of 1928, *Britain's Industrial Future*, the Liberal Party reiterated its support for giving Whitley Councils compulsory powers, while proclaiming that "we are already advancing towards a new industrial order" that "may be described as a system of industrial self-government under the regulation and encouragement of the State."[59] Leading Conservatives also praised the "new spirit of industrial solidarity, industry by industry" and called for transforming the existing system of joint industrial councils by providing them with "the formidable power" of making their decisions "implicit conditions of all civil contracts."[60] Advocates of rationalization of British industry such as Mond and Walter Meakin saw strengthened joint industrial councils as a particularly promising means of accomplishing their objective.[61]

Britain in the 1920s may have seemed a far more likely setting than America for the eventual implementation of a government-sanctioned and comprehensively applied form of meso-level corporatism. Ironically, for reasons discussed in the following chapter, in the decade to come it would be the United States—not Britain—that would engage in a full-blown experiment with such an approach.

Micro-level Developments

During the twenties, the micro-level of the individual firm remained the most important arena in America for new developments in labor-management relations. In fact, the growth of company unionism and welfare capitalism in the United States has probably received more attention from historians than any other trends affecting industrial relations in this period. Neither of these schemes was as prevalent in Britain, where employers had fewer managerial and financial resources to implement such programs, and where employers were more likely already to have well-established relations with independent unions. Although there were some parallels between developments in the field of personnel management in the United States and Britain, firm-specific approaches to industrial relations remained more significant in America. Whereas many British employers still exercised only limited control over the shop floor and continued to rely on unions to perform what in America might have been regarded as management tasks, American employers often adopted firm-specific industrial relations policies that were intended to strengthen their ability to control the shop floor and at the same time avoid either union or state interference with their managerial prerogatives. Moreover, while employers in many British industries had long engaged in multiemployer bargaining as a means of keeping wages out of competition, many American employers, especially in more technologically advanced industries, adopted what political scientist Peter Swenson refers to as a "segmentalist" approach to labor markets, offering high wages and welfare benefits as a means of attracting the most efficient workers.[62]

Employer hostility to unions in the United States was clearly a major factor in the growth of welfare capitalism and employee representation schemes during the 1920s; but it is impossible to understand the full meaning and significance of the growth of these developments in micro-level industrial relations if one dismisses them as nothing more than cynical union-busting tactics or as an essentially aberrant development in the history of American labor relations.[63] Recognizing the need to respond to some of the shortcomings in the conflict-based prewar system of labor relations and to the demands for some form of "industrial democracy" growing out of World War I if they wished to increase worker efficiency, and hence profits, employers sought to implement new measures to enhance employees' loyalty and identification with their companies. The new approaches to managing labor may well have contributed to the unprecedented increases in worker productivity that were especially noteworthy in the United States during the 1920s. During the decade output per worker-hour in manufacturing rose at a rate of 6.3 percent per year compared to annual rates of 0.8 percent, 1.6 percent, and 2.0 percent in the 1890s, 1900s, and 1910s, respectively. By 1929 labor productivity in American industry was more than twice the rate for Britain.[64]

Moreover, the development of welfare capitalism, though often assumed to have been halted by the onset of the Great Depression, had significant long-term consequences for the development of labor relations and the limited state provision of social welfare that now distinguishes the United States from Britain and most other industrial democracies. The welfare capitalist measures introduced in this period reinforced the tendency of American labor relations to be focused at the individual firm, rather than at the industry-wide level, as was the case in Britain. In addition, employers (as well as private insurance companies) in the 1920s developed various forms of group insurance and other welfare capitalist plans as a means of defusing the increasing calls for the state to become involved in the provision of such services. Even the later introduction of Social Security did not fundamentally alter the essentially private, company-based character of the American welfare system.[65]

Employer initiatives in the area of welfare capitalism and employee representation represented an alternative to state-sponsored corporatism, but they were influenced by many of the same concerns that motivated corporatist proposals for change in labor-management relations in this period. The question was not whether labor in some way ought to be organized and allowed some form of collective representation, but rather what form of labor organization would triumph in the emerging system of "self-government in industry" that business, union, and government leaders all sought to shape and define. Even as they sought to maintain or even enhance their control of the production process, American employers began to see the need to deal with their workers collectively and to allow them greater "voice" in determining certain aspects of their working conditions. Before the introduction of welfare capitalist measures, workers who became discontented with an employer often simply quit. Once welfare capitalist programs such as company pensions and insurance programs were introduced, an exit strategy became less attractive. Workers sought other means to give voice to their discontent. Company unions then came to play an important role in allowing workers to voice complaints about such issues as arbitrary foremen and unsafe working conditions, but in a way that was less threatening to employers than participation in strikes and independent unions.[66]

The development of company unionism in America thus reflected a more broadly based interest in workshop organization growing out of the First World War.[67] On both sides of the Atlantic by the end of the war, militant socialists favoring workers' control of industry, government officials seeking to maintain labor peace, and personnel management experts concerned with improving efficiency and productivity had all become promoters of shop committees or works councils. The various promoters of workshop organization may have had differing goals, but many of the proposals for such organization that were put forward during the 1920s had in common the assumption that it was necessary to create new mechanisms to foster a greater sense of common purpose among workers, as well as greater interaction between workers and managers.[68]

In stark contrast to the United States, where employers became the most powerful force for organizational innovation at the level of the individual firm or workshop, and where company unionism became a significant trend in the 1920s, in Britain the original impetus for workshop organization came from the radical, syndicalist-inspired, shop stewards' movement. Employer-dominated company unions never became a significant factor in Britain.[69] The militant shop stewards' movement lost momentum before the war ended, but the Whitley Committee gave official sanction to the general idea of workshop organization and called upon the government to encourage, but not to compel, the establishment of joint labor-management works councils as an essential means of achieving "industrial harmony and efficiency." The Whitley Committee envisioned such works councils as having to be fully integrated with the existing unions to be effective.[70] In practice, the British government's effort to encourage the establishment of Whitley Councils at the shop level proved to be both short-lived and disappointing. Nevertheless, the idea of workshop organization cutting across traditional lines of division in industry continued to have many supporters in Britain during the twenties.

A Conservative Party manifesto published in 1927 contended that works councils were of "immense value," because they provided "an essential basis" for the creation of a strong "fabric" of labor-management relations.[71] The Liberal Party's policy statement, *Britain's Industrial Future,* went even further in its advocacy of works councils, not only proclaiming that they were "the best way" of enabling labor and management to "take counsel together about their common interests," but even calling for legislation making the establishment of works councils compulsory in any concern employing more than fifty people.[72] Conservatives and Liberals continued to hope that joint works councils might ultimately contribute to the development of a system of industrial relations in which labor and capital, rather than fighting against each other, cooperated with each other to maximize efficiency.

The TUC also favored workshop organization, though not because it fully accepted the possibility of establishing a harmony of interests between labor and capital. In a resolution adopted in 1925, the TUC declared its belief that "strong well-organised shop committees" were "indispensable weapons in the struggle to force the capitalists to relinquish their grip on industry."[73] While British radicals sought to eliminate private capital's control of industry and therefore remained skeptical about the benefits of joint industrial councils, many socialists still envisioned the possibility that workshop organization could be used as a means of creating a new relationship between hand workers and brain workers. In their plan for the nationalization of the coal industry, the British miners' union called for the creation of pit committees consisting of both manual and technical workers.[74] Similarly, in their vision of a model socialist commonwealth, Sidney and Beatrice Webb argued that "Works Committees, Shop Committees, Pit Committees, or Office Committees" facilitating communication between foremen or works managers, on the one hand, and workers, on the other, would be an "essential" aspect of any nationalized industry.[75]

The growing importance of professionally trained managers and the increasing separation of ownership from managerial control were widely commented upon in both the United States and Britain, even before the publication in 1932 of Adolph Berle and Gardiner Means's pioneering study of the modern corporation highlighted the trend.[76] Although the process was much further advanced in the United States, British industry was beginning to mirror the American pattern in this regard by the late 1920s.[77]

Economist George Soule was but one of many progressives who echoed the views of those in the American business community who contended that the separation of ownership from control was opening up new possibilities of cooperation between labor and management. Not all spokespersons for labor in the United States and Britain agreed with Soule's assessment, but British union leader Ernest Bevin, following a visit to America, came away with a similar impression, expressing his admiration for the new managerial class: "I frankly confess in my job, the large-scale organisation of labour, I feel more akin with this type than I do with the so-called director."[78]

Personnel management, in particular, was developing as a new field at this time, with management professionals and academic experts in America taking the lead. Management specialists on both sides of the Atlantic argued that a new generation of professional managers might serve as an integrating link between labor and capital.[79] The role of the personnel manager, as Mary Parker Follett, a theorist influential in both America and Britain, conceived it, was not simply to adjust the conflicts arising from the different interests of labor and capital, but rather to serve as an instrument of "integration" in which a true "uniting of interests should take place."[80] Similarly, even though a large majority of American employers viewed personnel management as an alternative to unionism, in both America and Britain most leading management theorists who extolled the virtues of workshop institutions as a means of encouraging greater interaction between managers and workers also advocated a policy of cooperation with trade unions. As historian Sanford Jacoby has argued, personnel management and trade unionism had much in common as both sought to decrease labor turnover, limit the arbitrary power of foremen, and assure greater job security.[81]

Still, it is true that in contrast to Britain, where a wide range of groups actively supported the growth of workshop organization, in the United States antiunion employers clearly had the initiative in this field. Writing in the mid-1920s, W. Jett Lauck, former secretary to the National War Labor Board, observed that the American movement to establish shop committees and joint industrial councils actually had drawn heavily from the British experience, especially the government-sponsored program to create so-called Whitley Councils. However, as Lauck himself pointed out, America did not usually follow the British example of having the labor representatives serving on works councils be union members.[82] The leaders of the AFL thus remained hesitant to support the creation of shop committees or works councils, in part because they feared that to do so might give legitimacy to employer-controlled company unions, and in part because their rigid commitment to traditional craft-based organization made them less open to organizational innovation than their British counterparts, who successfully co-opted shop stewards into the existing union bureaucracy. As Clarence Hicks and other experts in personnel management pointed out at the time, employee representation schemes, therefore, often filled the void created by the existing trade unions' failure to organize workers outside of the recognized crafts.[83]

There were, however, a few highly publicized cases of union involvement in the implementation of joint industrial councils in the United States during the 1920s. Sidney Hillman's ACW union participated in such councils at both the shop and industry levels, but "the foremost union-management cooperative program of its day" was the Baltimore & Ohio Railroad Cooperative Plan, first proposed in 1919.[84] Management expert Otto Beyer and International Association of Machinists leader William H. Johnston developed the plan, which had clear parallels to Britain's Whitley Councils scheme. They hoped their idea might be applied to the entire railroad industry, which was then still under government control. The plan was predicated on the assumption that scientific management undertaken in cooperation with organized labor could result in greater efficiencies while also leading to a harmonizing of the interests of labor and capital that would be to the advantage of both. Not long after the contentious railway strike of 1922, Beyer and Johnston successfully convinced B & O president Daniel Willard (who had at one time been a union member himself and who had taken a conciliatory position toward the unions in the shopcrafts strike) to implement the plan on the B & O. The railway unions supported the plan, because it explicitly excluded all issues that were normally dealt with in collective bargaining from the purview of the joint councils and because it recognized the unions as "necessary, constructive . . . agencies." At its 1925 convention, the AFL formally endorsed the plan.[85]

A number of academic and management experts in the United States during the 1920s, including Lauck, Sam Lewisohn, James Myers, Ben Selekman, and Edward Filene, wrote books to help bring added attention to a number of other employee representation plans that in their view provided good models for a more collaborative approach to workshop organization precisely because they were not initiated as antiunion devices. The "progressive" plans of employee representation most often mentioned were those of the Filene Department Store, the Dutchess Bleacheries, the Mitten Transit Company, the Dennison Manufacturing Company, and the A. Nash Company.[86] Interestingly enough, Ramsay Muir, a member of the Liberal Party's Industrial Inquiry, found much to praise in some of these plans when he visited the United States in mid-decade, singling out the B & O and clothing industry schemes, and describing Sidney Hillman as "probably the most striking figure in the American Trade Union world." Muir, and a number of other people of influence in Britain, were particularly impressed with the extent to which American labor, in exchange for wages that were much higher than those enjoyed by workers in Britain, was willing to cooperate with management efforts to use scientific methods in order to increase efficiency and productivity.[87]

Still, workshop organization of any kind remained limited to a small minority of firms in the United States. There were only a few isolated examples of employee representation plans conducted with union cooperation, and employer-dominated company unions, though growing relative to independent unions, covered less than 2 million workers by the end of the 1920s.[88]

Conclusion

The American experience in this period underscores several key points. The most dynamic developments in American labor relations were taking place at the level of the firm. In contrast to Britain, American industrial relations continued to be conducted in a highly decentralized system that was a legacy of the high degree of concentration and intensive use of technology that had emerged by the turn of the century in many American industries. Decentralization also clearly went hand in hand with the hostility of American employers to unions. Welfare capitalism and employee representation plans thus reflected the desire of many of the nation's most influential employers to develop an alternative to union-based collective bargaining that would reinforce or strengthen their control of the shop floor but at the same time move beyond the conflict-ridden industrial relations regime of the prewar era. The employer vision of integrating workers into an all-encompassing corporate structure free of either union or state interference was certainly self-serving. It also had little in common with a strictly pluralist conception of industrial relations.

In the decade to come, the Great Depression would prove a major impetus in both the United States and Britain to a renewal of interest in state-sponsored corporatist initiatives that would encompass all three levels of industrial relations. Ironically, it would be the American state—not the British—that would actually experiment with a comprehensive system of meso-corporatism. The New Deal would also end up using state power to reshape micro-level industrial relations by banning employer-dominated company unions. Yet, as the following comparison with Britain will show, the legacy of America's early concentration of corporate power and of the employer initiatives of the 1920s would help to shape the form of New Deal state intervention and the environment in which post–New Deal industrial relations would occur.

CHAPTER FOUR

The Great Depression and the Failure
of New Initiatives at Corporatist Planning

The Great Depression of the 1930s posed a dramatic challenge to existing patterns of state-labor-management relations throughout the industrialized world. In both the United States and Britain, the economic crisis generated extensive debate about the possibility of utilizing state power to foster the development of meso- and macro-level corporatist institutions to restore order and stability to economic life.[1] Yet by the end of the Depression decade, the British system of industrial relations remained largely unchanged, and the British state had experimented with only piecemeal efforts to implement corporatist mechanisms of economic stabilization in a few selected industries. In contrast, the United States proved willing, at least temporarily, to implement a far more thoroughgoing experiment in corporatism—the National Industrial Recovery Act (NIRA)—and subsequently adopted permanent legislation in the form of the National Labor Relations Act (NLRA) that involved unprecedented state intervention in labor-management relations at the micro-level of the political economy. No legislative enactment in Britain in this period compared in scope or significance to either the NIRA or NLRA.

In the United States, for what turned out to be a relatively brief period of time, the weakness of labor (and of the state) made the prospect of a business-dominated system of conservative corporatism sufficiently enticing to win the support of crucial sectors of the business community. This chapter will examine various proposals made on both sides of the Atlantic during the Depression for macro- and meso-level economic planning and industrial cooperation. In both cases of American legislative innovation (the NIRA and NLRA), the greater weakness of organized labor in the United States contributed significantly to the American state's more interventionist approach. Although the weakness of American unions in the early 1930s does not by itself explain America's decision to try a comprehensive experiment in corporatism, the consensus in behalf of the NIRA that emerged in 1933 would not have been possible had organized labor in the United States been as strong as its British counterpart.

Most scholars of post–World War II corporatism tend to focus on the development of macro-corporatism and thus argue that the creation of liberal corporatist institutions depends on the preexistence of strong governments and strong peak organizations representing both labor and capital. Examining the origins of the NIRA from a comparative perspective, however, reveals that key sectors of the American business community proved willing to support government sponsorship of a meso-corporatist experiment precisely because organized labor's weakness meant that unions could be excluded from any formal role in the system of industrial self-government that was to be created.

The status of micro-level labor-management relations in both Britain and the United States before the coming of the Depression directly affected the fate of proposals for broader-based reform at the meso- and macro-levels of the economy during the 1930s. Conversely, the failure of the NIRA to create a permanent structure of meso- or macro-corporatism in the United States set the stage for the subsequent creation of a form of state-sponsored industrial pluralism in the United States that differed significantly from the system of collective laissez-faire that continued to characterize micro-level industrial relations throughout most of the British economy on the eve of World War II. While it is convenient to treat micro-level developments in a separate chapter, it is important to bear in mind that such developments both influenced and were affected by what transpired at broader levels of the political economy.

Early Responses to the Depression

In both the United States and Britain, the debate over using corporatist measures to respond to the Depression took place in similar ideological contexts characterized by widespread antipathy to the expansion of centralized state powers. Given the antistatist attitudes in both countries during the 1920s, it is hardly surprising that on the eve of the Depression neither the United States nor Britain had in place any permanent macro-level institutions involving the state, capital, and labor for the purpose of economic planning. The limited experiments of the First World War remained as memories without any institutional legacy. Fairly extensive industry-wide collective bargaining and isolated instances of state involvement in establishing minimum wages for a few "sweated industries" existed in Britain; but in the United States, except in the railway industry, the state played almost no direct role in industry-wide labor-management relations. Industry-wide collective bargaining remained a rarity, even though trade associations, which usually shunned dealings with organized labor, grew in importance during the twenties.

The economic and political contexts in which issues of industrial restructuring were discussed in the early years of the Depression were in several respects quite different in the two countries. The years 1929–1933 witnessed a sudden and shocking turnaround for the American economy. Certain sectors of the economy had not shared in the prosperity of the 1920s, but just prior to the Depression the unemployment rate in the United States stood at only 3 percent after six years of steady economic growth. The drastic decline in economic activity between 1929 and 1933 cut industrial production in half and left more than one-quarter of the labor force unemployed.[2] In Britain between 1929 and 1933, the effects of the worldwide depression were less dramatic, not only because Britain began to recover more quickly than the United States, but also because so much of Britain's economy had already suffered from a long-term decline that the British initially had less far to fall following the crash of 1929. Throughout the 1920s the rate of unemployment in Britain remained above 10 percent; and while it jumped significantly after 1929, unemployment never quite reached the same high levels experienced by the United States at the nadir of the Depression. At its lowest point in 1931–1932, industrial production in Britain did not fall below 85 percent of 1929 levels.[3]

On both sides of the Atlantic, organized labor had already experienced a decade of dramatic decline prior to the onset of the Great Depression. The percentage of nonagricultural workers belonging to unions had dropped by just over 40 percent in both Britain and America during the 1920s, a decline that was much more severe than the drop that occurred after 1929. Union density in Britain in 1929, however, remained significantly higher than in the United States (26% as compared to 11%). The onset of the Depression resulted in a further reduction of union membership in both nations between 1929 and 1933, though a substantial reduction in the overall size of the nonagricultural labor force in the United States produced a slight rise in the level of union density in this period.[4]

Coincidentally, new governments came to power in both America and Britain in the first half of 1929, but Ramsay MacDonald's minority Labour government, with its philosophical commitment to socialism, appeared to be poles apart ideologically from Herbert Hoover's Republican administration. Nevertheless, as the Depression worsened in 1930 and 1931, both the Republican administration in the United States and the Labour government in Britain found that the ambiguous concept of "self-government in industry" had broad appeal.

During the early stages of the Depression, the strongest support in America for the development of a state-sanctioned system of "industrial self-government" came from the business community, especially from such labor-intensive and highly competitive industries as cotton textiles, which had fared poorly in the 1920s and found it even more difficult to turn a profit after 1929.[5] In these demoralized industries, business leaders favored some version of corporatism as a means of achieving stability through cartel arrangements to limit production and maintain prices. The most visible business proponents of industrial self-government, former War Industries Board head Bernard Baruch, Henry Harriman of the United States Chamber of Commerce, and General Electric president Gerard Swope, contemplated the development of a meso-level system of economic planning and coordination that would be based on existing trade associations. In favoring the establishment of government-authorized cartels to control production and prices, Baruch, Harriman, and Swope argued that the government's role ought to be limited to ratifying agreements arrived at by deliberations among participating business firms.[6] At its annual meeting in 1931, the United States Chamber of Commerce adopted a resolution favoring legislation to empower the Federal Trade Commission "to receive, approve, and enforce under judicial review, agreements on the part of business men seeking to eliminate wasteful practices and trade abuses in the course of their competitive relations, provided such agreements do not tend unreasonably to restrain trade or to create monopoly."[7] As one business supporter of the Swope Plan put it, the plan offered a method of "group control" that under the circumstances of 1931 provided industry's "only alternative" to an externally imposed form of "governmental control" or "State Socialism."[8]

Not only did these business plans for industrial self-government envision little active direction or involvement by the state, but they were also predicated on the assumption that organized labor would play no role in the industry-wide organizations that were to be granted cartelistic authority. Given Americans' traditional antistatism and the weakness of organized labor, which in 1931 enrolled fewer than one out of ten potential union members, business calls for a business-dominated system of industry-wide organizations did not seem politically unrealistic.[9] Swope's widely publicized proposal did go well beyond those of Baruch and Harriman in addressing some issues of concern to workers. It required participating firms to take part in industry-wide life, disability, old age, and unemployment insurance, and workmen's compensation programs that would be supervised by a "General Board of Administration" with equal representation from employers, employees, and the government. Swope was himself sympathetic to industrial unionism as a complement to the development of stronger trade associations.[10] Business support for government action to authorize cartel arrangements, however, came largely from industries that were hostile to unions and that would have resisted creating a tripartite corporatist system in which organized labor would have been equally represented with organized capital.[11]

In Wisconsin, Governor Philip LaFollette unsuccessfully offered a plan to guarantee adequate representation of nonbusiness interests in a state-sanctioned scheme of industrial self-government. He proposed state legislation to authorize groups of employers in the same industry "to associate themselves in a board of trade for the purpose of stabilizing employment," if every such organization established "a public policy committee" consisting of representatives of consumer and employee interests. This public policy committee, as well as the governor and each house of the state legislature, would retain veto power over the operations of an industry's system of self-government. LaFollette's proposal failed to win legislative approval before he was defeated for reelection in 1932.[12]

For most American unions, whose already-weak position was being further eroded by the Depression, meso-corporatist schemes of interfirm cooperation were less of a priority than more direct measures to prevent additional losses in union membership and bargaining power. Still, in the fall of 1931, the American Federation of Labor (AFL) voiced interest in the Swope Plan, while urging President Hoover to convene a national economic conference to consider both Swope's proposal and other plans for industrial reorganization.[13] Union leaders such as M. H. Hedges and leftists sympathetic to labor's interests such as Norman Thomas naturally were skeptical about the prospect of industrial self-government dominated solely by business interests.[14] Donald Richberg, legal counsel for the Railway Labor Executives' Association, reflected a widespread feeling in labor circles when he advised RLEA chair D. B. Robertson that he thought the Depression necessitated some form of voluntary economic planning, but he warned that a certain degree of government oversight or involvement would be necessary to guard against the improper exercise of monopoly power and to ensure adequate representation for workers in the planning process.[15]

In general, whereas industrialists tended to view the Depression as a problem of surplus production and destructive competition requiring sectoral cooperation among firms to limit supply and maintain prices, labor leaders saw the Depression as a problem of underconsumption resulting from inadequate earnings that could be solved if stronger unions were able to guarantee uniformly high wages. Representatives of organized labor, therefore, argued that legislation to remove impediments to effective unionism would be necessary to achieve authentic industrial self-government and to restore prosperity. Focusing primarily on the micro-level of industrial relations, the AFL made a ban on labor injunctions its highest legislative priority.[16]

While American labor put forth no comprehensive plans for meso-level industrial self-government comparable in scope and public notice to the Harriman and Swope plans, in one industry, bituminous coal, John L. Lewis and the United Mine Workers (UMW) took the lead in pressing for a government-sanctioned scheme of rationalization. Lewis was unusual among union leaders in that he had long before accepted the necessity of reducing excess capacity (and hence jobs) in the depressed coal industry in order to make possible the maintenance of union standards. The UMW-sponsored Davis-Kelley Bill sought to end cutthroat competition, including the low-wage policies of nonunion operators in the South, by offering mine owners government-sanctioned selling pools in exchange for a guarantee of industry-wide collective bargaining. The bill called for a direct role for the federal government through the creation of a presidentially appointed nonpartisan commission to oversee the plan's implementation. In spite of the legislation's potentially beneficial impact on profits, most operators strongly opposed the UMW's version of corporatism, fearing that it would create "unionization by fiat" and an "undesirable extension of government activity in the field of private enterprise."[17]

The coal industry was unique, not only because the UMW was one of the few important American unions organized along industrial lines, but also because it was the only major American industry in which the union was more effective than employers in speaking for the industry as a whole. W. Jett Lauck, former secretary to the National War Labor Board and later a close adviser to John L. Lewis, urged Lewis to support not only an industry-specific plan for reorganizing the coal industry but also a more comprehensive proposal to establish tripartite boards composed of employer, labor, and public representatives for all industries. Lewis rejected Lauck's advice, arguing that "it is debatable that I could undertake, with propriety, to act as a spokesman for industries other than coal."[18] Although some craft unionists supported industry-wide schemes of planning and cooperation, it is not surprising that the strongest advocates of such an approach in the labor movement were the leaders of the nation's most important industrial union. Sidney Hillman's Amalgamated Clothing Workers union played an analogous role in the garment industry, but on a regional, rather than nationwide, basis.[19]

Public pressure thus mounted in the early years of the Depression for some form of federal legislation to enable specific industries, such as coal, or industry in general to explore corporatist solutions to the nation's growing economic problems. Most of the proposals for legislation being discussed in 1930 and 1931 were still based on the belief that government intervention should be limited to using state power to support industry's own efforts to restore economic stability. Hoover remained committed to a narrow conception of industrial self-government that permitted the state to encourage greater cooperation in the private sector, but which rejected any direct use of the federal government's authority to mandate or sanction such cooperation. While Hoover was president, Congress failed to pass legislation giving direct government sanction to any scheme of industry-wide planning.[20]

In Britain, as in the United States, the first years of the Depression witnessed growing support across party and class lines for various schemes of industrial self-government. The economic problems that many Britons believed could be addressed by corporatist reforms resembled those plaguing the United States, but they were not identical. Even before the onset of the Depression in 1929, many British businessmen and economic commentators had voiced deep concerns about British industry's inefficiency and lack of productivity in comparison to its American and German competition. Thus, calls for rationalization of industry to eliminate long-term excess capacity and technologically obsolete plants were much more widespread in Britain both before and after the start of the Depression. As a result, whereas most American corporatists envisioned industrial self-government as a means of limiting production and controlling cutthroat competition in prices and labor standards without permanently eliminating plant capacity or forcing mergers, British corporatists usually viewed such proposals as a means of rationalizing production through amalgamations, the elimination of redundant plants, and the encouragement of technological innovation.

Lloyd George's wartime government had earlier encouraged the development of joint industrial councils on a purely voluntary basis, but by 1930 most observers agreed that the so-called Whitley Councils had achieved little.[21] A number of public figures thus concluded that a more direct use of government authority was necessary. Whereas in the United States the most outspoken advocates of government action to foster the development of meso-corporatist institutions came from certain sectors of business, in Britain state actors took the lead in supporting such proposals, because they doubted industry's capacity to rationalize and modernize production on its own initiative.

Liberal MP Geoffrey Mander claimed that the Whitley Councils had proved disappointing in part because they lacked enforcement powers, and he once again introduced a bill in Parliament to enable joint councils to obtain legal sanction for their agreements.[22] Voices for change in the other two major parties offered more comprehensive proposals for industry-wide planning in 1931. Conservative MP Eustace Percy published a proposal for industrial self-government; while fellow Tory Harold Macmillan argued that tariff protection could be used to foster industrial reorganization and rationalization if it were granted on an industry-by-industry basis on the condition that each industry create a representative body "with full representation of labor as well as management" to develop plans to restore economic stability.[23] Oswald Mosley, then a junior member of the Labour government and soon to become the leader of British fascism, offered a similar proposal for "commodity boards" with trade union, consumer, and producer representatives.[24] Journalist Max Nicholson's call for "A National Plan for Great Britain" also attracted considerable attention with its advocacy of "extensive devolution" of state authority onto a newly constructed system of "flexible self-government for industry." Nicholson's plea helped inspire the organization of a private research society called Political and Economic Planning (PEP) that became a leading advocate of industrial self-government.[25]

The Labour government, however, remained as reluctant as the Hoover administration to seek a legislative mandate to compel industry to experiment with any form of corporatism. When Mander pressed the government to seek ways of encouraging or compelling employers to develop profit-sharing or copartnership schemes, Minister of Labour Margaret Bondfield voiced the government's view that such schemes "can only be put into successful operation as the result of voluntary action by the parties directly concerned."[26] Similarly, in response to Mander's later query as to why the government had not expanded the system of Trade Boards whereby tripartite bodies were empowered to set minimum wages in low-wage industries lacking effective union organization (affecting approximately 1.25 million workers in 1930), a Labour government spokesperson argued that no action could be taken until appropriate "representations" were made by "responsible people" from the industries in question.[27] Such views were consistent with the Labour government's earlier rejection of legislation to compel employers to recognize unions, as well as with the position of the leadership of the Trades Union Congress (TUC), which was quite hesitant to support any form of state intervention that might detract from the centrality of collective bargaining.[28] In spite of their commitment to a socialist future for Britain, Labour's leaders continued, in the existing capitalist world, to uphold an essentially voluntarist conception of industrial relations.

Although no general enabling legislation was adopted while Labour was in power between 1929 and 1931, Parliament did pass one bill, the Coal Mines Act of 1930, that applied the notion of industrial self-government to Britain's ailing coal industry. Britain's coal industry confronted many of the same problems as America's. Overproduction, which began well before 1929, not only made many mines unprofitable, but also caused drastic reductions in the labor force, as a whole, and in union membership, in particular. Like its American counterpart, the Miners' Federation of Great Britain (MFGB) nevertheless remained the most powerful industrial union in the country.[29]

The MFGB was less willing than Lewis's UMW to accept the necessity of a reduced labor force, but it sought legislation mandating a seven-hour day throughout the industry and national wage agreements backed up by a national wage board. The miners' support for legislation to create national standards was due largely to their inability, in spite of their industrial form of organization, to establish such standards by collective bargaining. In most other British industries, though workers were not organized along industrial lines, collective bargaining took place between national employers' associations and the various national craft unions. For unions involved in this system, state intervention to establish maximum hours or other conditions of labor seemed unnecessary or even counterproductive. British employers outside the coal industry had come to favor national collective bargaining with a multitude of craft unions, because it undercut the grassroots power of workers on the shop floor, reinforced existing divisions within the working class, and took wages out of competition as a factor in production. Moreover, so long as overall unemployment remained high, the system clearly favored employers. The British coal industry was unusual in that the mine owners had resisted national collective bargaining and had, instead, established district-level bargaining as the industry's norm.[30]

The mine operators were unsympathetic to legislative remedies for their problems and opposed any reduction in hours or government mandate to establish wages on a national basis. They were, however, willing to consider a national levy to subsidize exports and a national quota system to reduce overproduction. Liberals favored government-sponsored compulsory amalgamations as the only means of rationalizing the industry.[31] The compromise legislation finally adopted established a seven-and-a-half-hour day; a relatively weak National Industrial Board, headed by a representative of the government, to protect wages; and government sanction for national and district production and marketing schemes voluntarily arrived at by the operators themselves.[32]

As was the case in the United States, there remained widespread opposition to any government intervention in the economy that compelled private industry to accept externally imposed state directives. Winston Churchill attacked the Labour government's proposal as "a most repulsive specimen of Syndicalism whereby the Government, under duress, joins forces with a powerful capitalist interest, and with a still more powerful vote interest, in the hope of fortifying their own political strength and with the callous intention of pillaging the wealth of the nation."[33] Ironically, the small minority of Liberals were the most insistent on a more direct role for the state in rationalizing production. But, as one contemporary observer concluded, the Coal Mines Act of 1930, by avoiding any direct government "voice either in the control of output or in the fixing of prices," was based on the assumption that "the industry should enjoy the sole authority and assume the whole responsibility in operating this machinery."[34]

Historian Barry Supple argues that the forces leading toward government stabilization of the depressed coal industry were quite similar in both Britain and the United States, and that ultimately industry-specific legislation derived primarily from the "*political* need to stabilize the economic condition of working miners," rather than from pressure from the coal operators for government to impose a solution to the problem of excessive competition.[35] Why, though, did Britain pass legislation specifically targeted at the coal industry as early as 1930 (before the Depression in Britain had reached its nadir), while in the United States legislation affecting the coal industry was initially subsumed under the comprehensive NIRA? Only after the NIRA was ruled unconstitutional did industry-specific legislation, the Guffey-Snyder Coal Act of 1935, pass Congress.

Certainly, political contingencies and state capacities played a role. MacDonald's Labour government was far more beholden to the MFGB than Hoover's administration was to the UMW (even though Lewis was a Hoover supporter). Prior to the 1929 election, the Labour Party leadership had promised the MFGB that once in power it would push for legislation limiting hours.[36] Civil servants in Britain were also more influential and more supportive of state action in this particular area than were their American counterparts.[37]

The existing state of industrial relations in the two industries was also a critical factor. Although there had been a long history of collective bargaining in the American coal industry before the Depression, by 1932 nonunion operators had come to dominate the industry. They forcefully resisted government intervention that would have required them to deal with the UMW. Since the UMW was the most powerful voice calling for government action to stabilize the coal industry and thus was unlikely to have been excluded in the operation of any state-sponsored corporatist scheme for the industry, most American coal operators opposed state action that would have applied to their sector of the economy. Only after the National Recovery Administration (NRA) was established as a comprehensive scheme of industrial reorganization, over the objections of the majority of mine owners, and the balance of power had been altered in the coal industry, with both the UMW and the unionized operators in the Central Competitive Field greatly strengthened, would it become possible for industry-specific legislation to get through Congress.[38]

In Britain, the MFGB's concentration on using state power to reduce the miners' hours of work set the stage for passage of industry-specific legislation, but the union's failure to involve itself actively in the campaign to cartelize the coal industry meant that the government could propose and subsequently enact legislation excluding the MFGB from playing any role in the state-sponsored marketing arrangements that were established. The MFGB was more powerful politically than the UMW. Although union density in Britain's coal industry fell substantially after reaching a peak of 77 percent in 1921, union membership at no time during the Depression went below 50 percent. By contrast, union density in the American mining, quarrying, and oil industries, which stood at 36 percent in 1920, fell to 23 percent in 1930.[39] Nevertheless, the MFGB's inability to achieve national collective bargaining on its own initiative had helped to cause the union to narrow its focus in such a way as to make a weak form of government-sponsored corporatism less objectionable to British coal operators than it might otherwise have been. British mine owners did not provide the main impetus for the Coal Mines Act of 1930. However, unlike most American operators who resisted state intervention because it might further legitimize unions, British operators who had already accepted unions had less reason to fear that legislation affecting their industry would spur additional unionization.

The debate in both the United States and Britain over the future of the coal industry demonstrated that for union leaders during the Depression the bottom line in any plan for restructuring industry was the guarantee of higher wages and shorter hours.[40] Lewis may have been more aware than the leaders of the MFGB of the need to support state controls over production and marketing to help the owners of the mines earn the profits out of which higher wages might be paid, but in seeking to use government power to guarantee nationwide collective bargaining, the miners in both countries envisioned a state-sponsored system of industrial self-government based on meso-level negotiations between organized labor and organized capital that would still be compatible with a voluntaristic conception of industrial relations. For both American and British coal operators, on the other hand, self-government in industry was appealing only insofar as it meant using state power to create a cartel to limit production and maintain prices. Meso-level industrial self-government had widespread appeal, but it had a different meaning for different groups.

Proposals for New Macro-level Initiatives

Most proposals for industrial self-government in the United States and Britain during the first years of the Depression were grounded in the assumption that planning would take place on an industry-by-industry basis. By 1931 an increasing concern with the need to achieve coordination between various parts of the economy led influential figures in both countries to call for some form of national industrial congress or economic council to deal with macro-level problems.[41] Although no significant macro-corporatist institutions were ultimately established prior to the outbreak of World War II, a review of the proposals that were made reveals how seriously traditional ideas about the organization of the political economy were being challenged. Moreover, a comparison of the macro-level plans that were advanced in the United States and Britain also highlights certain key differences in the status of organized labor in the two countries—differences that would profoundly affect the institutional innovations that were actually adopted in this period in the United States.

Two distinct conceptions existed of how a national planning or coordinating body ought to be organized and what functions it ought to serve. Susan Howson and Donald Winch have used the terms *representative* and *technocratic* to describe these two contending views.[42] The representative conception reflected a corporatist desire to create a functionally organized body whose membership would be selected by the nation's employers' associations and trade unions. The technocratic version favored the establishment of a small panel of nonpartisan experts to aid the development of rational economic planning.

The distinction between representative and technocratic conceptions of a national economic council is useful, but each of these categories can be further differentiated into statist and nonstatist varieties. Representative councils could exist either outside or within the structure of government, though nonstatist versions of this scheme were more common. Since a representative congress would retain an organizational base of support outside of the state, it could be as much a reflection of the state's dependence on organizations in the private sector as a vehicle for the state to co-opt private associations for its own purposes. Most proposals for a technocratic economic council had a clearly statist dimension in that they addressed the problem of limited state capacities for economic planning not by devolving state power onto existing private-sector organizations, but rather by enhancing the state's own independent expertise. An alternative nonstatist technocratic model was also possible, so long as the body of experts assembled under private auspices and remained formally outside the government.

In both countries, business supporters of either form of macro-level planning body tended to favor reliance on nonstatist approaches; support for either representative or technocratic mechanisms with a statist dimension was more likely to come from intellectuals, labor leaders, or government officials.

In Britain, the idea of a standing national economic council composed of representatives of the country's employers' associations and trade unions was discussed before World War I, but it gained particular prominence at the National Industrial Conference of 1919.[43] The Mond-Turner talks in the late 1920s produced another call for the creation of a permanent national industrial council composed of representatives of the TUC, the Federation of British Industries (FBI), and the National Confederation of Employers' Organizations (NCEO).[44]

Such proposals did not necessarily require state action. The Mond-Turner conference recommendation envisioned the TUC, the FBI, and the NCEO establishing a permanent council on their own initiative. During the Labour government between 1929 and 1931, several meetings between representatives from these three organizations took place, though they produced no significant results.[45] Shortly after becoming prime minister, Ramsay MacDonald responded to an inquiry about the government's willingness to take action to set up a national industrial council by arguing that he thought government action was not then appropriate, since those involved in the Mond-Turner talks were still seeking to establish a national industrial council "by direct negotiation." Minister of Labour Margaret Bondfield offered a similar response when Mander again raised the issue the following May. Ultimately, the NCEO proved unwilling to follow through on the idea.[46]

Although militant segments of the British labor movement opposed efforts to establish a formal macro-level collaborative relationship with employers, the most influential voices in the TUC, especially Ernest Bevin and Walter Citrine, saw such efforts as a useful means of continuing to restore labor's legitimacy in the wake of the abortive 1926 General Strike and of giving labor an opportunity to influence government monetary, fiscal, and trade policy.[47] The Mond-Turner talks were relatively harmonious, because the TUC leadership and the employers involved, who came principally from Britain's largest and most efficient and capital-intensive firms, agreed not only on the importance of union participation in efforts to rationalize production but also on the need for the Treasury and Bank of England to pursue monetary policies that would give greater priority to the interests of British industry than to the financial interests of the City of London. The attempts by the TUC, FBI, and NCEO to reach agreement, independent of the state, on the creation of a permanent national industrial council subsequently failed because of divisions and territorial jealousies between the two peak organizations representing capital, and because the dominant companies in the FBI and the NCEO were less willing to depart from monetary and fiscal orthodoxy than the aggressively expansionist industrialists represented in the Mond group.[48]

Many British supporters of the idea of a representative congress favored its having a more direct and formalized relationship with the state and favored legislation creating an industrial parliament with governmental standing. Economists John A. Hobson and Walter Layton, as well as TUC head Citrine, pushed the new Labour government to establish a representative council that might be entrusted with authority to determine whether government sanction ought to be given to specific joint industrial council agreements, and to encourage reorganization plans for particular industries.[49]

Although MacDonald initially showed interest in the idea of a large representative council exercising some executive functions, he ultimately decided in favor of creating a body that was more "technocratic" in conception. In February 1930 he established the Economic Advisory Council (EAC) under his own chairmanship, consisting of several cabinet members and fifteen experts "with special knowledge and experience of industry and economics" drawn from the ranks of organized labor, business, and academe. MacDonald's nominations to the EAC showed some deference to a "representative" conception of a national economic congress, but the new body was essentially "technocratic" in nature and was limited to an advisory capacity in which it spoke only for itself in private consultations with the Cabinet, rather than as a public deliberative body representing the organized interests of the entire country. The EAC provided a means by which economists with views differing from Treasury orthodoxy could have direct access to leaders of the government. The establishment of the new body thus constituted a small step toward enhancing the state's own economic expertise and capacity for action, but the EAC's problematic relation to the cabinet and the minimal resources at its command greatly limited the new body's effectiveness.[50]

In response to MacDonald's decision to establish a timidly conceived EAC, Winston Churchill proposed the creation of an "Economic Parliament . . . composed of persons of high technical and business qualifications" to make recommendations directly to the House of Commons.[51] Oswald Mosley soon called for a national planning council far more powerful than either the EAC or Churchill's Economic Parliament.[52] Conservative MP Eustace Percy observed that organized interest groups already exercised great influence on government through various forms of interaction with individual ministries, but he noted that as matters currently stood, the House of Commons had come to dislike and distrust the "growing tendency of Ministers to present it with foregone conclusions and almost accomplished facts" resulting from such behind-the-scenes contacts. He, too, advocated the creation of "a new deliberative body, representing local administration, commercial and industrial associations, agriculture and trade unions" with "the statutory right and duty" to report in an advisory capacity to Parliament.[53]

In the United States proposals for some form of national economic council went back at least as far as the Council of National Defense (CND) during World War I. The War Industries Board that grew out of the CND established a precedent that would later exert significant influence in the

Depression.[54] The National Industrial Conferences convened by Wilson in 1919, which closely paralleled in organization and purpose the British conference held earlier in the year, also recognized the principle of functional representation at the macro-level of the political economy.[55] Even before the Depression, the AFL had exploratory discussions with a committee of the American Bar Association (ABA) concerning a proposal for legislation authorizing the president to appoint a national industrial council with representatives of the AFL, Chamber of Commerce, ABA, and other peak organizations.[56] Hoover himself, both as secretary of commerce in 1921 and as president in 1929, was instrumental in summoning national conferences to which representatives of business, labor, and finance were invited to address the problem of unemployment.[57]

Nevertheless, *Nation's Business,* the organ of the United States Chamber of Commerce, found even MacDonald's cautious initiative creating the EAC a potentially dangerous step "toward further government control." The editors advised that if a permanent council were created in the United States, it ought to "be one brought together by business and inspired by business."[58] Business spokespersons were not alone in favoring an approach that would be free of direct government involvement. Matthew Woll, a member of the AFL Executive Council and acting president of the National Civic Federation (NCF), also favored a voluntaristic approach to the problem of macro-level organization. When he suggested in June 1931 that the NCF "summon a great American congress of industry," he proposed that it "be composed of representatives of all forms and characters of industrial organizations already in existence." The purpose of such a congress would be to allow "all functional groups" to "come into ordered relationship with each other" in order to promote the "coordination" needed to achieve "industrial balance" without the direct intervention of the federal government.[59] Woll's proposal thus had much in common with the call for a national industrial conference that the TUC and the Mond group of employers had favored in Britain.

As in Britain, however, many advocates of national coordination or planning in the United States saw a need for government involvement. In the Senate, Robert LaFollette introduced a bill in 1931 empowering the president to appoint a fifteen-person National Economic Council drawn from nominees suggested by "groups of associations and organizations representing the industrial, financial, agricultural, transportation, and labor interests of the United States." The bill charged the proposed council with making recommendations concerning the economy to the president and Congress.[60] LaFollette's proposal resembled Britain's EAC in that it combined elements of both "representative" and "technocratic" conceptions of a national council.

The leaders of organized labor were sympathetic to LaFollette's bill. Not long after LaFollette introduced his proposal, the *American Federationist* editorialized in favor of some form of national economic planning, arguing that there "must be cooperation by all functional organizations and coordination by some agency national in scope." The editorial argued that "without representation of Labor in national planning, just as in planning for plants and industries, there can not be balance because an essential group is not supplying the facts of its needs and progress."[61] Sidney Hillman had been particularly influential in convincing LaFollette of the need to draft a bill and to hold special hearings on the causes and consequences of the Depression as a means of drumming up support for the idea of a national economic council. George Soule and John Maurice Clark, two economists with ties to Hillman, helped draft LaFollette's legislative proposal, and William Green, John L. Lewis, D. B. Robertson, and Hillman all testified in behalf of the legislation during Senate hearings in late 1931.[62]

So, too, did General Motors president Alfred Sloan, but other business leaders were not so supportive. Gerard Swope argued that an effective national council required the existence of a solid base of functioning trade associations. Swope contended that once a scheme closely resembling his own plan was in operation, the various trade associations would then be able to select representatives to serve on a national council whose membership could be supplemented by representatives of banking and labor organizations. Henry Harriman, echoing the views expressed the previous year by *Nation's Business,* insisted that no new council could be effective unless it had the respect of the business community. Consequently, he advocated the establishment of a small economic council of three to five experts appointed and compensated by business itself to serve as an advisory body to the government.[63]

Few witnesses before the LaFollette committee went so far as to advocate a purely business-controlled council, but the notion of a technocratic group of experts serving in an advisory capacity to the federal government did have significant appeal, especially for those who considered themselves experts. Henry Kendall, one of the country's leading advocates of scientific management, testified against the LaFollette bill because it provided for a quasi-representative body, though he supported legislation creating a smaller council of technocrats. Several other technocrat witnesses, including John Maurice Clark, one of the economists who played a key role in drafting LaFollette's proposed bill, contended that it would be desirable to create both a small body with special expertise to serve as an economic general staff, and a larger, representative council that might meet only infrequently to review and assess the findings of the experts. LaFollette himself, with support from Lewis Lorwin of the Brookings Institution and Mary Van Kleeck of the Sage Foundation, argued that the economic council he envisioned would not be an essentially representative body, but that it could "be effective in helping to build up, within the various industries" self-governing "organizations" that would be able to carry out needed stabilization measures.[64] LaFollette's proposal therefore went well beyond what the British had attempted with the EAC, in that it called for the establishment of a body that, like the wartime Advisory Commission to the CND, would have organizational and administrative functions in addition to its planning and coordinating responsibilities.

The Seventy-First Congress ended without taking action on LaFollette's bill. Although the idea of an advisory council won general praise, the LaFollette committee hearings demonstrated the continuing strength and depth of resistance to direct state involvement in the economy. Throughout the hearings, LaFollette indicated his own ambivalence about government intervention when he voiced opposition to the state's sanctioning of trade association efforts to limit production, claiming that such a policy would require government to become involved in the morass of price-fixing to protect the public interest. Macro-level planning was appealing to many people as a general idea, but, in practice, in both Britain and the United States there was only limited support in the early 1930s either for creating a truly powerful technocratic council of experts within the state apparatus or for handing over state power to a national assembly based on functional representation.

Whereas in Britain the debate about establishing some form of national economic council took for granted labor's participation, business spokespersons in America remained reluctant to acknowledge the need for labor representation. By the late 1920s business leaders from some of Britain's most technologically advanced, capital-intensive growth industries had come to see the possible advantages of union representation in efforts to break the grip of the City of London and orthodox Treasury economists on monetary policy. Although, as Thomas Ferguson argues, comparable sectors of the American business community may have later come to similar conclusions about the advantages of accepting a more significant role for organized labor, in the early years of the Depression, hostility to unions was still far more important in virtually all sectors of American industry than visions of common ground between high-tech industry and organized labor.[65] Moreover, American labor leaders paid less attention to such macroeconomic issues as monetary policy and international trade, while focusing more on micro-level problems such as gaining union recognition, than did the leadership of Britain's TUC. Much of the testimony at the LaFollette committee hearings focused on the role of trade associations (or on the government's role in overseeing trade associations). During the hearings there was relatively little discussion of ways in which the state might institutionalize a role for organized labor in macro- or meso-level planning based on the idea of industrial self-government.

Britain's Piecemeal Efforts at Reform

A lack of legislative initiative and continuing economic deterioration in the early 1930s in the United States and Britain soon led to changes in government leadership in both nations. Only in the United States, though, did the change in leadership lead to a substantial change in policy involving a comprehensive experiment in meso-corporatism.

Because of Britain's parliamentary system, MacDonald's minority Labour government fell from power more quickly under the pressures of the

Depression than did the Hoover administration. Faced with defections in his own party over his decision to cut unemployment benefits as a means of reducing the deficit, MacDonald chose to remain in office by forming a coalition National government in which Baldwin Conservatives would play the leading role.[66]

With the Labour government's collapse, Harold Macmillan, Oswald Mosley, and a number of other prominent figures in politics and industry became more convinced than ever that corporatist measures were needed. Although support for the establishment of a macro-corporatist planning organization with representation from organized labor that would be far stronger than the EAC was expressed by members of all three political parties, discussions of economic planning focused largely on proposals for meso-level industrial reorganization.[67] Macmillan called upon the government to urge each of the country's major industries to establish its own national industrial council and then to create "the necessary statutory powers to carry through the scheme of integration" each council would draw up "to preserve stability." In contrast to the Harriman and Swope plans, Macmillan's proposal explicitly called for labor to play an important role in industrial self-government through the establishment of a "parallel structure" in each industry of "Trade Union Councils" to represent workers' interests. While opposing too much "central bureaucratic authority," Macmillan proposed a "Central Economic Council" or "Industrial Parliament" on which representatives from each industrial and trade union council, and from government and finance, would sit as a national coordinating body.[68]

In late 1933 Macmillan helped to organize the Industrial Reorganisation League (IRL) to rally support for his approach to planning. Several prominent business leaders, including Lord Melchett, the son of Sir Alfred Mond, became involved with the IRL, as did a number of Conservative politicians. The league worked together with PEP to push for parliamentary action to implement a more comprehensive system of industrial self-government.[69] Conservatives Sir Arthur Salter, Sir Basil Blackett, and Roy Glenday (who was an economic adviser to the Federation of British Industries) also published manifestos at this time outlining their own particular versions of industrial self-government. Salter thus proposed in 1933 the establishment of a new "self-governing and self-regulating economic structure, based upon specialised institutions and group organisations" that reflected a similarly corporatist outlook, even though it was less ambitious in scope than the PEP plan and made no explicit provision for the participation of organized labor.[70]

Oswald Mosley went much further than Macmillan in the quest for "corporate unity."[71] Disillusioned with the Labour Party, Mosley in 1932 issued a manifesto calling for the establishment of an explicitly fascist corporate state. Mosley still used the familiar phrase "self-government in industry" to describe the corporations he wished to see emerge for each industry, but in stark contrast to moderate corporatists such as Macmillan, he began to argue that Parliament itself ought to be based exclusively on functional rather than geographical representation and to emphasize the supremacy of the state as the sole embodiment of the national interest.[72]

Although one prominent scholar describes the "economic policy" of the coalition government that came to power in 1931 as "comprehensive and radically different from that of previous generations," most historians view the government's efforts at industrial reorganization as "piece-meal and opportunist."[73] At the macro-level of planning, the National government allowed the EAC to die a quiet death, thereby ending MacDonald's hesitant experiment with functional representation, and instead opted for a more purely technocratic body of economists and civil servants to provide it with economic information.[74]

The National government's most significant policy innovation involved a highly tentative effort at meso-level planning. The Import Duties Act of 1932 established an Import Duties Advisory Committee with the power to raise tariffs for industries willing to develop plans for eliminating excess capacity. The charge of the Advisory Committee, however, was ill-defined, and the scheme fell far short of being a comprehensive experiment with corporatism. The Conservative-dominated government rejected a Liberal- and Labour-backed proposal presented by Liberal MP Geoffrey Mander to broaden the mandate of the Advisory Committee by requiring that the committee "satisfy itself" that three conditions were met before granting additional tariff protection: (1) that the industry was "efficiently organised both on a national scale and in individual factories"; (2) that standard wage rates and hours of work were being observed; and (3) that "adequate facilities" existed "for joint consultation by employers and employed in the conduct of the industry through joint industrial councils, works councils, and similar machinery."[75] Because the government's primary objective in passing the Import Duties Act was to provide immediate tariff protection for British industries, the government failed to make the legislation anything more than a small and very halting step toward state-sponsored corporatism.

The most important industry to take advantage of the legislation was iron and steel. As early as 1930, the unions in the industry had favored creating a powerful industry-wide organization with labor representation to rationalize the industry. As part of their scheme, the unions called for an industry-wide levy to raise funds to compensate both factory owners whose plants would be taken out of production and the workers whose jobs would be lost through the reduction of excess capacity. With the lure of tariff protection, industry employers hesitantly organized the British Iron and Steel Federation (BISF) in 1934. The BISF's power and accomplishments proved to be quite limited because of continuing conflicts among member firms and because the government took a largely passive role in the industry's affairs. In 1934, once the unions realized that the employers were unwilling to form a strong central organization and that organized labor was to be excluded from the weak BISF that was established, the Iron, Steel and Kindred Trades Association began to support nationalization of the industry.[76]

In one case, cotton textiles, the National government did make more extensive use of state power to foster industrial self-government. Throughout the interwar period, cotton, along with coal, had suffered from a long-term problem of excess capacity and was among the most depressed sectors of the British economy (paralleling the situation in the United States). Even before the crash of 1929, support for some form of industrial self-government to rationalize production and reduce excess capacity had come from sources as diverse as the Bank of England and the industry's unions. In 1929 Montagu Norman of the Bank of England had been instrumental in the organization of the Lancashire Cotton Corporation, a large-scale amalgamation whose principal purpose was to achieve economies of scale and to eliminate redundant plants.[77] The cotton unions, which during World War I had secured an equal voice with employers on the state-sponsored Cotton Control Board and which in the 1920s enjoyed effective industry-wide bargaining on wages, sought to establish a system of joint control to deal with the industry's problems. In pursuit of this objective they became affiliated in 1928 with the employer-initiated Joint Committee of Cotton Trade Organizations.[78]

These earlier attempts to stabilize the cotton industry had not involved direct state action. One of Norman's main motives in pushing the industry toward voluntary amalgamations was to avoid more direct state involvement. The Bank of England played a similar role in the shipbuilding industry, helping to sponsor the National Shipbuilder Security corporation as a vehicle for eliminating excess capacity.[79] Under the additional pressures of the Depression, however, cutthroat competition led to the collapse of national wage standards and caused both the unions and the majority of employers to turn to the state to make industry-wide wage agreements reached through collective bargaining legally enforceable. Parliament responded to this consensus in the industry by enacting such legislation in the Cotton Manufacturing (Temporary Provisions) Act of 1934.[80]

The cotton unions, though, failed to win the establishment of a strong joint control board that might deal effectively with the industry's continuing difficulties. On the other hand, owners in the spinning section of the industry were also unsuccessful in getting the government to give legal sanction to their proposed system of pools and quotas, though in 1936 they did gain authority in the Cotton Spinning Industry Act to impose a levy on spinning firms to finance a buy-out of inefficient producers. Labour spokespersons objected to the law's failure to provide for compensation for the workers who would lose their jobs as a result of the scheme, but the Baldwin government did feel obliged to include a representative from the United Textile Factory Workers' Association on the Advisory Committee to the Spindles Board that the act created. The Cotton Industry Act of 1939 later provided for payments to operatives made redundant by rationalization and also allowed for union representatives on a reconstituted Cotton Board. The act was not implemented, though, because of the outbreak of war. As in the case of steel, the failure to establish effective industrial self-government in cotton led the unions involved to conclude that nationalization of the industry was necessary.[81]

Labour Party and trade union support for nationalization had expanded significantly by 1935, as hopes faded for labor effectively participating in the development of schemes of industrial rationalization that might be implemented in the context of private enterprise without increasing unemployment. In fact, it was becoming obvious that rationalization was unlikely to occur in any meaningful way with or without the participation of organized labor.[82] Whereas in 1929 the Labour Party platform called for nationalization only in the case of the coal mines, the Labour election manifesto of 1935 supported nationalization in coal, transport, iron and steel, gas, electricity, cotton, armaments, banks, and land.[83]

Leaders of the Labour Party and of the trade union movement were not in complete agreement about the form nationalization ought to take. The controversy within the labor movement echoed the debate that took place among the various schools advocating centralized planning over whether a technocratic or representative form of organization would be most effective in coordinating the economy as a whole. The labor movement itself was divided over whether nationalization should be carried out by establishing public corporations run by technocrats chosen strictly because of their managerial skills, or whether the trade unions of socialized industries should have the power to appoint a substantial portion of the newly constituted boards of directors. Although Herbert Morrison's vision of a nonpartisan public corporation ultimately triumphed, the issue of workers' control was continually revisited at the annual meetings of the TUC in the mid-1930s.[84]

Whereas nationalization seemed still to be a distant possibility for most British industries, in the months before Ramsay MacDonald stepped down in 1935 as head of the National government, the leading supporters of a state-sponsored system of meso-corporatism made their most concerted effort to win parliamentary approval of comprehensive enabling legislation to permit each of the nation's industries to establish a legally enforceable system of self-government. By late 1934, the IRL and PEP both developed comparable legislative proposals that would have allowed the majority of firms in an industry to seek government sanction to implement plans for controlling production and stabilizing market conditions. The House of Commons engaged in an extended debate over the issue in April 1935, with Conservatives Harold Macmillan, Hugh Molson, and Lord Eustace Percy, and Liberal Geoffrey Mander, all arguing in support.[85] Historian Daniel Ritschel describes the moment as "perhaps the one single instance of an attempt to legislate a corporatist economy in Britain."[86]

Although Macmillan, for one, had expressed support for including organized labor in his scheme for industrial self-government, the proposals that both PEP and the IRL ultimately put forward were at best vague on the issue. Partly as a result of this omission, the idea of an enabling act gained little support from the leadership of the trades unions or the Labour Party. Labour MP Sir Stafford Cripps warned that the proposal was comparable to fascism and would lead to a restriction of production and not an increase in wages.[87] The Liberal *Economist* also expressed a similar concern about the likely economic consequences of such an approach to planning.[88] During the debate on the House floor, Mander, who had long advocated legislation making possible some form of meso-corporatist arrangements, reiterated his belief in the necessity of including the trade unions in any new system of industrial self-government.[89]

Perhaps even more important than trade union, Labour, or Liberal opposition to the final IRL and PEP bills was the continuing reluctance of many Conservatives and the FBI to support the idea of a comprehensive scheme of government intervention. Small-scale independent companies that supported the FBI were concerned about being squeezed out in a system that would likely be dominated by their larger competitors. Many business and Tory leaders were also ideologically opposed to greater state involvement in the economy. Moreover, they also realized that even though both the PEP and IRL bills were vague on the issue of labor involvement in industrial self-government, the potential for union participation remained strong.[90]

Thus, the June 1935 manifesto of the so-called Next Five Years group, a loose coalition of over one hundred progressive business and labor leaders and politicians from all three parties that included such figures as Macmillan, Mander, Basil Blackett, Arthur Salter, J. A. Hobson, Arthur Pugh, R.D. Denman, and Seebohm Rowntree, acknowledged: "It is taken for granted in this country that the wage earners should organize themselves for collective bargaining in Trade Unions." The manifesto included a call to extend to other industries the provisions of the Cotton Manufacturing (Temporary Provisions) Act of 1934 that allowed for legal enforcement of wage agreements arrived at by collective bargaining. While supporting a form of industrial self-government similar to the one embodied in the bills then pending in Parliament, the Next Five Years group also recognized that its proposals would "have the natural effect of further consolidating the position of labour as an equal partner in industry."[91]

The MacDonald coalition government never pushed the proposed enabling legislation to a vote in Parliament, and during the remainder of the decade the National governments subsequently headed by Baldwin and Neville Chamberlain made no effort to resurrect the idea. During the Depression decade, the more limited system of Trade Boards, which dealt narrowly with the issue of minimum wages, was extended to several new industries, but such action was taken by the National government only in industries in which the majority of employers and the existing trade unions were able to reach agreement over the need for such action.[92] In the road haulage industry, which had long been characterized by intense competition among numerous small firms, including many that were owner-operated, and in which unions had traditionally been weak, the Conservative government did in 1938 adopt legislation supported by Ernest Bevin's Transport and General Workers' Union and the leading employers' organization in the industry that regulated wages and hours and contributed to growing union strength.[93]

British state intervention in the road haulage industry, and in coal and cotton nevertheless represented only piecemeal efforts to intervene in the field of industrial relations. These efforts were far less intrusive and less comprehensive than what would be attempted in the United States during the 1930s. Considering British industry as a whole, in spite of all the talk about planning and industrial reorganization during the Great Depression, little was accomplished or even tried. The government failed in its tentative efforts to use the tariff as a means of prodding ailing industries to rationalize production through amalgamations and ultimately rejected any comprehensive scheme of state-sponsored corporatism.

America's Experiment with Corporatism

With the continuing collapse of the American economy after 1931, Herbert Hoover's defeat in the 1932 election was all but a foregone conclusion. While Hoover continued to resist efforts to use state authority to mandate a restructuring of industry and labor-management relations, before leaving office, he did sign the Norris–La Guardia Anti-Injunction Act, thereby satisfying organized labor's highest priority for micro-level reform. Although the law would indirectly affect all levels of industrial relations, major legislation directly targeting the meso-level organization of industry would have to await the coming to power of Franklin Roosevelt and the New Deal.[94]

The culmination of the previous several years' discussion of industrial self-government came with the passage of the NIRA in June 1933. Although FDR did not come into office with a clear commitment to trying a corporatist solution to the problems of the Depression, the NIRA achieved remarkably widespread support from leaders of business, labor, and government.[95] The legislation's ambitious scope is in marked contrast to anything attempted in Britain in this period. The law empowered the president to sanction the creation of legally enforceable codes of fair competition for each of the nation's industries, with the requirement that each code include a Section 7a guaranteeing the right of workers "to organize and bargain collectively through representatives of their own choosing."[96] In order to carry out the codes that were to be drafted by industries themselves (subject to the approval of the presidentially appointed head of the NRA), each industry was to establish a standing code authority.

Why, then, at this time did the United States, but not Britain, adopt such a comprehensive approach to industrial self-government? Ideology was not a determining factor. The ideological context in which the subject of the government's possible role in industrial reorganization was discussed was remarkably similar on both sides of the Atlantic. Although a wide range of views existed in both countries, it could hardly be argued that Americans were generally more predisposed toward state intervention than the British, who even before the Depression had accepted considerably greater state involvement in the area of welfare. Nor could it be said that planning as an ideal had greater appeal in the United States. Under the impact of the Depression, the need for some form of planning had come to be almost a cliché in both nations.

Possible differences in state administrative capacities might offer an explanation. Theda Skocpol and Kenneth Finegold argue that the lack of state expertise and governmental mechanisms for economic planning and coordination help to explain not only the New Deal's need to turn to established trade associations as the institutional bulwark of the NRA but also the NRA's subsequent failure to become permanently institutionalized as part of an American corporatist state.[97] More broadly, some students of contemporary corporatism claim that the development of liberal forms of corporatism since 1945 is as much a product of the weakness of states and their need to rely upon private-sector organizations to legitimate and implement public policy as it is a reflection of the growing strength of statist institutions.[98]

Yet, as important as the issue of state capacities may be in helping to understand how the NRA actually functioned, it does not tell us why the United States, but not Britain, initiated so ambitious a corporatist scheme in the first place. Britain's state apparatus was to some extent better developed than America's, especially with regard to the quality and influence of the civil service, but Britain had at best only a marginal advantage over the United States in terms of its ability to use state power and authority to engage directly in meso- or macro-level economic planning and coordination. As Robert Skidelsky observes, in Britain too at this time "the central government controlled and administered virtually nothing."[99]

Perhaps differences in the nature and timing of the business cycle provide the answer. Although the Depression produced a serious political crisis in Britain in 1931, economic conditions in Britain were not then as bad, nor were they deteriorating as rapidly, as they were in the United States when a change in administration occurred in 1933. Contemporary accounts agree that there was much more of a crisis atmosphere in America when FDR became president than ever existed in Britain during the Depression. Thus, the pressure to try more far-reaching remedies was not as great in Britain when the new government took office as it was in the United States in 1933. This contrast in economic context cannot be ignored, but Britain's willingness to adopt industry-specific corporatist schemes for the coal and textile industries both before and after the Depression reached its nadir, in one case under Labour and in the other under a National government, supports the conclusion that more than the timing of the business cycle was involved in causing the divergence in American and British policy choices.

Political contingency, especially the nature of the party leaders who came into office as a result of the Depression, certainly was a factor. The Depression brought about a change in government in both countries, but Franklin Roosevelt provided a very different approach to governing than did either Ramsay MacDonald or Stanley Baldwin. Neither MacDonald nor Baldwin was personally receptive to innovation or experimentation. Baldwin even observed that he "dreaded Roosevelt's experiments" and thought they would quickly produce "an appalling mess up in America."[100] Ironically, in Britain the Depression had the effect of bringing to power a standpat coalition of the center at the expense not only of the Labour left but also of the progressive wing of the Conservative party represented by Macmillan. In the United States, though the election of 1932 gave little indication of FDR's intentions, the change of government at the low point of the Depression brought into office a man temperamentally willing to experiment.

Contingencies such as the timing of the business cycle and the nature of political leadership undoubtedly contributed to Britain's generally more conservative response to the Depression and, in particular, to its resistance to adopting unorthodox fiscal policies in the manner of Germany, Sweden, and the United States. However, a closer look at the immediate circumstances surrounding the adoption of the NIRA, including the political forces and particular interests that made the law's passage possible, demonstrates the need to go beyond contingencies to understand the contrast between the American and British experiences. The NIRA was an omnibus piece of legislation that seemed to offer something for every interest group, but to understand how a temporary cross-class coalition could be formed in the United States, but not in Britain, in support of such a seemingly radical experiment in corporatism, one must consider certain structural differences between the American and British political economies.

Ironically, the immediate impetus for the Roosevelt administration's drafting of the NIRA came from the ranks of organized labor. At its annual convention in November 1932, the AFL went on record as favoring a mandatory thirty-hour workweek as its priority response to the Depression. Soon thereafter Hugo Black introduced such a proposal in the Senate.[101] Senate passage of the Black Bill prompted FDR to speed action on an alternative recovery program that eventuated in the NIRA. The bill that won FDR's approval came much closer to reflecting the desires of the business corporatists than it did the approach favored by the AFL in the Black Bill, but the NIRA did hold out the promise of some form of industry-by-industry hours limitations, and, especially after Congress at the instigation of the AFL strengthened Section 7a, the law also included wording that seemed to protect labor's right to collective bargaining.[102]

For many American businesspeople the most attractive feature of the NIRA was its suspension of the antitrust laws for participating industries, a concern that did not exist for British employers. Especially for industries, such as cotton textiles, that had suffered from excess production and "destructive competition" even before 1929, the antitrust laws stood as a critical obstacle to effective industry-wide organization. Although most business supporters of antitrust law revision had earlier hoped to accomplish this objective without giving the state any direct role in meso-level coordination and planning, by early 1933 business advocates of industrial self-government had come to realize the political necessity of allowing the government at least some oversight role in exchange for a suspension of the antitrust laws.[103] British firms confronted no comparable legal barriers to cartel arrangements and thus had less incentive to accept state involvement in industry-wide planning.[104]

By 1933 the possibility of forming cartels not subject to the antitrust laws was so appealing to American industries suffering from uncontrolled competition that most were willing to accept some state involvement in the process. It is unlikely, though, that any substantial segment of the business community would have supported the NIRA had it also guaranteed organized labor a role as an equal partner with capital in the system of meso-level industrial self-government the law established. Of course, the NIRA made no such provision. This omission, which, given the strength of Britain's union movement, would have been politically impossible in any comprehensive experiment with corporatism in Britain, helps explain the law's ultimate passage.

For business supporters of the NIRA, the bill's empowerment of business remained far more significant than the uncertain protections afforded to labor. Writing in *Nation's Business,* Raymond Willoughby expressed the widely shared understanding that the bill's "obvious intent" was "to give business a larger measure of freedom for its cooperative powers" and that the adoption of the law marked a significant recognition of the maturity of the trade association as a device for industrial government, administration, and agreement."[105] Most business supporters of the NIRA understood the law to mean that trade associations would play the principal role in drafting and implementing "codes of fair competition," with labor representatives perhaps being consulted, though not as institutional equals and only on matters directly affecting wages, hours, and other conditions of employment.[106]

Business leaders were not alone in thus interpreting the law. Robert Wagner, perhaps labor's strongest supporter in Congress, said nothing about organized labor being assured a formal role in all aspects of code making and code enforcement when he appeared before the Senate Finance Committee to discuss the proposed legislation. Robert LaFollette did explicitly raise the prospect of amending the NIRA to guarantee labor representation, but nothing came of his suggestion. When Franklin Roosevelt spoke to the nation immediately following the enactment of the NIRA, he indicated that trade associations would have primary responsibility for carrying out the new system of industrial self-government.[107]

Donald Richberg, organized labor's principal representative in the drafting of the bill, who went on to become the NRA's general counsel, shared a similar view of the NIRA.[108] In spite of his earlier warning about the dangers of industrial self-government in which labor would not be adequately represented, in testimony at the Senate hearings on the NIRA he contended that since the codes envisioned in the legislation involved "practices . . . concerned with the management of operations," it would be appropriate that those drafting the codes for each industry be "representative of management." He explained that "insofar as the code only dealt with management problems, as to marketing or production, it would not necessarily follow that there would be labor representation" in the code-making and enforcement process. For those code sections dealing with matters of direct concern to workers, Richberg argued that labor might play a role either by participating at the invitation of the industry trade association in the drafting of such provisions or by advising the presidentially appointed administrator of the NRA as to the fairness of the labor provisions before they were given government sanction.[109]

Felix Frankfurter, who had initially suggested that Richberg help draft the NIRA so that someone having close contacts with organized labor be involved, expressed concern to Robert Wagner, the chief legislative sponsor of the NIRA, about the possible lack of protection for labor interests in the proposed law. Instead of arguing that the bill be amended to require direct representation of organized labor, Frankfurter suggested to Wagner an amendment providing that the secretary of labor be assured "real authority in the initiation and conduct of negotiations on all proposals affecting labor in the development of industrial codes."[110]

Although the AFL's leadership expressed concern that organized labor be treated as a "partner in industry" equal to management and enjoying the "right to participate in the decisions and duties of industry," during the debate in Congress over the proposed recovery program, the AFL's principal interest was not so much the composition of the code-drafting and code-enforcement bodies envisioned by the NIRA as it was the wording of Section 7a's protections for labor's right to collective bargaining.[111] It should come as no surprise, then, that in January 1935, when 775 codes were in operation, only 26 provided specifically for labor representation on the code authorities charged with enforcement responsibilities. Labor was represented in the coal and clothing industries, but not in such mass-production industries as autos, steel, rubber, or electrical manufacturing.[112]

Although historian Colin Gordon claims that employers in some of the most competitive sectors of the economy favored Section 7 as a necessary means of bringing order to their industries, such an enlightened perspective was actually quite rare among businessmen prior to the passage of the NIRA.[113] Many American employers may have come to see the benefits of limiting destructive wage cutting and other predatory forms of competition that undermined labor standards. However, most preferred state enforcement of labor standards that were part of a broader business-generated plan to restore profits, rather than relying on the spread of collective bargaining with independent unions to enforce uniform standards.[114] Employers, therefore, generally opposed the inclusion in the NIRA of Section 7a's protection of workers' rights to collective bargaining at the level of the individual shop or firm. This was especially true after the AFL successfully lobbied Congress to modify Richberg's original version of Section 7a by adding wording taken from the Norris–La Guardia Act banning "interference, restraint, or coercion" by employers in their workers' designation of collective-bargaining agents, and by changing wording that initially prohibited employers from requiring workers to join "any organization" as a condition of employment to a ban applying only to compulsory membership in a "company union."[115]

The labor provisions of the NIRA thus proved to be much more of a sticking point for business than the bill's granting of great potential powers to the state.[116] However, as the trade journal of the coal industry editorialized just prior to the passage of the NIRA, it would have been "naive beyond understanding" to think that the recovery act could have been approved without any labor provisions at all.[117] Shortly after the NIRA went into effect, *Nation's Business* observed: "The apprehension that the Act would be a vehicle for unionization of industry through the power of Government seems to have been largely unfounded."[118]

The coal operators were still not enthusiastic about the NIRA, but they saw its provisions regarding labor to be less threatening than the industry-specific legislation that might have been an alternative.[119] In spite of industry's continuing fears about "compulsory unionization," Section 7a fell far short of banning open shops and guaranteeing that unions would universally be recognized as the sole representative of workers' interests. NRA administrators subsequently interpreted Section 7a in such a way that company unions grew quite rapidly while the law was in effect.[120]

The lack of national collective bargaining in the United States provided another incentive for certain sectors of American industry to support the NIRA experiment in corporatism. In Britain, employers' associations in most industries had come to accept multiunion national collective bargaining as a useful means of avoiding cutthroat competition regarding wages and working conditions and reducing the dangers of shop-floor militancy.[121] Except in rare circumstances, such as in cotton textiles and road haulage, British employers had little incentive to seek government assistance to help stabilize industry by establishing enforceable labor standards, especially since such state involvement might well have entailed an acceptance of a far broader role for labor in industry's affairs than currently existed. In the United States, especially in older labor-intensive industries, the NIRA may well have been appealing because it held out the prospect of achieving enforceable industry-wide norms relating to wages and hours without, as Gordon claims, necessarily requiring antiunion American employers to engage in traditional collective bargaining.

The weakness of organized labor in America was not the only factor that made possible America's experiment with a comprehensive scheme of meso-corporatism in the early 1930s, but it is highly unlikely that the NIRA would have been adopted with such widespread support if American unions had been as strong as organized labor in Britain. Some of the New Deal reformers who favored the NIRA may have had a vision of corporatist harmony transcending individual or sectarian interests, but the business and labor support that was essential in making the passage of the NIRA politically feasible was predicated on each group's calculation of the recovery program's benefit to its own interests. For each group, the weakness of organized labor entered critically into its calculations. Union leaders concluded that the weakness of organized labor required some form of state protection to help them establish labor's right to collective bargaining. For business corporatists, on the other hand, labor's weakness meant that it was possible to create a system of meso-level industrial self-government in which labor could be virtually excluded.

In both the United States and Britain, the persistence of antistatist attitudes and relatively underdeveloped centralized state bureaucracies continued during the early 1930s to be major obstacles to the establishment of any state-dominated corporatist system. Some intellectuals and individuals within the governments of both countries perceived a need to create state macro- or meso-level planning institutions that could put the interests of the nation ahead of any sectarian interests, but even in the crisis of the early 1930s they had little chance of gaining sufficient support to implement corporatism on their own terms. The real question, then, was whether key sectors of business and organized labor might each be willing to support a corporatist experiment in the hope of using the power of the state to its own advantage.

Capitalist interests were by no means monolithic in either America or Britain, with obvious divisions between competitive and oligarchic sectors of the economy, capital- and labor-intensive industries, and manufacturing and international finance. Colin Crouch, however, observes: "The *central* reason why capitalist interests mistrust the state is not the fear that it will be other fractions of capital which gain its favour (though this may sometimes be the case) but that it will be responsive to class interests other than those of capital." Crouch concludes that "capitalist interests within liberal societies enter corporatist arrangements with great reluctance."[122]

For most sectors of British industry in the 1930s, the dangers of an expanded role for organized labor and for independent state actors in a comprehensive system of state-sponsored corporatism more than offset the possible gains they might have enjoyed, especially since there were no existing legal barriers to the development of purely nonstatist forms of industry-wide cooperation to be overcome and since multiunion national collective bargaining already limited cutthroat competition involving labor standards. In the United States, on the other hand, most industry leaders decided to support what proved to be a temporary experiment in conservative corporatism, not only because of their desire to be free of the restrictions of the antitrust laws, but also because they believed that the weakness of American unions would allow them to dominate the new system.

Historians agree, as did most contemporary participants and observers, that the NRA proved to be a failure. By the time the Supreme Court ruled the NIRA unconstitutional in the Schechter decision of 1935, leaders of business and labor, as well as many influential members of the Roosevelt administration, had developed serious doubts about the wisdom of America's experiment with corporatism. In spite of business dominance of the NRA code-making and code-enforcement process, Gerard Swope was calling as early as November 1933 for the NRA to be replaced by a new plan that, as historian Robert Collins describes it, "demanded pure and simple business self-government, without the concessions to labor and to a vaguely defined but bothersome 'public interest'" that characterized the NRA.[123] Both the Chamber of Commerce, which had strongly supported the initial passage of the NIRA, and the National Association of Manufacturers, which had somewhat more reluctantly backed the adoption of the recovery program, had become disillusioned about the actual economic benefits of state-sponsored corporatism and troubled by the impact Section 7a was having on labor-management relations. Even the Cotton Textile Institute, which initially had been among the earliest and strongest supporters of a state-sponsored system of industrial self-government, also turned against the NRA by 1935. Persisting fears of the potential threat to business interests posed by increased state authority also once again came to the fore, so that long before the Supreme Court struck down the NIRA, both of the nation's leading business organizations voiced their support for a thorough overhaul of the NRA along the lines advocated by Swope.[124]

The leadership of organized labor had strong objections to the way NRA administrators Hugh Johnson and Donald Richberg interpreted Section 7a's protections of workers' rights to organize and bargain collectively. Less than a year after the NRA had been created, the AFL called for revising the NIRA when it expired in 1935 in order to guarantee a fuller role for all "organized groups." The journal of the AFL also proclaimed that experience under the existing administration of the law made "plain" what had long been a central tenet of the AFL's ideology, "that political agencies are not a substitute for economic organizations mobilizing and directing economic power."[125] Yet, even with its shortcomings, Section 7a contributed to a significant growth in union membership during the life of the NRA. As a result, labor leaders remained generally more ambivalent than employers about the program.

In the months before the original NIRA was due to expire, the AFL supported the continuation of the recovery administration, albeit with a strengthened role for labor, including equal representation with employer interests on all boards, and more effective enforcement of the protections of Section 7a. After the Schechter decision, the annual convention of the AFL "reaffirmed its approval of the principles of the National Recovery Act with adequate labor representation in code making, administration, and modification," but organized labor, which had always been most concerned with gaining recognition and collective bargaining rights at the level of the individual firm, had already begun to concentrate its efforts on the passage and subsequent implementation of Wagner's Labor Disputes Bill.[126]

New Dealers in the Roosevelt administration also had become disenchanted with the NRA. Donald Richberg, the controversial figure who had become the de facto head of the recovery agency before its demise, concluded that the program needed to be scaled back significantly by eliminating price and production control provisions in the codes. Felix Frankfurter, one of FDR's closest advisers, actually saw the Schechter decision as a welcome opportunity to narrow the focus of government-sanctioned industry trade agreements so that they would deal only with minimum labor standards.[127] Wage and hour laws, in particular, might be used as a means of buttressing mass purchasing power and thereby contribute to getting the country out of the persisting Depression. Such an argument would come to play a central role in cementing the political alliance between New Dealers, the labor movement, and consumer advocates that was critical to the success of progressive reforms in the period.[128]

Post-NRA Labor Standards

The debate over what eventually became the Fair Labor Standards Act (FLSA) that was passed by Congress in 1938 sheds light on the lessons labor and business leaders, as well as state actors, drew from the NRA experience. The FLSA provided for the gradual implementation of a forty-hour week and forty-cent-per-hour minimum wage rate. Both the adoption of state-mandated labor standards and the limited nature of the standards that were established can be explained in good part as legacies of the NRA experience.

The American adoption of legislatively-mandated labor standards stands in sharp contrast to Britain, which in this period continued to reject comprehensive wages and hours legislation. The TUC ambivalently supported legislating a forty-hour workweek, but the widespread persistence of anti-statist attitudes and the lack of any precedent for departing so significantly from the philosophy of collective laissez-faire meant that comprehensive hours legislation lacked sufficient support to be adopted. With the Trade Boards system in place to establish minimum wages for "sweated" industries in which women workers predominated, a universally mandated minimum wage was never seriously considered.[129]

In the United States, in spite of the widespread dissatisfaction with the NRA, the precedent had been established for government-sanctioned labor standards. New Dealers Thomas Corcoran and Benjamin Cohen, who drafted the original version of the FLSA, as well as corporatist-minded labor leaders such as Sidney Hillman, not only hoped to salvage what they saw as the NRA's laudable effort to establish a bare "nonoppressive" minimum-wage and maximum-hours standard; they also sought to retain at least some elements of a meso-corporatist approach to economic planning by empowering a government board to set more generous "fair" wage and hours standards for individual industries. Hillman supported such a provision not as a substitute for collective bargaining, but rather as a means of allowing the government to enforce throughout an entire industry labor standards that had been achieved by some organized workers, but in which the "facilities for collective bargaining have proved inadequate or ineffective" in applying higher standards universally. The "fair wage" provision of the original bill held out the possibility of going much further than a limited "nonoppressive" standard in contributing to an increase in labor's share of the national income and thereby addressing the problem of the lack of mass purchasing power. Although the government was to have the authority to make a final determination as to what constituted a "fair wage," industry advisory boards with representatives of both employers and workers would play a central role in the process.[130]

The fair wage provision, though, was subsequently dropped from the final legislation. In the wake of the NRA experience, interest in any scheme to involve the state in meso-corporatist arrangements had dwindled. Not only did most employers oppose what they claimed was an unconstitutional extension of state authority, but the leadership of the AFL, as well as Secretary of Labor Frances Perkins, also objected to state efforts to establish anything other than a bare minimum for labor standards. Perkins specifically cited the British Trade Boards Acts as a model, arguing that it would be best to set standards on an industry-by-industry basis only for those industries in which collective bargaining was ineffective. Following the collapse of the NRA, the AFL once again revived the idea of a legislatively mandated thirty-hour workweek, while remaining generally opposed to any role for the state in setting wages for workers who had access to collective bargaining. AFL president William Green did grudgingly support a Fair Labor Standards Act with fixed minimums of a forty-hour workweek and a forty-cent-per-hour wage rate to protect those who did not enjoy the protections of collective bargaining, but in language very reminiscent of British labor's support for the Trade Boards system, he argued that once collective bargaining expanded to cover workers previously falling below the minimum standards established by law, then "Government interference, if I may put it that way, Government regulation [would] recede."[131]

Interestingly, John Lewis differed with fellow Congress of Industrial Organizations (CIO) leader Sidney Hillman and sided with the AFL on the issue of government-mandated fair wage standards. In an argument that reflected an essentially individualistic conception of the Fair Labor Standards Act focusing on the "rights" of individual workers, Lewis proclaimed that the bill was "really an extension in principle" of the Wagner Act's guarantee of labor's "right to organize and bargain collectively through representatives of its own choosing." That guarantee, he asserted, marked the beginning of an industrial bill of rights for workers as against industry, just as the so-called Bill of Rights in our political Constitution guarantees personal and civil liberties of the citizen or individual as against our State or Federal Governments. They safeguard the freedom of the citizen against arbitrary or tyrannical governmental action.

Similarly, the Wagner Act protects industrial workers as citizens of industry against arbitrary encroachments upon their freedom of association and action. They are assured the right of organization and representation in the determination of their compensation and working conditions.

The pending bill . . . builds up or extends the industrial bill of rights inaugurated by the Wagner Act. It declares it to be a matter of public policy that, (1) no "oppressive wage" or wage below a designated "minimum wage standard" shall be paid by industry; (2) that no "oppressive workweek" above a designated "workweek standard" shall be established.

Lewis contended that establishing bare minimum labor standards was thus appropriate, but that efforts by the state to establish fair or reasonable wages would be too complex and were best left to the workings of collective bargaining.[132]

In its final form, the Fair Labor Standards Act established a forty-hour week and forty-cent-per-hour minimum wage to be implemented gradually over a period of seven years, with forty-four hours being the maximum and twenty-five cents being the minimum in the first year of the bill's operation. In a slight concession to those supporting an industry-specific approach, provision was made for individual industries to implement the new standards more quickly if industry committees of employers and workers agreed that conditions permitted such action.[133]

Conclusion

Historians differ as to the underlying causes for the NRA's failure, with explanations variously emphasizing internal contradictions in the law, the lack of state capacity to make the program effective, or the lack of social consensus to make a system of "societal corporatism" workable.[134] Whatever the reasons for the NRA's failure, America's abortive experiment with corporatism left an important legacy. First of all, the experience significantly discredited the idea of direct state sponsorship and enforcement of meso-level agreements as a means of comprehensive economic planning. In a few special cases of natural resources industries such as agriculture, oil, and coal, NRA-type state intervention might continue, but insofar as broad-based corporatist thinking survived as an influential force in the United States, it did so in a form that had more in common with Herbert Hoover's voluntarism than with the statist approach of the NRA.[135] Whereas in Britain, piecemeal efforts to utilize corporatist arrangements did not yield much more positive results than America's experiment with the NRA, the lack of negative experience with a grand scheme meant that the idea of meso- and macro-level tripartite mechanisms retained a longer-lasting appeal. Moreover, since industry-wide collective bargaining was already much more common in Britain in the 1930s than in the United States, there was a foundation upon which to build a system of informal business-labor-government contacts through what came to be known as "quangoes" (quasi-nongovernmental organizations) that grew up without the necessity of coercive legislation. Britain did not develop into a fully corporatist society, but the possibility of building upon and extending what Keith Middlemas has described as the "corporatist bias" of the British political economy remained a potentially viable option for the future.[136]

America's short-lived experiment with the NRA also had a major impact on labor-management relations at the level of the individual firm. In addition to contributing to the enactment of the FLSA, it also set the stage for the passage of the NLRA and the creation of a system of collective bargaining that entailed a far more intrusive role for the state than was the case in Britain. Even as the notion of explicitly statist forms of macro- or meso-corporatist planning lost favor, backing for state involvement in establishing the framework for micro-level collective bargaining gained support in the United States. The following chapter, therefore, shifts the focus of discussion to the growing divergence that emerged during the Depression decade between the American and British approaches to direct state involvement in the collective bargaining process. Here too, as in the case of the NRA experiment in economic planning, the weakness of organized labor proved to be a critical factor shaping the state's response.

CHAPTER FIVE

The Great Depression and the Development of Diverging Paths in Micro-level Industrial Relations

The most important and long-lasting legacy of the Depression decade for American industrial relations was the establishment of a new role for the state, overseeing and regulating micro-level labor-management relations. Despite the persistence of antistatist values in both America and Britain, the United States' adoption of the National Labor Relations Act (NLRA) in 1935 established an enduring measure of state involvement in the collective bargaining process that contrasted sharply with the system of collective laissez-faire that would remain in place in Britain until the 1970s. The British approach in these years did not represent a wholly literal or absolute application of the doctrine of laissez-faire. British public policy and administrative practice at least indirectly supported collective bargaining. Nevertheless, as in the case of the National Recovery Administration (NRA) trial with meso-corporatist economic planning, it was again the United States that resorted to a much more direct and more intrusive use of state power—in this instance, to reshape the nation's industrial relations system.

Two important questions regarding the public policy developments of the Depression era are the focus of this chapter: Why, when the political climate for organized labor became more favorable, did the United States not simply follow the British example of adopting a generally abstentionist labor law regime as a means of fostering the growth of unions? Why did the Wagner Act entail the specific forms of state intervention in the collective bargaining process that it did?

As comparison with Britain demonstrates, both the greater strength of employer opposition to unionism and the emergence of company unionism in the United States as a serious alternative to collective bargaining proved to be crucial factors contributing to the divergence in the roles played by the state in American and British industrial relations after 1935. Because collective bargaining had become firmly institutionalized in Britain when industry was overwhelmingly competitive and conducted by small firms, British labor leaders still found no need to look to the state to compel employers to deal with unions, even as British industry began more closely to resemble American industry in structure. In the United States, on the other hand, the continuing legacy of the antiunion consensus that had formed among American employers following the turn of the century meant that the leaders of organized labor and their sympathizers finally turned to state power in the 1930s to force employers to engage in collective bargaining with independent unions. The efforts of leading American firms to develop company unions as an alternative to independent unions—an alternative that was almost nonexistent in Britain—would significantly affect the form of state involvement in industrial relations that would be institutionalized in the NLRA.

Micro-level Developments in Early Years of Depression

To a remarkable extent, micro-level labor-management relations in Britain, including the legal context in which those relations occurred, changed little during the Depression. For many years, most employers, as well as the political parties that exercised state power, had accepted unionization as a basic norm in industrial relations. Public policy continued to favor the spread of trade unionism through indirect means, such as by allowing public employees to organize and by directing public contractors to maintain "fair wages" and working conditions that did not undercut union standards.[1] Given the generally favorable environment for unions in Britain and the willingness of most employers to engage in collective bargaining, the leaders of organized labor continued to rely on a policy of collective laissez-faire as the best means of advancing workers' interests.[2]

Deteriorating economic conditions at the beginning of the decade did contribute to a decline in union membership, which by 1933 reached a post–World War I low of 23 percent of the labor force—a rate that was still considerably higher than any achieved in the United States up until that time. The rate of union decline in Britain in the early 1930s, though, was actually less steep than it had been in the years immediately following the abortive General Strike of 1926, and there were no signs of a major effort by employers to dismantle the system of collective bargaining that already existed.[3] Britain's economic recovery after 1932 subsequently paved the way for steady growth in union membership during the remainder of the decade. By the eve of World War II, nearly 32 percent of British workers belonged to unions—a figure higher than in 1929, though not so great as right after World War I. On the whole, the Depression of the 1930s had surprisingly little impact on the role of unions in Britain's economy or on the role of the state in labor-management relations.[4]

The same could not be said for the United States. State intervention in labor-management relations, at least in the form of antilabor injunctions, had long been more common in the United States, but what distinguished the developments of the 1930s was the form and impact of the new state role resulting from the decade's legislation. Not only did the state become more directly involved in certain aspects of the collective bargaining process, including the determination of appropriate bargaining units and the conduct of union certification elections, but the state also took affirmative action to protect the right of workers to organize from interference by employers. As a result, union membership, which had dropped below 3 million at the nadir of the Depression in 1933, had by 1939 come to exceed the figure reached at the peak of union strength immediately following World War I. While the total number of union members increased in Britain by 35 percent between 1929 and 1939, in the United States union membership doubled during the same period. Although union density in the United States still lagged behind that of Britain, for the first time in American history, more than one-fifth of potential union members belonged to unions.[5]

At the beginning of the Depression, the leaders of both the American and British labor movements continued to try to enhance their legitimacy by proclaiming their support for greater union-management cooperation as a means of increasing productivity. Increased productivity, union leaders argued, would allow for profits while also justifying improved living standards for workers. In 1930 and 1931, for example, the *American Federationist* printed numerous articles extolling the virtues of union-management cooperation, while the leadership of the Trades Union Congress (TUC) continued to pursue the prospect of a more collaborative relationship with employers through the Mond-Turner talks.

Even when the Mond-Turner talks collapsed, Walter Citrine and Ernest Bevin continued throughout the decade to support efforts to change the image of unions so that they would not be seen as obstacles to increased efficiency and productivity.[6] Similarly, in spite of a dramatic increase in labor strife in the United States after 1935 stemming in part from the rise of the Congress of Industrial Organizations, the leadership of the newly emerging industrial union movement frequently emphasized the ultimate gains to productivity that industry might enjoy once the labor force was organized on a more rational basis.[7]

The heads of the American Federation of Labor (AFL) and TUC also supported legislative initiatives reflecting their common commitment to the principle of collective laissez-faire. The TUC hoped the election of a Labour government in 1929 would make possible the achievement of its highest legislative priority, the repeal of the Trade Disputes and Trade Unions Act of 1927, which, in addition to requiring "contracting in" by individual trade union members regarding their contributions to union political funds, banned general strikes, imposed restrictions on other forms of sympathetic strikes, and prohibited public employees' unions from affiliating with the TUC. Repeal of the law thus would have removed the limited restrictions on unions that were the legacy of the General Strike.

Ironically, in introducing legislation in early 1931 to modify the 1927 law, Attorney General Sir William Jowitt referred favorably to the efforts then taking place in the United States Congress to end the use of labor injunctions when he declared:

> . . . the political genius of our people has evolved this system—that we have not sought to make strikes illegal but we have sought to control, and rigorously control, what was done during the strike. The American policy has been exactly the opposite. The Americans have sought to make strikes illegal, and it is an interesting reflection to the student of comparative history that just at the time when we are abandoning our old policy and having recourse to the American policy—that is the very time when the Americans are abandoning their policy and adopting ours.[8]

Because of its minority status and fear of appearing too much under the control of the British trade union movement, the Labour government was unable, before it fell in 1931, to push repeal or even substantial modification of the Trade Disputes Act through Parliament.[9] Nevertheless, in practice, the law had little impact on labor-management relations at the level of the individual firm or on the shop floor. As noted previously, the antiunion act was intended more as a means of undermining union funding of the Labour Party than of delegitimizing trade unionism itself. Moreover, in making "political" strikes illegal, the law prohibited a tactic that the trade unions themselves had come to view as counterproductive.

In the United States, the AFL finally succeeded in 1932 in getting Congress to act on its highest legislative priority: a bill that would prove more effective than the Clayton Act in limiting the power of judges to interfere in labor disputes through the issuance of injunctions. The worsening Depression, with its consequent undermining of the political position of employers and the strengthening of the power of Democrats in Congress, helped pave the way for the passage of the Norris–La Guardia Act, in spite of Hoover's behind-the-scenes opposition.[10] Although the legislation asserted as a matter of "public policy" the need for workers to have an unencumbered right to organize and engage in "collective bargaining" as a means of obtaining "acceptable terms and conditions of employment," the law sought to advance this right not through positive state action but rather by establishing tighter limits on the judiciary's one-sided use of injunctions restricting union organizing efforts and by making "yellow dog contracts" unenforceable in court.[11] One of the principal authors of the anti-injunction act, Edwin Witte, had long considered the British Trade Disputes Act of 1906 as a model for labor legislation and explained that he did "not advocate that government compel employers to deal with the labor unions" but instead favored "the policy of complete freedom to both sides, with strict neutrality on the part of the government."[12]

Although the Norris–La Guardia Act was clearly designed to move the United States closer to the British approach to labor law, it did not go so far as to extend full legal immunity to American trade unions. Legal historian Daniel Ernst argues that none of the other principal drafters of the law— Felix Frankfurter, Donald Richberg, Herman Oliphant, and Francis Sayre— fully shared Edwin Witte's strongly antistatist conception of "industrial pluralism," which sought simply to allow workers' collective organizations freedom of action. He claims that the "legal realists" in the group favored a more interventionist role for the state in defining appropriate behavior for both labor and management.[13]

Two differing approaches to the problem of labor law reform influenced the drafting of the Norris–La Guardia Act, but it is difficult to identify the individuals involved as belonging exclusively to one camp or the other. Especially in this volatile period of transition, it was possible for an individual simultaneously to embrace seemingly contradictory elements of both voluntarism and a more statist approach to labor relations. Neither Frankfurter nor Richberg supported a highly intrusive role for the state in labor-management relations; their views represented an unstable mixture of both pluralist and liberal corporatist ideas. Richberg, for example, opposed a universal system of government-provided old-age pensions, but was willing to have government mandate that each industry create its own pension plan.[14] Frankfurter, writing some years earlier in the wake of the infamous Wilkerson injunction issued during the national railroad shopmen's strike of 1922, had favorably contrasted Britain's rejection of the use of labor injunctions with American practice. However, he did not favor following the British precedent of making trade unions fully exempt from civil suits.[15] All those involved in drafting the Norris–La Guardia Act agreed at the time that for purely tactical reasons "a strictly proceduralist approach" focusing on the restriction of judges' injunctive powers was most likely to gain the support of organized labor, win votes in Congress, and survive constitutional scrutiny by the Supreme Court. The next few years would bring to the fore the inherent tensions between an essentially antistatist pluralist conception and a state-centered liberal corporatist vision of the future of American labor relations.[16]

For most Americans, the shift away from a purely individualistic understanding of liberalism, which had been under way for several decades, was not leading in a straight line toward either a fully corporatist or a consistently pluralist conception of the new collectivist political economy that was emerging. The national leadership of the AFL, which prior to the onset of the Depression had advocated a fairly strict version of voluntarism, had called in October of 1931 for the establishment of a "federal labor board" to "give labor federal assistance and service comparable to what is given farmers and industry," and by 1932 had come to support the idea of government-sponsored unemployment insurance. In the years immediately ahead, the American labor movement would begin more closely to resemble British labor by supporting further extensions of the very limited American welfare state. Clearly, the Depression was eroding support for a thoroughgoing voluntarism, even among those who continued to have deep reservations about the use of state power to recast labor-management relations.[17]

The evolving positions of American and British labor leaders on state-mandated wages and hours standards also demonstrate certain limits to their faith in the principles of completely free collective bargaining. Definite parallels exist in the stances taken by the two labor movements, with both favoring universally applied maximum-hours legislation while being more reluctant to support state-determined minimum wage standards that would apply to all workers. Even in the late nineteenth century, both American and British unions had been willing to seek state action in order to establish the eight-hour day. During the 1930s the leadership of the British trade union movement called upon Parliament to legislate a forty-hour workweek, even though the TUC was itself divided over the issue of how best to implement such a proposal. The persistence of antistatist sentiments, which contributed to the opposition of employers, the lack of support by the coalition and Conservative governments, and the ambivalence and internal divisions within the labor movement, prevented any legislative action in Britain to establish a universally applied norm for hours.[18] In the United States, William Green and the AFL, after initially waffling on the idea, actively supported the Black Bill to mandate a thirty-hour workweek, though Green continued to oppose government-determined minimum wage standards for all workers.[19]

Sections 7b and 7c of the National Industrial Recovery Act, which the Roosevelt administration developed as an alternative to the Black Bill, reflected labor supporters' evolving reinterpretation of voluntarism by establishing the possibility of a greater state role in the enforcement of fair labor standards, including maximum hours and minimum wages. The law did so in ways that paralleled exceptions to the principle of collective laissez-faire that had also gained acceptance in Britain in this period. Section 7b authorized the president to give legal sanction to wages and hours agreements arrived at in a particular industry through collective bargaining, even if the industry in question had not succeeded in drawing up a comprehensive code of fair competition. This provision, though never actually utilized by Roosevelt, was similar in approach, if not in potential breadth of coverage, to the law enacted in Britain the following year for the cotton textile industry [Cotton Manufacturing (Temporary Provisions) Act]. Section 7c gave the president the power to impose a standard for minimum wages and maximum hours on an industry that failed either by means of collective bargaining or by the adoption of a full industrial code to address the problem of fair labor standards. Such a provision was analogous to the British system of Trade Boards for industries lacking effective labor organization. The exercise of government power in such a case (as carried out subsequently through the President's Reemployment Agreement) was clearly intended to be a temporary expedient and a spur for labor and employers to reach agreements themselves on wages and hours.[20]

While in the early years of the Depression neither the AFL nor the TUC favored state-mandated wage standards that would be universally applied, both supported legislation that would have required government contractors to pay "prevailing" wage rates defined in terms of industry-specific or locally determined norms established through collective bargaining. Such an approach would not have surrendered to the state the authority to determine appropriate wage levels, but rather would have provided a means for preventing nonunion employers from gaining a competitive advantage by undercutting union wage rates. Support for "prevailing wage" legislation was not restricted to unions. Many building contractors also supported such measures as a means of eliminating the competitive advantage of low-wage "outside" firms. Similar considerations applied to the road haulage industry. Both the Transport and General Workers' Union and the leading employers' associations supported legislation in 1938 that provided for government regulation of wages. British unions continued to gain at least some indirect advantage from the less precise standard of "fair wages" that had long been applied in government contracts, but the TUC was unsuccessful in getting legislative or administrative action to strengthen existing public policy by making the union rate the explicit standard of fairness.[21] While the AFL was no more successful in getting full satisfaction in this area, it was able to help convince Congress in 1931 to pass the Davis-Bacon Act, which applied to federal construction contracts and bore a close resemblance to the approach to fair wages then embodied in British law. The Walsh-Healey Act, passed in 1935, extended the requirement of paying prevailing wages to all government contracts for awards of more than $10,000.[22]

Section 7a of the National Industrial Recovery Act

Although, as noted in the previous chapter, the debate over national economic planning in the early months of the new Roosevelt administration focused primarily on the potential of meso-corporatist schemes for business cooperation, the drafting of the National Industrial Recovery Act (NIRA) also brought renewed consideration of the state's role in micro-level labor-management relations. The inclusion of Section 7a in the final version of the law built on the recent precedents of the Norris–La Guardia and Railway Labor acts.[23] The intense controversy that quickly developed over the law's meaning and implementation, though, clearly highlighted the problems involved in the state trying to advance the ideal of collective bargaining without using its powers of coercion against resistant employers. Section 7a thus became a key milestone on the way toward Congress's later enactment of the NLRA's more interventionist approach.

Section 7a's attempt to protect workers' collective bargaining rights had no clear parallel in Britain. In contrast to the Norris–La Guardia Act, which, like British law, did not call upon the state to use its coercive powers to enforce collective bargaining rights for workers, the NIRA created the possibility for such intervention by requiring all industries seeking exemption from the antitrust laws through the adoption of a government-approved industrial code to include in that code a section legally establishing the right of workers "to organize and bargain collectively through representatives of their own choosing."[24]

The attempt to write this protection into law was clearly a response to the success American employers had enjoyed in avoiding collective bargaining. In addition to their recent introduction of welfare programs and company-sponsored employee representation plans, American employers had long used other, more aggressive methods to deter their workers from joining unions. Active union-avoidance behavior had become the norm throughout most of American industry following World War I. A federal government during the 1920s that was particularly responsive to the concerns of the business community had also helped to create an environment that tolerated or even encouraged hostility to unions among both large and small employers. By 1930 union labor had been virtually eliminated from American manufacturing. Total union membership in the entire country was only somewhat more than 3 million out of a nonagricultural labor force of over 30 million, and approximately 60 percent of those union members worked in mining, building construction, and railways. In manufacturing, only in the highly competitive, labor-intensive clothing and printing industries were unions able to maintain a significant presence.[25] With the advent of a new Democratic administration in Washington that was at least more sympathetic to the plight of workers than were its Republican predecessors, the leadership of the American labor movement concluded that the opportunity, as well as the need, now existed to call upon government power to prevent employers from actively interfering with union efforts to organize workers.

In Britain, in contrast, aggressive union-avoidance tactics by employers did not become widespread throughout industry. Unions had lost members during the 1920s, but collective bargaining remained solidly entrenched in many sectors of the British economy. Thus, for example, whereas only about 10 percent of American workers in the metals and machinery industry belonged to unions in 1930, in Britain the figure was approximately 30 percent.[26] British industry was becoming more concentrated, and the size of a typical plant was beginning to approach that of the typical American plant, but much of British manufacturing remained more dependent on skilled labor and was less geared to mass production. Britain's iron and steel industry became considerably more concentrated and efficient through the elimination of obsolete plants in the 1920s and 1930s; yet the average output of British blast furnaces in 1937 was still only 40 percent that of

American blast furnaces.[27] In many sectors of the British economy, employers continued to believe that their own interests were best served by maintaining the system of multiemployer collective bargaining with unions that had been established years earlier. Such bargaining seemed an effective way to keep wages out of competition. In addition, many employers continued to see national collective bargaining as a means of restricting the potential power of shop-floor militants. Union recognition in the context of national bargaining meant that negotiations with labor would focus on wages and hours, rather than on issues of shop-floor control that were unique to each firm, and bargaining would take place mainly with moderate and bureaucratic-minded trade union officials who would then be obliged to harness spontaneous expressions of shop-floor discontent.

In some of the newly emerging capital-intensive industries such as automobiles and chemicals, which developed with less dependence on skilled craftsmen with union traditions, British employers were successful in establishing union-free work environments. However, these firms were not yet numerous or powerful enough to determine the general climate in which industrial relations in Britain took place. Whereas in 1929 the automobile industry in the United States by itself accounted for nearly 13 percent of the value of manufacturing output, in Britain the "new" industries of automobiles, electrical goods and supply, chemicals, aircraft, silk and rayon, hosiery, and scientific instruments, taken all together, accounted for only about 16 percent of manufacturing output.[28]

Employers throughout British industry might use a variety of means to avoid employing radical activists, defend management prerogatives, or beat back labor's wage demands. Nevertheless, in contrast to the United States, in Britain the legacy of the past and the structure of the economy still created a reasonably favorable climate for unions. As a result, neither the leaders of organized labor nor their supporters saw any need for the direct use of state power to force employers to recognize and deal with unions.

Among the issues discussed relating to the final wording and later implementation of the labor provisions of the NIRA, none was more significant than the legitimacy of company unions. Some employers responded to the economic pressures brought on by the onset of the Depression by ending their support for employee representation plans (as well as other manifestations of welfare capitalism), but the number of workers covered by such plans did not drop dramatically between 1929 and 1933. For employers, one major attraction of company unions continued to be their utility as a defense against the spread of independent unionism. Especially for some large-scale employers in mass-production industries who had developed internal labor markets as part of a broader strategy of personnel management, employee representation plans also had the more positive appeal of offering a form of labor organization that might contribute to efficiencies of operation without endangering management control of the shop floor. No matter how constrained the authority of employer-sponsored workshop councils, so long as the AFL remained committed to a craft-based form of organization, such councils would be the only mechanism in most industries for bringing workers together to express their views across narrow craft boundaries.[29]

Such considerations were not entirely absent in Britain, where works councils and shop stewards sometimes played a role in micro-level industrial relations. However, even though the TUC, like the AFL, was organized largely along craft lines, British management's dealings with organized labor in the early 1930s were less fractionalized than was the case in the rarer instances of collective bargaining occurring in the United States. The frequency of national or regional multiemployer bargaining was particularly important in this regard, but the prevalence of so-called general unions and amalgamations among existing labor organizations, as well as the willingness of some unions to participate in workshop organizations either through the institution of shop stewards or as part of the Whitley Councils scheme, also lessened the possible appeal of American-style company unions for British employers. In addition, because British managers were still less likely than their American counterparts at this time either to have developed internal labor markets or to be willing to devote the time and resources to achieve total managerial control over the production process, the establishment of company unions did not become part of a larger management strategy.[30]

Company unions like those that existed in the United States were exceptional in Britain. A small number of employers, most notably Quakers such as the Cadburys and the Rowntrees, had established works councils that were in some ways analogous to American company unions; but rather than using these bodies to try to forestall the formation of independent unions, these employers generally sought to maintain good relations with organized labor.[31] The so-called nonpolitical trade union movement that developed in the aftermath of the General Strike of 1926 with support from employers in coal mining and, to a lesser extent in shipbuilding, was more clearly intended by management to serve as a form of competition for Britain's independent trade unions. This movement, which continued until the late 1930s, was largely inspired by concerns revolving around the Miners Federation's support for the Labour Party and nationalization, political issues that were of little relevance in the United States. In contrast to the company union movement in the United States, the nonpolitical trade unions in Britain had a very limited membership in only a few sectors of the economy and were organized on an industry-wide basis, rather than within the confines of individual plants or firms. In sum, company unionism as an alternative to independent trade unions never became an important issue in Britain's public debate about state-labor-management relations.[32]

As originally written by a drafting committee on which Donald Richberg was the principal representative of labor interests, Section 7a provided: "1) that employees shall have the right to organize and bargain collectively through representatives of their own choosing; 2) that no employee and no one seeking employment shall be required as a condition of employment to join any organization or to refrain from joining a labor organization of his own choosing."[33]

Even before the Depression, the AFL had begun to press for a legislative ban on company unions.[34] As noted in chapter 4, during the course of the debate over the NIRA, the labor federation successfully lobbied Congress to strengthen the protections against employers' unfair labor practices by modifying Richberg's original language through the addition of wording taken verbatim from the Norris–La Guardia Act, which banned "interference, restraint, or coercion" by employers affecting their workers' designation of collective-bargaining agents, and also by changing the wording that prohibited employers from requiring workers to join "any organization" as a condition of employment to a ban applying only to compulsory membership in a "company union."[35] The latter change left open the possibility of agreements establishing a closed shop. Though not creating an outright prohibition of company unions, the AFL leadership believed the new language held out the promise of government action to impede their development.

Colin Gordon claims that employers in a number of older competitive sectors of the economy hoped that organized labor could prove effective in limiting destructive wage competition and in bringing order to their industries and thus "saw Section 7 as the economic core of the act and not just a political expedient to its passage."[36] Ordway Tead, who was an active figure in the Taylor Society and coauthor of the first academic text in the field of personnel management, argued at the time that a strengthening of unions would "forward a desirable uniformity of labor standards," including a needed increase in wage rates to create more mass purchasing power, and would also contribute to "a more effective compliance with regulatory and code provisions on labor standards."[37] Such a perspective, though, remained far more prevalent among British than American employers, most of whom in 1933 continued to be strongly hostile to unions.[38]

Important elements of the business community were initially willing to accept Section 7a (even as worded following the AFL-suggested revisions) as a necessary trade-off in exchange for gaining exemption from the antitrust laws, but during Senate hearings on the proposed NIRA, business opposition to the labor provisions of the recovery act solidified. National Association of Manufacturers (NAM) spokesperson James Emery offered substitute language that would have restricted the development of the closed shop by prohibiting any agreement whereby an employee or anyone seeking employment "be required as a condition of employment to join or refrain from joining any legitimate organization." Ironically, Emery favorably cited the 1927 British Trade Disputes Act's prohibition of public employers requiring workers to belong to unions in supporting his argument against the closed shop. In spite of its claims to the contrary, NAM's proposal to use the power of the state to restrict closed shop agreements was itself hardly consistent with a strict notion of collective laissez-faire and reflected the lack of ideological consistency that was characteristic of both the supporters and opponents of organized labor at this time.[39]

Even more important given later developments was Emery's advocacy of substitute language in order to legitimize company unions by specifically permitting "any form" of collective bargaining that was "mutually satisfactory" to both employers and employees. Emery made the greatly exaggerated claim that "probably three times as many workers have operated over long periods of time under employee representation schemes" as had belonged to trade unions. In fact, in 1932 there were approximately 1.3 million workers covered by employee representation plans as compared to close to 3 million workers who belonged to independent unions.[40] Nevertheless, the concentration of company unions among the nation's largest employers gave greater prominence to the issue than might have been expected based on the actual numbers of workers involved. Emery argued that any provision that could be interpreted as limiting the constructive functioning of existing company unions would have a harmful effect on industry. At one point, the Senate voted favorably on an amendment to Section 7a, which Richberg was willing to accept, that would have allowed for the continuation of any existing "satisfactory relationships between employers and employees of any particular plant, firm, or corporation."[41]

In the end, due largely to the efforts of Senator George Norris, such language was removed because of concern that employers, in order to thwart the formation of independent unions, might use the wording to justify covertly pressuring workers into joining employee representation plans. Senator Huey Long colorfully referred to such plans as "the spider in the soup."[42] From the outset of discussions about the proposed recovery act, one of the bill's chief sponsors, Senator Robert Wagner of New York, had advanced the argument frequently made by the leadership of the AFL that only through the extension of meaningful collective bargaining would it be possible to achieve a proper balance between wages and profits and thus establish the level of mass purchasing power needed to restore the health of the nation's economy. Recognition of the need to increase mass purchasing power was emerging as a key factor in the consumer-labor alliance that would become central to the New Deal reform coalition, and Wagner, Norris, and a majority in Congress in 1933 recognized that company unions could not fulfill this purpose.[43]

Even with the AFL's success in strengthening Section 7a, the NIRA remained ambiguous. Stanley Vittoz describes the labor provisions as a "rhetorical concession" to organized labor but implies that leaders of the American business community may well have had assurances from the Roosevelt administration even before the final passage of the act that the law would not be used to prohibit company unions.[44] John L. Lewis himself assured the Senate that there was "nothing in Section 7 that will destroy the company union as it now exists in any plant," so long as membership was not made compulsory.[45] As would soon become apparent, the NIRA represented only a halting step away from a purely voluntarist approach to labor law.

The American labor movement had turned to the state with a certain degree of ambivalence in the hope that the power of government could be used to limit company unions and other antiunion employer practices. However, Hugh Johnson and Donald Richberg, who were appointed administrator and general counsel, respectively, of the newly established NRA, adopted an essentially voluntarist approach to implementing the law's protections of collective bargaining. Both men expressed strong misgivings about using government compulsion to force upon workers and employers any single model of labor relations, with Richberg insisting that the main purpose of Section 7a was to "protect individual liberty and voluntary collective action" and not to force on employers or workers the closed shop or to limit in any way the establishment of mutually satisfactory methods of structuring labor-management relations.[46]

Soon after the NIRA went into effect, crucial differences developed between the administrators of the NRA and the National Labor Board (NLB), which President Roosevelt appointed in August 1933 with Senator Wagner as chair to help settle the rapidly increasing number of labor disputes arising under the recovery act. The NLB had no clear statutory authority but was modeled upon the National War Labor Board of World War I. It attempted to serve as both a mediator in particular disputes and judicial interpreter of the meaning of Section 7a. Wagner was clearly sympathetic to organized labor and continually stressed the benefits to the entire economy that he thought would flow from increased unionization. At the same time, though, his belief in the need for a more active state role in labor-management relations led Wagner to proclaim that any "group which indulges in strikes or lockouts without first invoking the intervention of the National Labor Board violates every dictate of good policy and exhibits a complete oversight of the magnificent possibilities of our whole recovery philosophy and program." Wagner was thus willing at least to explore the possibility of an expanded state role in collective bargaining and establishing certain elements of a corporatist order, while Richberg and Johnson continued to remain committed to a more voluntaristic version of collective laissez-faire.[47]

The NLB and its system of regional labor boards had some success in mediating disputes, but because of lack of cooperation from the NRA, the NLB faced great difficulties in enforcing its interpretations of the protections afforded labor by the recovery act. In particular, the NRA failed to enforce the NLB's rulings on two key issues stemming from Section 7a, the legitimacy of company unions and the methods by which workers would determine their collective-bargaining agents. However, the NLB developed a "common law" on industrial relations through its interpretations of Section 7a that would have a major impact on subsequent New Deal labor policy.[48]

In spite of industry fears about the government's possible use of the NIRA to force employers to recognize independent unions, Section 7a, in practice, proved to be as much a spur to the spread of employer-sponsored employee representation plans as it did to the growth of independent trade unions. Leaders of organized labor such as John Lewis and Sidney Hillman were able to recruit new members, in part because of their rather disingenuous, but nonetheless effective, claim that President Roosevelt wanted workers to join unions. Roosevelt had shown no particular interest in fostering unionization as part of his recovery program, while Hugh Johnson proclaimed soon after the adoption of the NIRA that he did not consider it "the duty of the Administration to act as an agent to unionize labor in any industry" and that the NRA under his leadership would not "so act."[49] Membership in independent unions consequently increased by nearly 1 million between 1933 and 1935, yet the number of employees belonging to company-sponsored schemes rose even more rapidly (by approximately 1.25 million), as employers, eager to avoid having to deal with independent unions, chose to organize company unions as a means of claiming that they were satisfying the requirements of Section 7a for collective bargaining.[50]

Neither the Wagner labor board nor Johnson and Richberg interpreted Section 7a as a total ban on company unions, but the NLB adopted an interpretation of the law that, if strictly enforced, would have eliminated most company unions. The board held that employers illegally interfered with their workers' right to self-organization if they initiated or imposed on their workers an employee representation plan, or if they dominated the operation of a previously established plan.[51] The administration of the NRA proved far less restrictive than the NLB in its view of what constituted an unacceptable form of company unionism, with Richberg, in particular, warning against the government becoming too deeply involved in the "administrative enforcement" of "legislative rules."[52] Because the NLB itself had no enforcement powers, the organization of company unions, especially in mass production industries such as automobiles, soon outstripped the growth of independent unions. By 1934, some of the initial gains in membership made by AFL-affiliated or other independent unions in the first months of the NRA were being lost.[53] An editorial on the subject of company unions in *Nation's Business* in the spring of 1934 declared: "In the whole realm of industrial relations perhaps no other issue even approaches this in importance at this hour."[54]

Writing at about the same time, industrial relations consultant Edward Cowdrick perceptively summed up the uncertainties resulting from the adoption of Section 7a:

> The National Recovery Act, with its guarantee to workers of the right to bargain collectively, immensely enlarged the importance of both employee representation and trade unionism. There is little doubt that the old American custom of individual dealing between worker and boss has suffered a loss of favor

and prestige from which it scarcely will recover. . . . Whether unionism or employee representation will prove to be the dominant method of collective bargaining; whether both will survive and function competitively as in the past; whether there will be some integration in which the most useful features of each system will be retained; whether trade unions or industrial unions will be the more favored; whether works councils will be linked together throughout whole companies or whole industries—these are questions that must await answers in the near future. The current prominence of the National Labor Board indicates that some form of government supervision may become a permanent factor in collective dealing between employees and management.[55]

The second crucial area of NLB rulings involved the "majority rule" principle of representation. Employers had long argued in cynical fashion that every employee deserved the "right" to bargain "individually" and that unions could speak only for their own members and not for all workers in a particular plant or company. The NLB, on the other hand, held that in the determination of bargaining agents, the principle of majority rule needed to apply if collective bargaining was to be conducted in a meaningful way. In the crucial case of the automobile industry, President Roosevelt and Hugh Johnson failed to support the NLB position and instead backed the creation of a separate automobile labor board that allowed individuals, as well as company and independent unions, to bargain with management.[56]

During its short life, the NLB also handed down rulings that sought to clarify what forms of antiunion behavior by employers were unacceptable under the law, established the precedent of government-conducted secret-ballot elections to determine workers' choice of collective-bargaining agents, and encouraged the signing of written agreements as the final product of negotiations between employers and employees.[57]

Both the labor movement and its supporters faced a serious dilemma by 1934. The adoption of Section 7a, in combination with the upturn in the economy in the summer of 1933, had proved to be a boon to unionization, but the momentum that had been achieved following the establishment of the NRA was beginning to be lost. Although a more sympathetic state improved the chances for recruiting workers into the labor movement, employers' resistance to the organization of independent unions, and especially their increasing use of company unions to thwart the apparent intention of Section 7a, led to growing frustration in the labor movement and among labor's supporters in Congress over the NLB's inability to enforce its rulings. Without any support or encouragement from the White House, Wagner himself (with aid from economist Leon Keyserling and legal and industrial relations experts associated with the NLB) began to draft a bill that would give clear authority to a newly constituted labor board and write into statute law some of the principal rulings handed down by the NLB.[58]

AFL stalwarts such as Matthew Woll continued to express serious reservations about excessive reliance on the power of the federal government, arguing that the labor movement's "foundation principles" remained the "principles of American democracy," among which "decentralization" and a rejection of "any form of compulsion" were central. Reflecting his continuing commitment to the notion of collective laissez-faire, Woll reasserted his view that the "political program" of the AFL was "in some respects . . . similar to the political programs of the labor unions of Great Britain. Necessarily, first place is given to the legal rights and status of labor organizations."[59] Even as the conservative Woll came to support government involvement in the establishment of old-age pensions, unemployment insurance, and medical care that would have paralleled developments in the British welfare state, he still feared the consequences of the state becoming too directly involved in the collective bargaining process: "Any movement designed to compel employers and wage-earners to enter into collective agreements inevitably must lead to compulsory arbitration and where compulsory arbitration prevails, individual freedom or collective freedom no longer can prevail."[60]

An editorial in the *American Federationist* acknowledged that the "experience of the past few months under the National Recovery Administration makes plain that political agencies are not a substitute for economic organizations mobilizing and directing economic power" and that "the law and the Administration depend upon the workers to achieve their rights by their own initiative." While the leadership of the AFL recognized that the law could not force recalcitrant employers "to do something which implies volition," namely, to bargain voluntarily with "the chosen representatives of workers," the experience under the NIRA did not completely sour organized labor on the potential benefits of state action. The state could still "punish" employers for "non-compliance" with a clearly stated public policy favoring unionization. Writing before the Supreme Court struck down the NIRA, Matthew Woll warned against the danger of organized "labor's readiness to leave everything to the Government," an approach that, in his view, would lead to "certain failure." Woll, however, expressed his support for the government "giving full recognition to the legal right of labor to bargain collectively" and for the need for legislation to make the protections of Section 7a "more clear—more definite—less subject to confusing, misleading and conflicting interpretations." Consequently, the AFL and many industrial relations experts became active supporters of Wagner's efforts to draft legislation that would create stronger and more explicit government powers to protect workers' collective bargaining rights.[61]

National Labor Relations Act

It would not be until after the Supreme Court struck down the NIRA in 1935 and thus made null and void what little protection Section 7a did provide labor that Wagner's legislative initiative would bear fruit in the form of the NLRA. Wagner introduced his Labor Disputes Bill in the 1934 session of

Congress, but FDR convinced Wagner temporarily to relent on his initiative when he offered the alternative of Public Resolution 44 to authorize the president to establish a new National Labor Relations Board under executive authority. The failure of the new labor board, which was chaired by Francis Biddle and which also lacked clear powers of enforcement, to prove more effective than its predecessor convinced Wagner to reintroduce a modified version of his bill in Congress in February of 1935. FDR did not initially indicate any interest in the bill, but indications that Wagner's bill would pass with or without the president's active support helped convince Roosevelt of the political wisdom of backing the legislation. The Schechter decision further eased the passage of the Wagner Act, since many members of Congress concluded that they could vote for the bill with the assurance that the Supreme Court would ultimately rule the law unconstitutional.[62]

In its final form, the NLRA went further than Section 7a by explicitly stating that "encouraging the practice and procedure of collective bargaining" was "the policy of the United States." The NLRA called for the establishment of a three-person National Labor Relations Board (NLRB) to carry out the provisions of the law, including proscriptions of several specifically designated "unfair labor practices" by employers. An employer was prohibited from dominating, interfering with, or financially supporting "any labor organization"; refusing to "bargain collectively with the representatives of his employees"; or in other ways interfering with or obstructing the employees' "right to self-organization." In contrast to the labor boards that existed under the NIRA, the new NLRB was given direct access to the courts to enforce its orders, and its findings as to facts were to be considered "conclusive." The NLRB also was given the authority to determine the appropriate bargaining unit ("employer," "craft," "plant," or "subdivision thereof") and to conduct secret-ballot elections "or utilize any other suitable method to ascertain" who, if anyone, the majority of workers in the unit wanted as exclusive agents in collective bargaining with management. Such language would make possible the growth of industrial unions, but it ruled out the development of industry-wide collective bargaining.[63]

Radical critics of the law, both at the time of its passage and since, have argued that the Wagner Act was a direct response to the wave of strikes and labor protests that had occurred since the summer of 1933 and that the law was intended to defuse an increasingly militant labor movement by incorporating the more moderate elements of organized labor into a newly stabilized system of American capitalism. Emmett P. Cash of the Steel and Metal Workers Industrial Union and William F. Dunne, who represented the communist Trade Union Unity League, both testified in Congress against the bill, which was also opposed by Roger Baldwin of the American Civil Liberties Union.[64] Some radical scholars have emphasized the role played by experts and state actors who were more farsighted in their understanding of what was needed to preserve American capitalism than were the capitalists themselves, most of whom opposed the law.[65]

Other historians and social scientists espousing a "corporate liberal" interpretation have argued that key elements of the business community did appreciate the long-term benefits from an accommodation with organized labor and therefore provided crucial support for the NLRA. Advocates of a corporate liberal interpretation differ as to whether business support grew out of a recognition of the potential of "regulatory unionism" to limit excessive wage competition within highly competitive labor-intensive industries, or whether it came primarily from multinational firms in capital-intensive industries that accepted the idea of a high-wage economy, not only because wages were a less significant element of their production costs than they were for labor-intensive firms, but because these firms looked forward to the expansion of markets at home and abroad.[66]

There is virtually no evidence that directly supports the corporate liberal interpretation of the Wagner Act. Business opposition to the NLRA was even stronger and more unified than business opposition had been earlier to the incorporation of Section 7a into the NIRA. More plausible, though still not fully convincing, is the claim that a political and intellectual elite acting in behalf but without the direct support of capitalists was responsible for the passage of the NLRA because it saw the need for state action that would have the effect of deradicalizing an increasingly threatening labor movement. Although such a view correctly identifies the key group in the drafting and enactment of the NLRA, it offers a rather misleading explanation of the motives that guided Wagner and his allies.[67]

William Connery, who chaired the House Committee on Labor and Education, did argue in May of 1934 that legislative action along the lines of the Wagner Act was necessary to halt the spread of labor radicalism and that a strengthened AFL would serve as "the bulwark against communism in the United States."[68] Nevertheless, left-wing militancy among workers in 1934–1935 was not so widespread as to create sufficient political pressure on legislators to convince Congress of the need to pass new labor legislation in order to co-opt the labor movement. Wagner and his associates were not principally motivated by a desire to use state power to prevent the American working class from turning in wholesale fashion to radicalism. Rather, the NLRA can best be understood as stemming from the conclusion drawn by Wagner and other policy intellectuals that without collective bargaining as a means of improving wages and hence mass purchasing power, the American economy might never fully recover from the Depression, and that without more effective state intervention, American employers would continue effectively to resist unionization. Supporters of the NLRA were also genuinely disturbed by the coercive methods many employers utilized to prevent workers from freely choosing their own representatives for purposes of collective bargaining, so that Wagner and other reformers envisaged the new labor law much more as a means of constraining the behavior of employers than as one curtailing a threat posed by labor radicalism.[69]

The issue of company unionism was at the heart of the Wagner Act. Wagner himself described company unions as the "greatest obstacle to collective bargaining." Seeing the initiation of such plans as the most effective tactic used by employers to frustrate the intent of Section 7a, Wagner incorporated explicit language in the NLRA making it an "unfair labor practice" for an employer to "dominate or interfere with the formation or administration of any labor organization or contribute financial or other support to it." In addition, he sought to establish a mechanism by which the state would be able to review and affirm the legitimacy of workers' choices of their collective bargaining representatives.[70]

The ban on company unions naturally elicited strong opposition from employers. James Emery attacked the provision, claiming: "It ignores successful and practical experiments in new forms of collective relationship" and "would cast all labor relations in one mold, granting a labor monopoly to those who employ it."[71] Some individuals associated with the business community who had a reputation for being relatively progressive in the area of labor relations, such as Henry Dennison and Dean Wallace Donham of the Harvard Business School, argued against the prohibition, repeating the view expressed by Emery, as well as by NRA General Counsel Richberg, that the state should not attempt to impose a single model of labor relations on industry.[72]

The rush by employers to create company unions as a response to Section 7a, though, had only confirmed the claims made by the labor movement that employers sought to use company unions largely as a means of avoiding the establishment of more effective representation for their workers. Even James Myers, who had served as director of one of the most progressive employee representation plans of the 1920s (Dutchess Bleacheries) and in 1935 was industrial secretary for the Federal Council of the Churches of Christ in America, strongly defended the ban on company unions. He informed the chair of the Senate Committee on Education and Labor that he had learned from his own experience that company unions, no matter how sincere or generous the motives of their organizers, were incapable of matching the effectiveness of independent unions, because they prevented employees from pooling their resources with "workers throughout an industry" and because they forced employees to "get along without a spokesman engaged and paid by themselves" who could "speak fearlessly during negotiations with employers."[73]

The enforcement of a prohibition on company unions by itself would have involved the American state more directly in setting the conditions for collective bargaining than was the case in Britain. Even more important, the perceived need to have the state assume responsibility for determining the legitimacy of labor organizations led directly to the NLRA provisions calling for government determination of appropriate bargaining units and workers' choice of representatives. The AFL had traditionally established the jurisdictional lines for union representation and remained wary about the state becoming in any way involved in such matters, particularly because of the possibility that a government board might issue rulings favoring indus-trial over craft unionism.[74]

Wallace Donham had actually cited the AFL's craft-based form of organi-zation as a justification for his opposition to a ban on company unions. He maintained that so long as the AFL continued to be organized largely along craft lines, a system of government-mandated collective bargaining involv-ing existing unions would prevent the development of the kind of coherent planning for "continuity of production" that either company or industrial unions might allow.[75] Of course, in the months and years ahead, the labor movement itself would become bitterly divided between proponents of in-dustrial unionism and the upholders of the AFL's craft-based traditions.

At the time of the debate over the Wagner Act, the American labor move-ment had not yet splintered, and the leadership of the AFL had good reason to transcend its concerns about the potential consequences of granting the NLRB additional authority over what had previously been considered inter-nal union affairs. The problem of employers rejecting the principle of ma-jority rule and insisting on the right of any individual or any group of em-ployees to engage in "bargaining," as well as the possibility that employers themselves would attempt to determine bargaining units, led the drafters of the NLRA to give the new labor board the power to designate appropriate units and final authority in establishing the majority preference of workers in their choice of bargaining agents.

In spite of AFL concerns about relinquishing its authority in jurisdic-tional disputes between unions, William Green found it expedient in his testimony before the Senate Committee on Education and Labor to support a supervisory role for the proposed labor board as a counter to employers' obstructionist tactics:

> There is only one satisfactory way of determining by whom employees want to be represented when an employer challenges the right of a union to bargain for all of the employees in a certain class or craft. That is by Government-supervised election—by secret ballot. If the employees and the employer are not able to agree as to what constitutes the bargaining unit, I believe that National Labor Relations Board should decide what the bargaining unit shall be.[76]

Francis Biddle, a member of the newly emerging group of legal and pol-icy experts in the field of industrial relations, who served as chair of the original NLRB, also argued strongly in behalf of the "necessity for the Board deciding the unit." He warned that allowing employers to establish bargain-ing units "would invite unlimited abuse and gerrymandering" as employers sought to "defeat the aims of the statute." On the other hand, permitting the employees themselves to "make the decision without proper considera-tion of the elements which should constitute the appropriate units" would raise the possibility that "the practical significance of the majority rule" principle might be vitiated, and that "by breaking off into small groups," workers would "make it impossible for the employer to run his plant."[77]

AFL legal counsel Charlton Ogburn, William Leiserson, and some of the other industrial relations experts involved in the influential Twentieth Century Fund's study of industrial relations favored amendments to Wagner's bill that would have given greater protection to the organizational autonomy of the AFL and granted unions legal standing in controversies coming before the proposed board.[78] Economist Sumner Slichter favored the general aims of the proposed legislation, but he warned that entrusting the NLRB with the power to determine bargaining units meant giving the state the "discretion to determine in a significant number of cases the organization and structure of the American labor movement."[79] The Twentieth Century Fund Committee on the Government and Labor concluded that "a statute can and should assure to the employees the right to determine their bargaining units for themselves, free from coercion or restraint on the part of employers." Yet the committee acknowledged that employees would not always agree among themselves upon the scope of appropriate bargaining units, so that the proposed labor board, and not the AFL, would ultimately have to exercise final authority to give substance to the "principle of majority representation."[80]

Historian Christopher Tomlins correctly points out that once trade unions became invested with legitimacy provided by the state and were charged with carrying out what amounted to public functions, it seemed necessary to most advocates of labor law reform to grant the state the ultimate authority to determine the appropriate unit for collective bargaining and to supervise the application of the principle of majority rule by overseeing the process by which workers would designate their representatives. The state, in other words, would protect the "rights" of workers as individual "citizens" of industry in much the same way it established political jurisdictions and voting procedures in the political arena.[81]

In the end, the key factor convincing most supporters of the NLRA to accept a greatly expanded role for the state in industrial relations was not a desire to control workers' previously autonomous organizations, but rather the need they felt to justify government efforts to overcome employer resistance to unionization in terms of political values that were widely accepted among the American people. Advocates of labor law reform, in other words, were more concerned with the threat from the right than from the left. The language of individual rights that backers of the Wagner Act often used to defend the law should not, therefore, be viewed simply as an indication of their unwavering commitment to individualism. They were, after all, trying to devise a means by which the state could facilitate unionization. The obstacles to be overcome in achieving that goal, entrenched employer opposition and courts that still threatened to strike down pro-union legislation as unconstitutional, shaped not only the final form of the legislation but also the language that the advocates of reform used.

The complexity of contemporary attitudes toward the issue of state involvement in industrial relations is further demonstrated by the decision of the drafters of the NLRA to forgo granting any legal status to collective bargaining agreements. The NLB and the old NLRB had both favored policies that encouraged labor and management to codify collective bargaining agreements in writing. In both the United States and Britain, the corporatist idea of giving legal sanction to agreements negotiated between labor and management had been discussed since before the First World War, but such discussions focused on meso-level agreements that might apply to an entire industry as a means of avoiding cutthroat competition between employers, rather than on micro-level agreements between individual employers and unionized workers.

In Britain, the 1934 legislation concerning wages in the cotton textile industry did apply this principle to one sector of the economy in which collective bargaining took place on a national scale. Nevertheless, opposition from the peak organizations of both labor and employers, which reflected the continuing appeal of the ideal of collective laissez-faire, including the assumption by labor leaders that workers' interests were best served by avoiding state recognition of unions as legal entities with corporate responsibilities, prevented Parliament from extending the principle of state enforcement of collective bargaining agreements beyond the cotton textile industry.[82]

As noted above, in the United States, Section 7 of the NIRA did authorize the president to give legal force to collective bargaining agreements dealing with wages and hours, but the focus under the NRA on codes of fair competition between employers resulted in Roosevelt failing to utilize this authority. Wagner's proposed NLRA made no reference to the potential legal status of agreements arrived at through collective bargaining. The Twentieth Century Fund committee on labor law reform urged Wagner and the Congress "to offer a positive inducement to labor and industry to enter into collective agreements by means of permitting the registration" with the NLRA of such voluntary contracts, so that if both parties wanted to register these agreements with the board, the agency would "have power to issue cease and desist orders in support of those agreements."[83]

Nevertheless, as in Britain at this time, there was no widespread support in the United States from either business or the labor movement for giving the state the power to enforce collective bargaining agreements, since most employers still sought to avoid any dealings with unions, while union leaders feared anything that smacked of "compulsory arbitration." Wagner had even hesitated to include in the NLRA a provision making it an unfair labor practice for an employer "to refuse to bargain collectively with the representatives of his employees," because of his fear that critics of the law would claim that such wording would have mandated employers to reach agreement and sign written contracts with unions. Although Congress added to the NLRA the duty to engage in collective bargaining (but not to come to an agreement or to put agreements into writing), the Twentieth Century

Fund committee's proposal to allow for voluntary registration and enforcement of agreements met the same fate as similar proposals in Britain in this period and was not incorporated into the final version of the law.

Conclusion

The Wagner Act institutionalized a new role for the state in American industrial relations that entailed a degree of state involvement that went far beyond anything contemplated at the time in Britain. Yet it is not easy to characterize the underlying philosophy that guided the supporters of labor law reform. While the NLRA was being debated, some informed observers who remained committed to a philosophy of collective laissez-faire warned that the law had the potential to start America down the road to becoming a corporate state. Sumner Slichter noted how "paradoxical" it was that the AFL, which was "created for the express purpose of preserving the autonomy of its member unions, should be advocating a planned or managed economy in which the trade unions would inevitably lose much of their freedom," while "the Government, at the very time that it is seeking to develop its activities as a manager, should foster powerful bodies which are bound to limit its ability to subject the economic system to central control."[84] NLRA opponent Wallace Donham offered an assessment of the law that ironically foreshadowed the views of later leftist critics of the Wagner Act. He argued that if trade unions were to "remain healthy," then they needed to continue to be "voluntary organizations not creatures of the State."

> If the State now steps in and makes trade unions compulsory I believe there is no stopping point short of State control of the union and State control of industry. This . . . means State control of trade-union organizations, jurisdiction, elections; indeed, the death of trade-unionism as we know it. If State control develops, as I believe it must if this bill passes, rebel organizations outside the official organization will lose all opportunity to function or will be considered revolutionary. Trade-union officials will in the long run become part of our political machinery.[85]

In light of later developments it was also ironic that in attacking the NLRA, *Nation's Business,* the voice of the U.S. Chamber of Commerce, also warned that unions were foolish to think they had "nothing to fear from this entering wedge of government domination of wages and working conditions," because "administrations change, boards change."[86]

A number of scholars have subsequently adopted this view of the NLRA as marking the triumph of a liberal form of corporatism in which unions, in essence, became agents of the state. Tomlins thus contends that the Wagner Act marked a major departure from earlier legislation intended to "promote collective bargaining." The purpose of previous laws such as the Railway Labor and Norris–La Guardia acts, according to Tomlins, had been "stabilizing relations between existing organized parties," with the under-standing that unions "were assumed to be private organizations, perform-ing no public function." In contrast, Wagner's new approach was predicated on viewing "collective bargaining [as] an expression of the public interest in the terms of individual contracts of employment."[87] In a similar vein, histo-rian Clarence Wunderlin observes that the NLRA "marked a significant pol-icy change toward a state-administered industrial relations system," because it transformed "unions into agents of public policy[,] circumscribed their role as voluntary associations, and institutionalized a permanent federal government role in industrial relations."[88]

Wagner and Keyserling did offer their legislation as a means of contribut-ing to economic recovery, sharing the view expressed by NLB member Francis Haas that Americans henceforth needed to "abandon the notion that the wage contract concerns only an employer and an employee" and to recognize that such a contract "concerns everybody else," since a healthy economy depended upon sufficiently high wages to guarantee mass pur-chasing power.[89] To some degree, at least, the authors of the NLRA were in-fluenced by the liberal corporatist approach to the political economy that had been widely discussed in America since the First World War. Wagner's chief aide in drafting the labor disputes bill, Leon Keyserling, later insisted that although the senator always put the greatest emphasis on the need to give labor more effective representation in collective bargaining as a means of raising mass purchasing power, Wagner's

> . . . vision of the role of the American labor movement . . . was not limited to the idea that collective bargaining, based upon equality of bargaining power, would operate merely as a system of checks and balances. His was no simple doctrine of countervailing power. He envisaged the collective bargaining process as a cooperative venture guided by intelligence rather than a mere test of relative strength. And even beyond this he foresaw that this process within our enterprise system could become an integral part of an every [sic] larger co-operative process guided by intelligence which would animate the whole econ-omy, including the governmental sector.[90]

While favoring a more active role for the state in industrial relations and being attracted to many of the ideas associated with corporatism, Wagner and his allies stopped far short of supporting the development of a liberal corporatist order. The NLRA's exclusive focus on micro-level industrial rela-tions meant that it was completely silent on any possible role for the peak organizations of workers and employers at the macro-level of the economy. More important, in contrast to the views of Father Charles Caughlin, who called for the government to become more directly involved in organizing workers into industrial unions, the NLRA actually foreclosed the possibil-ity of meso-level or industry-wide collective bargaining.[91] Even as Wagner and other supporters of labor law reform accepted the need for state involvement in determining bargaining units and conducting union certification elections, they did not envision the state becoming involved in the internal affairs of unions or even using its power to enforce collective bargaining contracts.

The persistence of a pluralist fear of the state becoming too powerful is reflected in the frequent use that Wagner and other defenders of the proposed NLRA made of the image of checks and balances. Economist and future senator Paul Douglas testified in behalf of the first Wagner bill that it was "essential to build up organizations of labor as a counterpoise [to employers' associations]. For only so shall we obtain balance and prevent the domination of capital which seems to be the economic essence of Fascism." Both Francis Biddle, then chair of the old NLRB, and H. A. Millis, who also served on the old NLRB and later served on the NLRB under the Wagner Act, expressed very similar views about the need for creating a balance of power and influence between employers and employees. Even a business opponent of the law such as Arthur Young of U.S. Steel implicitly acknowledged the elements of pluralistic thinking underlying the Wagner Act when he attacked the law for being based on the "vicious" assumption that there was a "certain and complete clash of interest . . . between employer and employee."[92]

Shortly before the NIRA experiment was ruled unconstitutional, Wagner asserted:

> This process of economic self-rule must fail unless every group is equally well represented. In order that the strong may not take advantage of the weak, every group must be equally strong. Not only is this common sense; but it is also in line with the philosophy of checks and balances that colors our political thinking. It is in accord with modern democratic concepts which reject the merger of all group interests into a totalitarian state. It is necessary to avert the advent of fascistic devices.[93]

Wagner hoped, in the words of legal scholar Mark Barenberg, to achieve "a legislatively nurtured culture of cooperation," even if he did not envision the establishment of a corporatist order in which organized labor and organized capital would actually become extensions of the state, or in which all workers and employers would be compelled to join together in groups to facilitate coordination and cooperation in the political economy. As Barenberg notes, "Wagner's unwavering premise that workers would remain free not to organize—the hallmark distinguishing a contractualist from a corporatist labor law regime—reflected the bedrock voluntarism of the Wagner Act."[94]

Britain's abstentionist labor law regime at this time still remained more consistent with a pluralist ideal of collective laissez-faire than the industrial relations system established by the NLRA. Wagner's move beyond such an approach was clearly not the result of a greater ideological predisposition on his part toward statist solutions than existed among supporters of labor in Britain. The debate over labor law reform in the United States took place within an antistatist ideological context that was quite similar to the ideological context in which British labor law had developed over the previous three decades.

However, given the historic weakness of organized labor and the continuing hostility of employers to collective bargaining in the United States, factors that resulted in large part from the structure of American business, an abstentionist approach to labor law reform held out little promise of being effective in creating a greater balance between capital and labor and thereby restoring the health of the economy. Wagner thus supported state intervention that was on its face one-sided, proscribing certain employer but not union behaviors, to compensate for the weakness of unions. Had there been no state intervention in the 1930s, it is just as likely that organized labor would have languished as it is that it would have effectively challenged the organization of American industry. Although the Wagner Act was certainly not the only factor in the doubling of union membership in the United States between 1936 and 1938, public policy and the more favorable political environment created by the New Deal contributed significantly to this dramatic increase.[95]

The subsequent decline of unions and erosion of the collective bargaining regime that had emerged as part of the New Deal order was less a product of state repression or state control made possible by the NLRA than it was the result of the ultimate ineffectiveness of the law's protections against hostile employers, an ineffectiveness that was exacerbated by subsequent court interpretations and later antilabor amendments to the law, and by the fact that most American employers never really renounced their desire to operate in a union-free environment.[96] In the long run, the greatest failure of the NLRA was not so much that it attempted to use state power to recast labor-management relations, but rather that it did so in such a halting fashion. It neither created the foundation for a truly liberal corporatist political economy in which organized unions and organized employers cooperated with the state in the formulation and implementation of economic planning, nor, alternatively, did it create a truly level playing field in which employers and unions could compete as equals in a pluralist system of collective laissez-faire. The continuing hostility of most American employers toward unions was at least partially countered by the New Deal state, but the institutional legacy of the Wagner Act was not sufficient to sustain a system of industrial pluralism once the New Deal political order began to disintegrate after World War II.

Conclusion

On the eve of the Second World War, the American system of industrial relations operated in an environment that differed in several important respects from the setting in which labor relations were conducted in Britain. Although the British economy witnessed growing industrial concentration in the 1920s and 1930s, the large industrial firm, in which substantial resources were devoted to issues relating to personnel management and human relations, was still more characteristic of the American economy. As a consequence, both employers and workers in America were more likely than their counterparts in Britain to focus on strictly micro-level labor-management relations, and American employers would continue to be far more reluctant than employers in Britain to accept unions as a positive force in industry. Employer resistance to dealing with unions was at least partially overcome only when state intervention was made possible by the unique circumstances of the Great Depression and the vacuum created by the end of the National Recovery Administration experiment.

The adoption of the Wagner Act marked a critical milestone in the history of American industrial relations and created a significant divergence between American and British public policies. World War II and its immediate aftermath, however, were also critical in solidifying the system of "workplace contractualism" that came, at least for a time, to dominate American industry.[1] From the passage of the Wagner Act in 1935 until the Supreme Court upheld the constitutionality of the law in 1937, American labor under the leadership of the newly organized Congress of Industrial Organizations undertook an intensive organizing campaign that led to the establishment of unions in most of the nation's major mass-production industries. The surge in union membership, though, slowed substantially after 1937. Employers finally had to accept the reality of the Wagner

Act, but they developed an unholy alliance with the leaders of the AFL in attacking the National Labor Relations Board and calling for changes in the law. The AFL complained of the board's preference for industrial as opposed to craft organization and joined with business interests at the end of the decade in calling for revisions of the Wagner Act to limit the NLRB's discretion in determining bargaining units and to make it easier for employers to recognize AFL unions as a means of avoiding dealing with industrial unions affiliated with the CIO. The Smith Bill incorporating these and other changes to the Wagner Act passed the House in 1940 but failed to make it out of the Senate.[2]

The coming of war put calls for revision of the Wagner Act on hold and led to a new surge in union membership. As occurred in the First World War, mobilization for total war created conditions that favored the growth of unions in both the United States and Britain. Not only did shortages of labor enhance the bargaining power of unions, but both the American and British governments also looked to unions to bring order and stability to labor markets and to constrain shop-floor militancy and work stoppages. Given workers' less organized status and the greater hostility of employers to collective bargaining in prewar America, the war had what was in many ways an even more beneficial impact on unions in America than in Britain. The number of union members in the United States jumped by 63 percent between 1939 and 1945, whereas in Britain the increase was a more modest 29 percent. By 1945, for the first time since the early years of the century, American union density again came close to matching union density in Britain (34.3% as compared to 38.6%).[3]

Yet, in other respects, American unions emerged at war's end both more dependent on the state and in a considerably weaker political position than their British counterparts. Both nations relied on a variety of tripartite corporatist bodies to facilitate war production and brought prominent union leaders into positions of authority in government. In both nations the official leadership of organized labor supported the war effort by trying to limit strikes and by exercising restraint in wage demands. Yet in Britain tripartism entailed a greater degree of equality in the influence exercised by organized labor and organized employers than was the case in the United States, where business regained much of the power and popular respect it had lost in the previous decade. In comparison to the major role played by Ernest Bevin in Winston Churchill's war cabinet, Sidney Hillman exercised far less power in Franklin Roosevelt's business-dominated war administration.[4] Union membership grew substantially in America, in part because of rulings by the National War Labor Board that Roosevelt established shortly after Pearl Harbor, but the NWLB's efforts to foster a responsible form of unionism would have the lasting effect of reinforcing the legalistic and bureaucratic framework that came to distinguish the American from the British system of industrial relations after the war. Formalized grievance procedures codified in written agreements and enforceable by recourse to the state would become integral to the institutionalization of an American approach to labor relations that differed from the essentially collective laissez-faire model that continued to characterize British labor relations.[5]

The contrast in the war's lasting impact on the status of organized labor in the two countries is best illustrated by political developments immediately after the war. The growing power and status of unions in Britain led not only to the victory of the Labour Party in the national election of 1945 but also to the subsequent repeal by Parliament in 1946 of the Trade Disputes Act of 1927. The British state continued, largely by indirect means, to support the institutions of collective bargaining, but the repeal of the Trade Disputes Act was symbolic of a rejection of any intrusive state involvement in industrial relations and reflected the reinvigorated appeal of what could still be described as a flexible version of collective laissez-faire.[6] In the United States, on the other hand, a Republican victory in the 1946 Congressional elections set the stage for the passage in the following year of the Taft-Hartley Act. This law had the effect of institutionalizing some of the practices that had been encouraged by the NWLB, while also incorporating many of the proposals that had first been advanced by business interests before the outbreak of the war. Although the AFL had earlier joined business in attacking the NLRB, it now backed off its earlier support for amending the NLRA because it was clear that the Republican sponsors of the bill intended it as a means of curbing the power of organized labor as a whole, not just that of the CIO.

The Taft-Hartley Act was a complex and even self-contradictory set of amendments to the NLRA. The law was, nevertheless, largely consistent with the approach promoted by the National War Labor Board, though it did go beyond the Wagner Act by making it an unfair labor practice, enjoinable by the courts, for either employers or unions to violate the terms of collective bargaining contracts. It also allowed for state intervention in imminent strikes that might affect the national interest by giving the president the power to require a mandatory eighty-day cooling-off period.

In general, the law was predicated on the assumption that labor organizations, as well as employers, sometimes acted in ways that ran contrary to the public interest, so that it was necessary to ban "unfair practices" not just by employers, but also by unions. In the effort to "equalize" the impact of the law, the act banned certain forms of coercion by union agents, as well as secondary boycotts, while reasserting the free speech rights of employers to present their employees with arguments against unionization. The act also granted employers the right to request the NLRB to conduct certification elections. The law constrained union development in several other ways, including an outright ban on closed shops and a grant to individual states under Section 14b's so-called right-to-work provision of the authority to prohibit the union shop. Further, the Taft-Hartley Act excluded supervisory personnel, including foremen, from coverage under the nation's labor law and denied the law's protections to any union whose officials refused to sign an anti-communist oath.[7]

Pro-union opponents of the law described it as a "slave labor law" and predicted dire consequences would quickly ensue for organized labor. Union membership, however, was not significantly affected in the period immediately following the law's passage, with union density increasing slightly in the late 1940s and early 1950s and reaching a peak in 1954.[8] Although the Taft-Hartley Act was clearly intended as a means of putting a brake on the growth of union power and was strongly opposed by those who had been the most avid supporters of New Deal labor law reform, the legislation did not involve a fundamental repudiation of the approach institutionalized by the original Wagner Act. It was, after all, in the two decades following the passage of the Taft-Hartley Act that industrial relations experts most prominently proclaimed the triumph of a system of industrial pluralism they considered to be the natural expression of traditional American values. Living conditions for American workers did significantly improve in these years, and, especially after the merger of the AFL and CIO in 1955, organized labor once again seemed to be speaking with one voice.

Still, the collective bargaining regime that the Wagner Act helped to foster was, at best, only grudgingly tolerated by most American employers. The passage of the Taft-Hartley Act, and the enactment of the Landrum-Griffin Act in 1959, revealed the growing political potency of attacks on union power that did not bode well for the future of organized labor in America. Thus, trade union membership as a percentage of the labor force began a steady decline in the United States after the mid-1950s—a decline that turned into a collapse after 1980 when an overtly antiunion administration took power in Washington. By the beginning of the twenty-first century, fewer than 14 percent of all American workers belonged to unions. Although public-sector workers such as teachers joined unions in unprecedented numbers, in the private sector unionization rates actually fell below 10 percent.[9] From a present-day vantage point, it is now clear that the two decades following the passage of the Wagner Act were an anomaly in the history of American industrial relations.

In contrast to the United States, union membership in Britain continued to rise more or less steadily until the end of the 1970s. At that time, 57 percent of British workers were unionized—a density rate that was once again more than twice the figure for the United States.[10] Throughout the 1960s and most of the 1970s, a powerful TUC played a significant role in efforts by various British governments to implement a liberal corporatist incomes policy. As early as the 1960s, though, developments in the British economy were setting the stage for the dramatic change in Britain's system of industrial relations that would take place after 1979. Increasingly after 1979, Britain's approach to industrial relations would turn away from a collective laissez-faire model and come more closely to resemble the American pattern of labor-management-state relations.

Although a merger wave had occurred in Britain in the 1920s, it would not be until well after World War II that Britain's economy would take on a structure very much like that of the United States, with large firms and considerable concentration in industry.[11] The more "Americanized" structuring of business enterprise, including the development of a greater commitment by British employers to assert their control over all aspects of the production process, contributed to the ultimate collapse of the consensus that had formed earlier in the century in behalf of a collective laissez-faire approach to industrial relations. Even as unions maintained their overall strength in the 1960s, Britain's long tradition of centralized collective bargaining began to give way to more localized firm-specific forms of bargaining that mirrored the American focus on micro-level, as opposed to meso-level, industrial relations. Employers were finding that national agreements were proving less useful in containing the shop-floor militancy that developed in response to their increasing efforts to assert control over production.[12] Concerns about the apparent proliferation of unofficial strikes, interunion disputes, and the declining competitiveness of the British economy led the Labour government of Harold Wilson to appoint a Royal Commission in 1965 to examine the status of labor relations in the country. In its 1968 report, the Donovan Commission rejected Conservative calls to adopt a more American-style approach to state involvement in industrial relations, instead reaffirming its support for the idea of collective laissez-faire, but pressures for change were clearly building.[13]

When the Conservatives returned to power in 1970, they responded to the developing changes in British industry by attempting a fundamental reorientation of British public policy in the field of industrial relations. The abortive Industrial Relations Act of 1971 in many ways paralleled the Taft-Hartley Act. It established an Industrial Relations Court that had the authority to impose a cooling-off period in industrial disputes and to require a strike ballot in cases affecting the national interest. Even more important, the act virtually banned the closed shop, made collective bargaining agreements legally enforceable, and attempted to force unions to register with the government, which thereby was to gain oversight of some aspects of their internal affairs. The labor movement's resistance to the new law was fierce, with almost all unions refusing to register and strikes reaching a postwar high in 1972. The restoration of a Labour government in 1974 led to the repeal of the act, but as a result of the continuing Americanization of British firms and growing international pressures on British industry, the reassertion of union power and the growth in union membership of the 1970s proved temporary phenomena.[14]

Margaret Thatcher's Conservative victory in 1979 led to the piecemeal adoption of most of the measures the Conservatives had attempted to implement in one fell swoop in 1971. Thus, a series of laws adopted between 1980 and 1990 severely restricted the closed shop and secondary boycotts, made union officers liable for many kinds of union activities that had been protected ever since the passage of the Trade Disputes Act of 1906, and established extensive government oversight and regulation of the internal affairs of unions. These measures would remain in place even after Labour regained power in 1997. The Thatcher administration did not, however, try to revive the earlier Conservative effort to emulate the American system of making collective bargaining agreements legally enforceable contracts.[15] Ironically, whereas the initial impetus for the New Deal's intrusive state involvement in industrial relations was the need to overcome the obdurate resistance of employers to unions, in Britain direct and comprehensive state intervention after 1970 would be more clearly driven by a desire of both employers and state officials to bring militant unions under greater control.

By the end of the twentieth century, there was a growing convergence between the American and British systems of industrial relations, as Britain became more like the United States in business structure and in state involvement in labor-management relations. Both states had moved away from an essentially collective laissez-faire approach to public policy, and both nations had come to emphasize micro-level industrial relations over organized labor's possible involvement in meso- or macro-level institutional arrangements. Moreover, union membership had fallen dramatically in both countries over the previous two decades. The growing hostility of the state under the Reagan and Thatcher administrations was clearly a major factor in the fate of both American and British unions. Although no new major labor legislation was passed in the United States in the 1980s, Reagan's crushing of the air traffic controllers' strike and the administrative rulings of his appointees to the NLRB undermined the power of unions and allowed employers to adopt union avoidance strategies with virtual impunity.[16]

In addition to the development of less hospitable labor law regimes and more hostile state authorities, a number of other factors also contributed to the rapid decline of union strength on both sides of the Atlantic in the late twentieth century. Major changes in the composition of the labor force undermined the position of unions. Many basic manufacturing industries that had been the most highly unionized in both countries in the mid-twentieth century suffered substantial job losses resulting from either globalization or technological innovation. Public-sector and white-collar unions expanded, but not quickly enough to make up for the losses in what had been previous union strongholds. More and more women and people of color, groups that unions historically had done a poorer job of recruiting than of white males, entered the labor force, so that unions faced the problem of recruiting out of a much larger and much more diverse pool of workers. Globalization put added pressure on organized labor by making it increasingly difficult for unions to maintain labor standards in competition with nonunionized employers in other parts of the world.[17]

Even with the growing convergence in business structure and public policy, and similar patterns of declining power for organized labor in the United States and Britain, British unions continued at the beginning of the twenty-first century to be in a stronger position than their American counterparts. The legacy of past differences had not been totally eradicated. In spite of all the forces now working against organized labor in both Britain and America, the union density rate in Britain was twice that of the United States, as one-third of British workers still belonged to unions. Moreover, studies of the attitudes of British employers demonstrate that they remain less hostile toward unions than do American employers.[18]

Differences in the structure of corporate enterprise that emerged in the United States and Britain by the early twentieth century had a continuing influence on American and British approaches to labor relations. Differing economic contexts, not differences in ideological or cultural predispositions, ultimately allowed unions to establish a more secure foothold in Britain and made Britain, not the United States, the more congenial environment for the development of an approach to industrial relations that can broadly, though not literally, be characterized as collective laissez-faire. While an essentially pluralistic vision of industrial relations usually dominated public policy debates in both the United States and Britain throughout the first half of the twentieth century, beginning with World War I corporatist proposals for restructuring state-labor-management relations provided an important and recurring alternative model, which at times served as the basis for institutional experiments with tripartite arrangements. Moreover, in the United States, many Americans who might have been favorably inclined toward a collective laissez-faire model ultimately found it necessary to turn to the state to intervene in labor-management relations, even if they did not adopt a full-blown version of corporatism.

Britain industrialized well before the United States, but the United States pioneered in the development of large-scale, bureaucratically organized corporations. The growth of large-scale enterprise in the United States was fostered by a variety of economic factors, as well as by a legal environment that especially after 1890 had the effect of encouraging consolidation rather than the kind of cartel arrangements among smaller companies that remained legally permissible in Britain. In contrast to their British counterparts, who operated in a less highly rationalized economic setting and remained more dependent on the expertise of skilled workers with strong union traditions, American businessmen by the first decades of the twentieth century had invested significant resources in the creation of managerial hierarchies in an effort to limit their dependence on skilled labor and to gain full control over the production process. The end result was that prior to World War I the most influential leaders of corporate America had adopted a strongly antiunion perspective. In contrast, many employers in Britain had concluded that working with unions had more advantages than trying to eliminate them, and that working together with other firms in the same industry to negotiate with organized labor could be an effective means of limiting the potential of shop-floor militancy. The decentralized federal structure of the American state and the power of an independent judiciary contributed to the effectiveness of employers' antiunion efforts. Yet what most clearly distinguished the American from the British system of industrial relations by the early twentieth century was the economic setting that fostered a more active and determined hostility to unions among American employers and a far more decentralized, firm-based, approach to labor relations.

Later in the twentieth century, the organization of British firms would come more closely to resemble the American pattern of bureaucratic large-scale enterprise with extensive managerial hierarchies, and pressures would build that would ultimately have a significant impact on Britain's approach to industrial relations. Yet reversing the trends that had been established early in the century would not be easy. Because of what political scientists often refer to as "path dependency," once established, economic and state structures can shape subsequent historical development. Once unions had become more solidly entrenched institutionally and politically in Britain than in the United States, it proved difficult for employers to challenge their legitimacy or to construct a widely accepted alternative model of industrial relations. Thus, even in the wake of the General Strike of 1926, the idea of an aggressive open-shop campaign similar to the one that had so weakened unions in America in the twenties had little appeal for British employers. Even today, the greater strength of British as compared to American unions, and the greater willingness of British employers at least to tolerate the existence of unions, may best be explained as a legacy of earlier developments.

Conversely, although during the national emergencies created by World War I and the Great Depression, the opposition of American employers to unions would be at least partially offset by state action that worked to the advantage of organized labor, employer hostility to unions, which was rooted in the well-established structure of American industry, remained a determinative feature of American industrial relations. In fact, the nature and degree of state intervention entailed in the passage of the National Labor Relations Act becomes understandable only in the context of the historic opposition of American employers to unionization. American labor leaders and their political supporters were ideologically inclined to support a British-style, essentially abstentionist approach to labor law as a means of removing the obstacles to union growth, especially since the history of state intervention in the late nineteenth and early twentieth centuries had been so generally negative for the labor movement. However, by 1935 it had become clear that an abstentionist approach was as likely to lead to the expansion of company unionism as to the institutionalization of truly effective and independent unions. Ironically, the United States, the nation perhaps most identified with a philosophy of limited government, thus implemented a more intrusive role for the state in industrial relations than would have been conceivable at the time in Britain.

The structure of the American economy has generated a consistent hostility to unions among American employers, but such hostility has at cer-

tain times in the nation's history been partially offset by positive state action in behalf of organized labor. The New Deal is the most noteworthy example of such action, but the substantial advances made by unions during
World Wars I and II were also due, in part, to the policies of a more friendly
federal government. In contrast, since the end of World War II, organized
labor has been subject to a variety of actions and inactions by the federal
government that have, in effect, marked the end of meaningful state support for unions. Perhaps even more significant than the restrictions imposed by the Taft-Hartley and Landrum-Griffin acts has been the failure of
the National Labor Relations Board effectively to enforce the Wagner Act's
remaining protections for unions. American unions have declined not so
much because they have become entrapped in a web of federal regulations,
but rather because employers have become freer over the last several
decades to enact union avoidance strategies, including many that the
Wagner Act had attempted to ban.[19]

Even when unions were at their peak of strength in the United States,
collective bargaining continued to be more decentralized in America than
in Britain. The persisting focus on the individual firm, as well as the negative legacy of the failed NRA experiment, blunted the possibility of developing effective meso- or macro-level institutional arrangements in the postwar
period. Pattern bargaining developed in the United States in some oligopo-
listic industries such as automobile manufacturing, but Britain's more centralized system of collective bargaining and the nationalization of several
key industries after World War II made possible more concerted, if ultimately unsuccessful, attempts by the government to enlist unions in the
implementation of a form of quasi-corporatist incomes policy.[20] Although
Britain has now moved away from industry-wide collective bargaining, the
legacy of this past contrast between the American focus on micro-level labor-
management relations and the British emphasis on meso-level relations can
still be seen in the dramatically different approaches each nation developed
to social welfare provision.

The continuing emphasis in the United States on the individual firm was
a key factor in thwarting the development of a more generous and equitable system of social welfare that might have been comparable to the welfare state that emerged in postwar Britain. Whereas British employers generally sought to limit competition among themselves in wages and other
forms of compensation and were glad to pass on to the state the responsibility for social welfare benefits, in the United States dominant business
enterprises both before and after the Great Depression saw company welfare programs as a means of shaping the labor market. The federal government in America did supplement the various forms of social insurance
that at least some workers had access to through their place of employment, but even with the expansion in the 1960s of the limited American
welfare state, the individual employer would remain the primary provider
of health insurance and pension opportunities. Welfare capitalism would,

in fact, come to be more widespread in the late twentieth century than it had ever been in its supposed heyday during the 1920s.[21]

Postwar proponents of industrial pluralism in the United States often proclaimed that the success of the collective bargaining regime they saw emerging was based on its essentially voluntaristic nature. Ironically, however, state intervention was a critical aspect of that regime. In fact, at least since the late nineteenth century and continuing through the Depression, state intervention had long been more characteristic of the American than of the British system of industrial relations. Such intervention—either against unions in most of the pre-Depression period or in behalf of them in the thirties—was, at bottom, a product of the weakness of the American labor movement. State intervention during World War I and the Great Depression aided organized labor, but it is clear that it did so in a way that failed to bring about a permanent change in the historic hostility of American employers to unions. The ideal of industrial pluralism was thus never realized in practice. It is hard to imagine organized labor ever achieving parity with employers, or even regaining what limited influence and strength it once had, without a new form of state intervention that would more effectively redress the fundamental imbalance in power between labor and capital in America.

Notes

Introduction

1. Stephen Skowronek, *Building a New American State: The Expansion of National Administrative Capacities, 1877–1920* (New York, 1982); Bob Jessop, *The Capitalist State: Marxist Theories and Methods* (New York, 1982); J. P. Nettl, "The State as a Conceptual Variable," *World Politics* 20 (1968): 559–92.

2. Kenneth H. F. Dyson, *The State Tradition in Western Europe: A Study of an Idea and Institution* (New York, 1980).

3. Otto Kahn-Freund, "Intergroup Conflicts and Their Settlement," *British Journal of Sociology* 5 (1954): 193–227; Paul Davies and Mark Freeland, *Labour Legislation and Public Policy: A Contemporary History* (Oxford, 1993); Roy Lewis, "The Historical Development of Labour Law," *British Journal of Industrial Relations* 14 (1976): 1–17; K. D. Ewing, "The State and Industrial Relations: 'Collective Laissez-Faire' Revisited," *Historical Studies in Industrial Relations* 5 (Spring 1998): 1–31.

4. Howell John Harris, "Between Convergence and Exceptionalism: Americans and the 'British Model' of Industrial Relations, c. 1870–1920" (paper presented at "Justice at Work: A Conference Honouring David Brody," University of California at Santa Barbara, August 9, 2002).

5. Katherine Stone, "The Post-War Paradigm in American Labor Law," *Yale Law Journal* 90 (June 1981): 1511; Christopher L. Tomlins, "The New Deal, Collective Bargaining, and the Triumph of Industrial Pluralism," *Industrial and Labor Relations Review* 39 (1985); and *The State and the Unions: Labor Relations, Law, and the Organized Labor Movement in America, 1880–1960* (New York, 1985).

6. David B. Truman, *The Governmental Process: Political Interests and Public Opinion* (1951; repr., New York, 1971); Robert A. Dahl, *Pluralist Democracy in the United States: Conflict and Consent* (Chicago, 1967).

7. U.S. National Labor Relations Board, *Legislative History of the National Labor Relations Act* (Washington, 1949), 3270.

8. Seymour Martin Lipset, ed., *Unions in Transition: Entering the Second Century* (San Francisco, 1986); Thomas A. Kochan, Harry C. Katz, and Robert B. McKersie, *The Transformation of American Industrial Relations* (New York, 1986); Charles C. Heckscher, *The New Unionism: Employee Involvement in the Changing Corporation* (New York, 1988); Richard Edwards, *Rights at Work: Employment Relations in the Post-Union Era* (Washington, 1993); Nelson Lichtenstein, *State of the Union: A Century of American Labor* (Princeton, 2002).

9. John P. Diggins, *Mussolini and Fascism: The View from America* (Princeton, 1972).

10. Larry G. Gerber, "Corporatism and State Theory: A Review Essay for Historians," *Social Science History* 19 (Fall 1995): 313–32; Suzanne Berger, ed.,

Organizing Interests in Western Europe: Pluralism, Corporatism, and the Transformation of Politics (New York, 1981); Alan Cawson, *Corporatism and Political Theory* (Oxford, 1986); Colin Crouch, ed., *State and Economy in Contemporary Capitalism* (New York, 1979); Gerhard Lehmbruch and Philippe C. Schmitter, eds., *Patterns of Corporatist Policy-Making* (Beverly Hills, Calif., 1982); R. E. Pahl and J. T. Winkler, "The Coming Corporatism," *Challenge* 18 (March–April 1975): 28–35; Leo Panitch, "Recent Theorizations of Corporatism: Reflections on a Growth Industry," *British Journal of Sociology* 31 (June 1980): 159–87; Philippe C. Schmitter and Gerhard Lehmbruch, eds., *Trends toward Corporatist Intermediation* (Beverly Hills, Calif., 1979).

11. Colin Crouch, "Pluralism and the New Corporatism: A Rejoinder," *Political Studies* 31 (1983): 452–60.

12. Ellis W. Hawley, "Social Policy and the Liberal State in Twentieth-Century America," in *Federal Social Policy: The Historical Dimension,* ed. Donald T. Critchlow and Ellis W. Hawley (University Park, Penn., 1988), 123; and "The Discovery and Study of a 'Corporate Liberalism,'" *Business History Review* 52 (Autumn 1978): 309–20.

13. Robert H. Salisbury, "Why No Corporatism in America?" in *Trends toward Corporatist Intermediation;* Graham K. Wilson, "Why Is There No Corporatism in the United States?" in *Patterns of Corporatist Policy-Making.*

14. Crouch, "Pluralism and the New Corporatism."

15. Cawson, *Corporatism and Political Theory.*

16. Cawson, *Corporatism and Political Theory,* 118–19.

1—The American and British Systems of Industrial Relations on the Eve of World War I

1. Aristide Zolberg, "How Many Exceptionalisms?" in *Working-Class Formation: Nineteenth-Century Patterns in Western Europe and the United States,* ed. Ira Katznelson and Aristide R. Zolberg (Princeton, 1986), 399–400.

2. Werner Sombart, *Why Is There No Socialism in the United States?* trans. Patricia M. Hocking and C. T. Husbands (1906; repr., White Plains, N.Y., 1976); Selig Perlman, *A Theory of the Labor Movement* (New York, 1928).

3. Gerald Friedman, *State-Making and Labor Movements: France and the United States, 1876–1914* (Ithaca, N.Y., 1998), 40, 94; Foster Rhea Dulles and Melvyn Dubofsky, *Labor in America: A History* (Arlington Heights, Ill., 1984), 154, 173; Kim Voss, *The Making of American Exceptionalism: The Knights of Labor and Class Formation in the Nineteenth Century* (Ithaca, N.Y., 1993), 78; H. A. Clegg, Alan Fox, and A. F. Thompson, *A History of British Trade Unions since 1889,* vol. 1, *1889–1910* (Oxford, 1964), 466; Philip S. Bagwell and G. E. Mingay, *Britain and America, 1850–1939: A Study of Economic Change* (London, 1966), 5; U.S. Department of Commerce, Bureau of the Census, *Historical Statistics of the United States, Colonial Times to 1957* (Washington, 1960), 74.

4. Leon Fink, *Workingmen's Democracy: The Knights of Labor and American Politics* (Urbana, Ill., 1985), 5; Voss, *Making of American Exceptionalism;* Gary Marks, *Unions in Politics: Britain, Germany, and the United States in the Nineteenth and Early Twentieth Centuries* (Princeton, 1989), 41, 199–200.

5. George Sayers Bain and Robert Price, *Profiles of Union Growth: A Comparative Statistical Portrait of Eight Countries* (Oxford, 1980), 39, 63, 67–69, 88; Friedman, *State-Making,* 265.

6. Julie Greene, "'The Strike at the Ballot Box': The American Federation of Labor's Entrance into Election Politics, 1906–1909," *Labor History* 32 (Spring 1991): 165–92; and *Pure and Simple Politics: The American Federation of Labor and Political Activism, 1881–1917* (New York, 1998).

7. John V. Orth, *Combination and Conspiracy: A Legal History of Trade Unionism, 1721–1906* (Oxford, 1991).

8. Ross McKibbin, "Why Was There No Marxism in Great Britain?" in McKibbin, *The Ideologies of Class: Social Relations in Britain, 1880–1950* (Oxford, 1990).

9. Henry Pelling, *The Origins of the Labour Party* (London, 1965); John Lovell, "Trade Unions and the Development of Independent Labour Politics 1889–1906," in *Trade Unions in British Politics*, ed. Ben Pimlott and Chris Cook (London, 1982); David Butler and Anne Sloman, *British Political Facts, 1900–1975* (London, 1975), 182.

10. Lovell, "Trade Unions and Independent Politics," 51; Michael J. Klarman, "The Judges versus the Unions: The Development of British Labor Law, 1867–1913," *Virginia Law Review* 75 (1989): 1487–1602.

11. Klarman, "Judges versus Unions," 1536–47; D. F. Macdonald, *The State and the Trade Unions* (London, 1960), 63–66; Hugh Armstrong Clegg, *A History of British Trade Unions since 1889*, vol. 2, *1911–1933* (Oxford, 1985), 217–19.

12. Henry Pelling, *A History of British Trade Unionism*, 4th ed. (Houndmills, Eng., 1987), 314.

13. James Hinton, "Voluntarism versus Jacobinism: Labor, Nation, and Citizenship in Britain, 1850–1950," *International Labor and Working-Class History* 48 (Fall 1995): 68–90; Alan Fox, *History and Heritage: The Social Origins of the British Industrial Relations System* (London, 1985); Robert Currie, *Industrial Politics* (Oxford, 1979).

14. Pelling, *History of British Trade Unionism*, 126–27; Pat Thane, "The Working Class and State 'Welfare' in Britain, 1880–1914," *Historical Journal* (1984): 877–900; Hugh Heclo, *Modern Social Politics in Britain and Sweden: From Relief to Income Maintenance* (New Haven, Conn., 1974), 85–90; Marks, *Unions in Politics*, 105–6.

15. Vivien Hart, *Bound by Our Constitution: Women, Workers, and the Minimum Wage* (Princeton, 1994); Pelling, *History of British Trade Unionism*, 102–3, 142–43; Marks, *Unions in Politics*, 105; M. W. Kirby, *The British Coalmining Industry, 1870–1946: A Political and Economic History* (Hamden, Conn., 1977), 15–16.

16. Congressional Quarterly, *Guide to U.S. Elections* (Washington, 1976), 284; Butler and Sloman, *British Political Facts*, 182.

17. James Weinstein, *The Decline of Socialism in America, 1912–1925* (New York, 1967), 36.

18. Greene, "Strike at the Ballot Box," 180.

19. Marc Karson, *American Labor Unions and Politics, 1900–1918* (Carbondale, Ill., 1958); Greene, *Pure and Simple Politics;* and "'Strike at the Ballot Box'"; Craig Phelan, *William Green: Biography of a Labor Leader* (Albany, N.Y., 1989), 20–21.

20. Wayne L. McNaughton and Joseph Lazar, *Industrial Relations and the Government* (New York, 1954), 95–100; Christopher L. Tomlins, *The State and the Unions: Labor Relations, Law, and the Organized Labor Movement in America, 1880–1960* (New York, 1985), 84–86; John Lombardi, *Labor's Voice in the Cabinet: A History of the Department of Labor from Its Origins to 1921* (New York, 1942), 96–97; David Montgomery, *The Fall of the House of Labor: The Workplace, the State, and American Labor Activism, 1865–1925* (New York, 1987), 279.

21. Rodney Lowe, *Adjusting to Democracy: The Role of the Ministry of Labour in British Politics, 1916–1939* (Oxford, 1986), 117.

22. Julius Henry Cohen, *Law and Order in Industry: Five Years' Experience* (New York, 1916), 202, 225–26, 288–92.

23. George Ranken Askwith, *Industrial Problems and Disputes* (1920; repr., New York, 1974), xi; Clegg, *History of British Trade Unions,* vol. 2, 99–100.

24. Clegg, *History of British Trade Unions,* vol. 2, 99–100.

25. Dulles and Dubofsky, *Labor in America,* 173, 194; Graham Adams, Jr., *Age of Industrial Violence, 1910–15: The Activities and Findings of the United States Commission on Industrial Relations* (New York, 1966); Clarence E. Wunderlin, Jr., *Visions of a New Industrial Order: Social Science and Labor Theory in America's Progressive Order* (New York, 1992).

26. Lombardi, *Labor's Voice in the Cabinet,* 52–58.

27. James Weinstein, *The Corporate Ideal in the Liberal State, 1900–1918* (Boston, 1968); Bruno Ramirez, *When Workers Fight: The Politics of Industrial Relations in the Progressive Era, 1898–1916* (Westport, Conn., 1978); Christopher J. Cyphers, *The National Civic Federation and the Making of a New Liberalism, 1900–1915* (Westport, Conn., 2002).

28. Seymour Martin Lipset and Gary Marks, *It Didn't Happen Here: Why Socialism Failed in the United States* (New York, 2000), 86.

29. Bain and Price, *Profiles of Union Growth,* 39, 88.

30. Bain and Price, *Profiles of Union Growth,* 76; Leo Wolman, *Ebb and Flow in Trade Unionism* (New York, 1936), 197.

31. Clegg, *History of British Trade Unions,* vol. 2, 7–10.

32. George E. Barnett, "National and District Systems of Collective Bargaining in the United States," *Quarterly Journal of Economics* 26 (1912): 425–43; W. Jett Lauck, *The Development of Collective Bargaining on a National Basis* (Chicago, 1921); Jeffrey Haydu, "Trade Agreements vs. Open Shop: Employers' Choices before WWI," *Industrial Relations* 28 (1989): 159–73; Ramirez, *When Workers Fight.*

33. Ira Katznelson, "Working-Class Formation and the State: Nineteenth-Century England in American Perspective," in *Bringing the State Back In,* ed. Peter B. Evans, Dietrich Rueschemeyer, and Theda Skocpol (New York, 1985); Lipset and Marks, *It Didn't Happen Here.*

34. William E. Forbath, *Law and the Shaping of the American Labor Movement* (Cambridge, Mass., 1991); and "Courts, Constitutions, and Labor Politics in England and America: A Study of the Constitutive Power of Law," *Law and Social Inquiry* 16 (Winter 1991): 1–34; Victoria Charlotte Hattam, *Labor Visions and State Power: The Origins of Business Unionism in the United States* (Princeton, 1993).

35. Karen Orren, *Belated Feudalism: Labor, the Law, and Liberal Development in the United States* (New York, 1991).

36. Roy Lewis, "The Historical Development of Labour Law," *British Journal of Industrial Relations* 14 (1976): 1–17; Klarman, "Judges versus Unions."

37. David Brian Robertson, *Capital, Labor, and State: The Battle for American Labor Markets from the Civil War to the New Deal* (Lanham, Md., 2000), 65–93; Greene, *Pure and Simple Politics;* Gary M. Fink, *Labor's Search for Political Order: The Political Behavior of the Missouri Labor Movement, 1890–1940* (Columbia, Mo., 1973); Michael Kazin, *The Barons of Labor: The San Francisco Building Trades and Union Power in the Progressive Era* (Urbana, Ill., 1987).

38. Daniel R. Ernst, *Lawyers Against Labor: From Individual Rights to Corporate Liberalism* (Urbana, Ill., 1995).

39. Marks, *Unions in Politics,* 233.

40. Marks, *Unions in Politics,* 204–10.

41. Marks, *Unions in Politics;* Ruth L. Horowitz, *Political Ideologies of Organized Labor: The New Deal Era* (New Brunswick, N.J., 1978), 55–58; George G. Higgins, *Voluntarism in Organized Labor in the United States, 1930–1940* (1945; repr., New York, 1969).

42. Clegg, *History of British Trade Unions,* vol. 2, 1–6; Pelling, *History of British Trade Unionism,* 93–98; Larry Peterson, "The One Big Union in International Perspective: Revolutionary Industrial Unionism, 1900–1925," in *Work, Community, and Power: The Experience of Labor in Europe and America, 1900–1925,* ed. James E. Cronin and Carmen Sirianni (Philadelphia, 1983), 56.

43. Peter R. Shergold, *Working-Class Life: The "American Standard" in Comparative Perspective, 1899–1913* (Pittsburgh, 1982), 56–57; Charles More, *Skill and the English Working Class, 1870–1914* (New York, 1980), 171–73.

44. Haydu, "Trade Agreements vs. Open Shop"; and *Between Craft and Class: Skilled Workers and Factory Politics in the United States and Britain, 1890–1922* (Berkeley, 1988), 45–49, 86–87; William Lazonick, *Competitive Advantage on the Shop Floor* (Cambridge, Mass., 1990).

45. John Benson, *The Working Class in Britain, 1850–1939* (London, 1989), 17.

46. Lazonick, *Competitive Advantage on the Shop Floor;* Haydu, "Trade Agreements vs. Open Shop"; and *Between Craft and Class.*

47. Haydu, "Trade Agreements vs. Open Shop," 165–66; Montgomery, *Fall of the House of Labor,* 259–69.

48. Peter A. Swenson, *Capitalists against Markets: The Making of Labor Markets and Welfare States in the United States and Sweden* (New York, 2002), 21, 49; Ramirez, *When Workers Fight;* Howell John Harris, *Bloodless Victories: The Rise and Fall of the Open Shop in the Philadelphia Metal Trades, 1890–1940* (New York, 2000), 74–160.

49. Haydu, "Trade Agreements vs. Open Shop."

50. Zolberg, "How Many Exceptionalisms?" 438–41; George Sayers Bain, *The Growth of White-Collar Unionism* (Oxford, 1970), 15.

51. Leslie Hannah, *The Rise of the Corporate Economy,* 2nd ed. (London, 1983), 8–26; Mansel G. Blackford, *The Rise of Modern Business Enterprise in Great Britain, the United States, and Japan* (Chapel Hill, N.C., 1988), 51–76; Bagwell and Mingay, *Britain and America,* 153–84.

52. Hannah, *Rise of the Corporate Economy,* 22; Blackford, *Rise of Modern Business Enterprise,* 75; Ralph L. Nelson, *Merger Movements in American Industry, 1895–1956* (Princeton, 1959), 129–38.

53. Alfred D. Chandler, Jr., *The Visible Hand: The Managerial Revolution in American Business* (Cambridge, Mass., 1977), 1.

54. Leslie Hannah, "Visible and Invisible Hands in Great Britain," in *Managerial Hierarchies: Comparative Perspectives on the Rise of the Modern Industrial Enterprise,* ed. Alfred D. Chandler, Jr., and Herman Daems (Cambridge, Mass., 1980); Hannah, *Rise of the Corporate Economy;* Blackford, *Rise of Modern Business.*

55. Lance Davis, "The Capital Markets and Industrial Concentration: The U.S. and U.K., a Comparative Study," *Economic History Review,* n.s., 19 (1966): 255–72.

56. Sydney Checkland, *British Public Policy, 1776–1939: An Economic, Social, and Political Perspective* (New York, 1983), 174; Herman Levy, *Monopolies, Cartels and Trusts in British Industry* (1927; repr., New York, 1968).

57. Tony Freyer, "The Sherman Antitrust Act, Comparative Business Structure, and the Rule of Reason: America and Great Britain, 1880–1920," *Iowa Law Review* 74

(July 1989): 991–1017; and *Regulating Big Business: Antitrust in Great Britain and America, 1880–1990* (New York, 1992); Morton Keller, "The Regulation of Large Enterprise: The United States Experience in Comparative Perspective," in *Managerial Hierarchies*, 165–66.

58. Harris, *Bloodless Victories*, 159–60.

59. Lloyd Ulman, "Who Wanted Collective Bargaining in the First Place?" in *Thirty-Ninth Annual Proceedings of the Industrial Relations Research Association* (New York, 1986).

60. James Hinton, *The First Shop Stewards' Movement* (London, 1973); Chris Wrigley, *David Lloyd George and the British Labour Movement: Peace and War* (New York, 1976).

61. Sanford M. Jacoby, "American Exceptionalism Revisited: The Importance of Management," in *Masters to Managers: Historical and Comparative Perspectives on American Employers*, ed. Sanford M. Jacoby (New York, 1991); Kathleen Thelen, "The Political Economy of Business and Labor in the Developed Democracies," in *Political Science: The State of the Discipline*, ed. Ira Katznelson and Helen V. Milner (New York, 2002).

62. Voss, *Making of American Exceptionalism*, 232.

63. James Holt, "Trade Unionism in the British and U.S. Steel Industries, 1890–1914: A Comparative Study," *Labor History* 18 (Winter 1977): 5–35.

64. Jacoby, "American Exceptionalism Revisited," 199.

65. Pelling, *History of British Trade Unionism*, 314; Currie, *Industrial Politics*, 26–56; Leon Fink, "Labor, Liberty, and the Law: Trade Unionism and the Problem of the American Constitutional Order," *Journal of American History* 74 (December 1987), 916.

66. Louis S. Reed, *The Labor Philosophy of Samuel Gompers* (1930; repr., Port Washington, N.Y., 1966).

2—The Impact of World War I

1. Robert D. Cuff, *The War Industries Board: Business-Government Relations during World War I* (Baltimore, 1973); Paul A. C. Koistinen, *Mobilizing for War: The Political Economy of American Warfare, 1865–1919* (Lawrence, Kans., 1997); Samuel J. Hurwitz, *State Intervention in Great Britain: A Study of Economic Control and Social Response, 1914–1919* (1949; repr., New York, 1968); Kathleen Burk, ed., *War and the State: The Transformation of British Government, 1914–1919* (London, 1982); Gerry Rubin, *War, Law, and Labour: The Munitions Acts, State Regulation and the Unions, 1915–1921* (Oxford, 1987).

2. U.S. Department of Commerce, Bureau of the Census, *Historical Statistics of the United States, Colonial Times to 1957* (Washington, D.C., 1960), 98; George Sayers Bain and Robert Price, *Profiles of Union Growth: A Comparative Statistical Portrait of Eight Countries* (Oxford, 1980), 37.

3. Ralph L. Nelson, *Merger Movements in American Industry, 1895–1956* (Princeton, 1956), 140–41; Leslie Hannah, *The Rise of the Corporate Economy*, 2nd ed. (London, 1983), 27–28.

4. Hurwitz, *State Intervention in Great Britain*, 155; Llewellyn Woodward, *Great Britain and the War of 1914–1918* (London, 1967), 467.

5. David Lloyd George, *War Memoirs of David Lloyd George*, vol. 1, *1914–1915* (Boston, 1933), 215; Great Britain, Ministry of Munitions, *History of the Ministry of Munitions*, vol. 2, pt. 1 (London, 1922), 17; Chris Wrigley, "The Ministry of Munitions: An Innovatory Department," in *War and the State: The Transformation of*

British Government, 1914–1919, ed. Kathleen Burk (London, 1982); Peter K. Cline, "Eric Geddes and the 'Experiment' with Businessmen in Government, 1915–22," in *Essays in Anti-Labour History,* ed. Kenneth D. Brown (Hamden, Conn., 1974).

6. Rodney Lowe, *Adjusting to Democracy: The Role of the Ministry of Labour in British Politics, 1916–1939* (Oxford, 1986), 14.

7. Grosvenor B. Clarkson, *Industrial America in the World War: The Strategy behind the Line, 1917–1918* (Boston, 1923), 180.

8. Clarkson, *Industrial America in the World War;* Cuff, *War Industries Board.*

9. Clarkson, *Industrial America in the World War,* 91–92, 170, 276.

10. John Lombardi, *Labor's Voice in the Cabinet: A History of the Department of Labor from Its Origin to 1921* (New York, 1942).

11. Bernard Waites, *A Class Society at War, Britain, 1914–1918* (Leamington Spa, Eng., 1987), 213. Hugh Armstrong Clegg, *A History of British Trade Unions since 1889,* vol. 2, *1911–1933* (Oxford, 1985), 209.

12. Joseph A. McCartin, *Labor's Great War: The Struggle for Industrial Democracy and the Origins of Modern American Labor Relations, 1912–1921* (Chapel Hill, N.C., 1997), 12–24; Graham Adams, Jr., *Age of Industrial Violence, 1910–15: The Activities and Findings of the United States Commission on Industrial Relations* (New York, 1966), 44–46.

13. Ross M. Martin, *TUC, The Growth of a Pressure Group, 1868–1976* (Oxford, 1980), 149.

14. James Weinstein, *The Decline of Socialism in America, 1912–1925* (New York, 1967).

15. Koistinen, *Mobilizing for Modern War,* 140–46.

16. Cuff, *War Industries Board,* 155–57; David Montgomery, *The Fall of the House of Labor: The Workplace, the State, and American Labor Activism, 1865–1925* (New York, 1987), 353–56; Albion Guilford Taylor, *Labor Policies of the National Association of Manufacturers* (1928; repr., New York, 1973), 12, 28; Joseph L. Naar, *The Conference Board: An Historical Celebration of the Conference Board's 75th Anniversary* (New York, 1991).

17. Stephen Blank, *Industry and Government in Britain: The Federation of British Industries in Politics, 1945–1965* (Lexington, Mass., 1973), 14–15.

18. Sarah Vickerstaff and John Sheldrake, *The Limits of Corporatism: The British Experience in the Twentieth Century* (Aldershot, Eng., 1989), 18.

19. Lloyd George, *War Memoirs,* 226.

20. *History of the Ministry of Munitions,* vol. 2, pt. 1, 7; Lloyd George, *War Memoirs,* 242.

21. *History of the Ministry of Munitions,* vol. 2, pt. 1, 7–8; vol. 2, pt. 2, 10.

22. Hurwitz, *State Intervention in Great Britain,* 165–204; D. F. Macdonald, *The State and the Trade Unions* (London, 1960), 87.

23. Cuff, *War Industries Board,* 162–90. Gosling is quoted in Waites, *Class Society at War,* 63.

24. *History of the Ministry of Munitions,* vol. 1, pt. 2, 78–99; vol. 1, pt. 4. See also Chris Wrigley, *David Lloyd George and the British Labour Movement: Peace and War* (Hassocks, Eng., 1976), 91–121.

25. David M. Gordon, Richard Edwards, and Michael Reich, *Segmented Work, Divided Workers: The Historical Transformation of Labor in the United States* (Cambridge, 1982); Harry Braverman, *Labor and Monopoly Capital: The Degradation of Work in the Twentieth Century* (New York, 1974).

26. Wrigley, *Lloyd George and the British Labour Movement,* 121.

27. Jeffrey Haydu, *Between Craft and Class: Skilled Workers and Factory Politics in the United States and Britain, 1890–1922* (Berkeley, 1988), 127–29; Jeffrey Haydu, *Making American Industry Safe for Democracy: Comparative Perspectives on the State and Employee Representation in the Era of World War I* (Urbana, Ill., 1997), 36–47; John Child, *British Management Thought: A Critical Analysis* (London, 1969).

28. Rubin, *War, Law, and Labour;* Joseph Melling, "Work, Culture and Politics on 'Red Clydeside': The ILP during the First World War," in *The ILP on Clydeside, 1893–1932: From Foundation to Disintegration,* ed. Alan McKinlay and R. J. Morris (Manchester, 1991); Alan McKinlay and Jonathan Zeitlin, "The Meanings of Managerial Prerogative: Industrial Relations and the Organisation of Work in British Engineering, 1880–1939," *Business History* 31 (April 1989): 38.

29. Rubin, *War, Law, and Labour,* 17.

30. Melling, "Work, Culture and Politics," 98; Alastair Reid, "Dilution, Trade Unionism and the State in Britain during the First World War," in *Shop Floor Bargaining and the State: Historical and Comparative Perspectives,* ed. Steven Tolliday and Jonathan Zeitlin, (Cambridge, 1985), 69.

31. James Hinton, *The First Shop Stewards' Movement* (London, 1973); Branko Pribiâceviâc, *The Shop Stewards' Movement and Workers' Control, 1910–1922* (Oxford, 1959); G. D. H. Cole, *Workshop Organization* (London, 1923).

32. Hinton, *First Shop Stewards' Movement,* 337; Haydu, *Between Craft and Class;* Waites, *Class Society at War.*

33. James E. Cronin, "Labor Insurgency and Class Formation: Comparative Perspectives on the Crisis of 1917–1920 in Europe"; Larry Peterson, "The One Big Union in International Perspective: Revolutionary Industrial Unionism, 1900–1925"; and Carmen Sirianni, "Workers' Control in Europe: A Comparative Sociological Analysis," all in *Work, Community, and Power: The Experience of Labor in Europe and America, 1900–1925,* ed. James E. Cronin and Carmen Sirianni (Philadelphia, 1983); Carter L. Goodrich, *The Frontier of Control: A Study in British Workshop Politics* (New York, 1920), 264–65; Cole, *Workshop Organization,* 93–94.

34. Reid, "Dilution, Trade Unionism and the State"; Iain McLean, *The Legend of Red Clydeside* (Edinburgh, 1983); Rubin, *War, Law, and Labour.*

35. Gerd Hardach, *The First World War, 1914–1918* (Berkeley, 1977), 186.

36. The phrase, "statization of trade unions," comes from Rubin, *War, Law, and Labour,* 248.

37. Melling, "Work, Culture and Politics," 103.

38. Quoted in Hinton, *First Shop Stewards' Movement,* 129.

39. Marc Stears, *Progressives, Pluralists, and the Problems of the State: Ideologies of Reform in the United States and Britain, 1909–1926* (New York, 2002).

40. Waites, *Class Society at War.*

41. Hinton, *First Shop Stewards' Movement,* 277–78; Pribiâceviâc, *Shop Stewards' Movement,* 10–11.

42. Cole, *Workshop Organization,* 133–38, 170–84.

43. The quotation is from a pamphlet entitled *Towards Industrial Democracy: A Memorandum on Workers' Control* (1917), reprinted in Ken Coates and Anthony Topham, comps., *Industrial Democracy in Great Britain: A Book of Readings and Witnesses for Workers' Control* (London, 1968), 108–9. Pribiâceviâc, *Shop Stewards' Movement,* 50–53, 150–51; Hinton, *First Shop Stewards' Movement,* 279–80.

44. Rodger Charles, *The Development of Industrial Relations in Britain,*

1911–1939: Studies in the Evolution of Collective Bargaining at National and Industry Level (London, 1973), 77–226; John Barton Seymour, *The Whitley Councils Scheme* (London, 1932); Elie Halevy, "The Policy of Social Peace in England: The Whitley Councils (1919)," in Halevy, *Era of Tyrannies: Essays on Socialism and War* (Garden City, N.Y., 1965).

45. *The Industrial Council Plan in Great Britain* (Washington, 1919), 35–36.

46. *Industrial Council Plan,* 19–20, 22, 36.

47. Sirianni, "Workers' Control in Europe," 298–99. See also McLean, *Red Clydeside,* 240.

48. W. Jett Lauck and Claude S. Watts, *The Industrial Code* (New York, 1922), 18.

49. Haydu, *Making American Industry Safe.*

50. John S. Smith, "Organized Labor and Government in the Wilson Era; 1913–1921: Some Conclusions," *Labor History* 3 (Fall 1962): 265–86; Melvyn Dubofsky, "Abortive Reform: The Wilson Administration and Organized Labor, 1913–1920," in *Work, Community, and Power.*

51. Lauck and Watts, *Industrial Code,* 97.

52. W. Jett Lauck, *Political and Industrial Democracy, 1776–1926* (New York, 1926), 131–32.

53. Haydu, *Making America Safe;* Lombardi, *Labor's Voice in the Cabinet,* 296.

54. David Montgomery, "New Tendencies in Union Struggles and Strategies in Europe and the United States, 1916–1922," in *Work, Community, and Power,* 104–5; Haydu, *Making American Industry Safe,* 48–84; McCartin, *Labor's Great War,* 99–119; Valerie Jean Conner, *The National War Labor Board: Stability, Social Justice, and the Voluntary State in World War I* (Chapel Hill, N.C., 1983), 108–125; Alexander M. Bing, *War-Time Strikes and Their Adjustment* (New York, 1921), 161–64.

55. John Leitch, *Man to Man: The Story of Industrial Democracy* (New York, 1919); John D. Rockefeller, Jr., *The Personal Relation in Industry* (New York, 1923); Daniel Nelson, "The Company Union Movement, 1900–1937: A Reexamination," *Business History Review* 56 (Autumn 1982): 335–57; Stuart D. Brandes, *American Welfare Capitalism, 1880–1940* (Chicago, 1976).

56. Nelson, "Company Union Movement," 338.

57. Clegg, *History of British Trade Unions,* vol. 2, 441–42; Chris Smith, John Child, and Michael Rowlinson, *Reshaping Work: The Cadbury Experience* (Cambridge, 1990), 65–70.

58. Clarence J. Hicks, *My Life in Industrial Relations: Fifty Years in the Growth of a Profession* (New York, 1941), 82–83.

59. McCartin, *Labor's Great War,* 100.

60. Milton J. Nadworny, *Scientific Management and the Unions, 1900–1932: A Historical Analysis* (Cambridge, Mass., 1955); Steve Fraser, "Dress Rehearsal for the New Deal: Shop-Floor Insurgents, Political Elites, and Industrial Democracy in the Amalgamated Clothing Workers," in *Working-Class America: Essays on Labor, Community and American Society,* ed. Michael H. Frisch and Daniel J. Walkowitz (Urbana, Ill., 1983); Bruce Irving Bustard, "The Human Element: Labor Administration and Industrial Mobilization during the First World War" (Ph.D. diss., University of Iowa, 1984), 180–215.

61. Hinton, *First Shop Stewards' Movement,* 129–31, 332–36; Sirianni, "Workers' Control in Europe," 301–2; Seebohm Rowntree, "My Dream of a Factory," in Arthur Gleason, *What the Workers Want: A Study of British Labor* (New York, 1920), 306–16.

62. David Montgomery, *Workers' Control in America: Studies in the History of Work, Technology, and Labor Struggles* (New York, 1979), especially 91–112; Bing, *War-Time Strikes.*

63. Montgomery, "New Tendencies in Union Struggles," 104–5; Haydu, *Between Craft and Class,* 176–79; Montgomery, *Fall of the House of Labor,* 411–38; Montgomery, *Workers' Control in America,* 91–112; Peterson, "One Big Union," 59.

64. Steve Fraser, "The 'New Unionism' and the 'New Economic Policy,'" in *Work, Community, and Power,* 174. McCartin, *Labor's Great War;* essays by McCartin, Montgomery, and Harris in Nelson Lichtenstein and Howell John Harris, eds., *Industrial Democracy in America: The Ambiguous Promise* (Cambridge, 1993).

65. Paul Barton Johnson, *Land Fit for Heroes: The Planning of British Reconstruction, 1916–1919* (Chicago, 1968).

66. Michael Freeden, *Liberalism Divided: A Study in British Political Thought, 1914–39* (Oxford, 1986), 59–64.

67. *Industrial Council Plan,* 19–22; Haydu, *Making America Safe,* 45–47.

68. *Industrial Council Plan,* 7, 32, 28.

69. *Industrial Council Plan,* 27–28; V. L. Allen, *Trade Unions and the Government* (London, 1960), 59–60.

70. 107 *H.C. Deb.,* col. 72–73.

71. 107 *H.C. Deb.,* col. 95–96.

72. *Industrial Council Plan,* 18.

73. Charles, *Development of Industrial Relations,* 205–7.

74. Docker's aspirations for the newly formed FBI are spelled out in a speech he gave at the federation's first annual meeting, reprinted in *The Economist,* March 10, 1917, 479–80. R. P. T. Davenport-Hines, *Dudley Docker: The Life and Times of a Trade Warrior* (Cambridge, 1984).

75. Cited in John Turner, *British Politics and the Great War: Coalition and Conflict, 1915–1918* (New Haven, Conn., 1992), 353. John Turner, "Servants of Two Masters: British Trade Associations in the First Half of the Twentieth Century," in *Trade Associations in Business History,* ed. Hiroaki Yamazaki and Matao Miyamoto (Tokyo, 1988), 186–87.

76. Blank, *Industry and Government in Britain,* 16–19.

77. Alan Fox, *History and Heritage: The Social Origins of the British Industrial Relations System* (London, 1985), 295–99; Lowe, *Adjusting to Democracy,* 92–96.

78. Carl F. Brand, *The British Labour Party: A Short History,* rev. ed. (Stanford, Calif., 1974), 55–56.

79. Pribiâceviâc, *Shop Stewards' Movement,* 8.

80. For excerpts from Hodges's plan for nationalization, see Coates and Topham, *Industrial Democracy in Great Britain,* 259–63; and Gleason, *What the Workers Want,* 173–83.

81. Robert Currie, *Industrial Politics* (Oxford, 1979), 101–3; Susan Armitage, *The Politics of Decontrol of Industry: Britain and the United States* (London, 1969), 110–57; A. W. Wright, *G. D. H. Cole and Socialist Democracy* (Oxford, 1979).

82. Armitage, *Politics of Decontrol,* 110–57; Gleason, *What the Workers Want,* 422–40.

83. K. Austin Kerr, *American Railroad Politics, 1914–1920: Rates, Wages, and Efficiency* (Pittsburgh, 1968); House Committee on Interstate and Foreign Commerce, *Return of the Railroads to Private Ownership,* 66th Cong., 1st sess., 1919.

84. House Committee on Interstate and Foreign Commerce, *Return of the Railroads,* 602, 680.

85. Senate Committee on Interstate Commerce, *Extension of Tenure of Government Control of Railroads,* 65th Cong., 3rd sess., 1919, 1083.

86. J. B. S. Hardman, ed., *American Labor Dynamics: In the Light of Post-War Developments* (1928; repr., New York, 1968), 25; Colin J. Davis, *Power at Odds: The 1922 National Railroad Shopmen's Strike* (Urbana, Ill., 1997), 44.

87. Glenn E. Plumb and William G. Roylance, *Industrial Democracy: A Plan for Its Achievement* (New York, 1923), 203; Montgomery, "New Tendencies in Union Struggles," 98–99.

88. Sidney Webb and Beatrice Webb, *A Constitution for the Socialist Commonwealth of Great Britain* (1920; repr., Cambridge, 1975), 178; Kerr, *American Railroad Politics,* 161–64.

89. House Committee on Interstate and Foreign Commerce, *Return of the Railroads,* 1561.

90. Stanley Shapiro, "The Great War and Reform: Liberals and Labor, 1917–19," *Labor History* 12 (Summer 1971): 328–29; Steven Fraser, *Labor Will Rule: Sidney Hillman and the Rise of American Labor* (New York, 1991), 124–25.

91. Rockefeller is quoted in the *New York Times,* December 6, 1918, 13. *Industrial Council Plan;* Malcolm Sparkes, "Britain's Building Trades Parliament," *Nation* 110 (January 24, 1920): 102–3; Ordway Tead, "National Organization by Industries," *New Republic* 18 (February 8, 1919): 48–51; Arthur Gleason, "New Constitutionalism in British Industry," *Survey* 41 (February 1, 1919): 594–98; Arthur Gleason, "Whitley Councils," *Survey* 42 (April 5–19, 1919): 27–28, 75–77, 109–11; G. D. H. Cole, "Industrial Councils of Great Britain," *Dial* 66 (February 22, 1919): 171–73; Arthur Greenwood, "Development of British Industrial Thought," *Atlantic Monthly* 124 (July 1919): 106–15.

92. Quoted in McCartin, *Labor's Great War,* 189.

93. Fox, *History and Heritage,* 295.

94. George Bell, the chairman of the New York conference, is quoted in Fraser, "Dress Rehearsal for the New Deal," 218. Fraser, "The 'New Unionism,'" and *Labor Will Rule;* J. M. Budish and George Soule, *The New Unionism in the Clothing Industry* (1920; repr., New York, 1968), 149–50; Matthew Josephson, *Sidney Hillman: Statesman of American Labor* (Garden City, N.Y., 1952), 196; George Soule, *Sidney Hillman: Labor Statesman* (New York, 1939), 40–42, 100–101.

95. Robert F. Himmelberg, "Business Antitrust Policy and the Industrial Board of the Department of Commerce, 1919," *Business History Review* 42 (Spring 1968): 1–23; Koistinen, *Mobilizing for Modern War,* 279–87.

96. Wayne L. McNaughton and Joseph Lazar, *Industrial Relations and the Government* (New York, 1954), 47; Charles Loch Mowat, *Britain between the Wars, 1918–1940* (Chicago, 1955), 124.

97. Rodney Lowe, "The Failure of Consensus in Britain: The National Industrial Conference, 1919–1921," *Historical Journal* 21 (1978): 649–75; Charles, *Development of Industrial Relations,* 229–57; Chris Wrigley, *Lloyd George and the Challenge of Labour: The Post-War Coalition, 1918–1922* (New York, 1990), 139–41; Johnson, *Land Fit for Heroes,* 376–82; Kenneth O. Morgan, *Consensus and Disunity: The Lloyd George Coalition Government, 1918–1922* (Oxford, 1979), 57–59.

98. Industrial Conference, *Report of Provisional Joint Committee Presented to Meeting of Industrial Conference* (London, 1920); Charles, *Development of Industrial Relations,* 246–52; Keith Middlemas, *Politics in Industrial Society: The Experience of the British System since 1911* (London, 1979), 146–47.

99. H. M. Gitelman, "Being of Two Minds: American Employers Confront the Labor Problem, 1915–1919," *Labor History* 25 (Spring 1984): 189–216; and "Management's Crisis of Confidence and the Origin of the National Industrial Conference Board, 1914–1916," *Business History Review* 58 (Summer 1984): 153–77.

100. U.S. Department of Labor, *Proceedings of the First Industrial Conference* (Washington, 1920); Haggai Hurwitz, "Ideology and Industrial Conflict: President Wilson's First Industrial Conference of October 1919," *Labor History* 18 (Fall 1977): 509–24; Larry G. Gerber, "The United States and Canadian National Industrial Conferences of 1919: A Comparative Analysis," *Labor History* 32 (Winter 1991): 42–65.

101. U.S. Department of Labor, *First Industrial Conference,* 141.

102. U.S. Department of Labor, *First Industrial Conference,* 144; Charles E. Harvey, "John D. Rockefeller, Jr., Herbert Hoover, and President Wilson's Industrial Conferences of 1919–1920," in *Voluntarism, Planning, and the State,* ed. Jerold E. Brown and Patrick D. Reagan (New York, 1988); H. M. Gitelman, *Legacy of the Ludlow Massacre: A Chapter in American Industrial Relations* (Philadelphia, 1988), 305–29.

103. U.S. Department of Labor, *First Industrial Conference,* 81–82, 233, 240–44.

104. U.S. Department of Labor, *First Industrial Conference,* 59. Hurwitz, "Ideology and Industrial Conflict," 514–18; Gerber, "United States and Canadian Conferences"; David Brody, *Labor in Crisis: The Steel Strike of 1919* (Philadelphia, 1965).

105. *Report of Industrial Conference Called by the President* (n.p., 1920), 9–12; Gary Dean Best, "President Wilson's Second Industrial Conference," *Labor History* 16 (Fall 1975): 505–20.

106. Kerr, *American Railroad Politics,* 204–27; Ruth O'Brien, *Workers' Paradox: The Republican Origins of New Deal Labor Policy, 1886–1935* (Chapel Hill, N.C., 1998), 63–95.

107. Waites, *Class Society at War,* 14–17.

108. Bain and Price, *Profiles of Union Growth,* 37, 88.

109. Stanley Lebergott, *The Americans: An Economic Record* (New York, 1984), 380; Waites, *Class Society at War,* 120.

110. Andrew A. Procassini, *Competitors in Alliance: Industry Associations, Global Rivalries and Business-Government Relations* (Westport, Conn., 1995), 60; Herman Levy, *Monopolies, Cartels, and Trusts in British Industry* (1927; repr., New York, 1968), 177.

111. Harwood Lawrence Childs, *Labor and Capital in National Politics* (Columbus, Ohio, 1930), 28; Blank, *Industry and Government in Britain,* 15–18.

112. Kathleen G. Donohue, *Freedom from Want: American Liberalism and the Idea of the Consumer* (Baltimore, 2003).

3—The Twenties

1. George Sayers Bain and Robert Price, *Profiles of Union Growth: A Comparative Statistical Portrait of Eight Countries* (Oxford, 1980), 37, 88.

2. Joseph A. McCartin, "'An American Feeling': Workers, Managers, and the Struggle over Industrial Democracy in the World War I Era," in *Industrial Democracy in America: The Ambiguous Promise,* ed. Nelson Lichtenstein and Howell John Harris (Cambridge, 1993), 79; Chris Wrigley, *Lloyd George and the Challenge of Labour: The Post-War Coalition, 1918–1922* (New York, 1990).

3. Bain and Price, *Profiles of Union Growth,* 72, 77, 78, 95.

4. George Soule, *Prosperity Decade: From War to Depression, 1917–1929* (1947; repr., White Plains, N.Y., 1975), 96–106; Derek H. Aldcroft, *Inter-War Economy: Britain, 1919–1939* (New York, 1970), 23–37; U.S. Department of Commerce, Bureau of the Census, *Historical Statistics of the United States, Colonial Times to 1957* (Washington, 1960), 73; B. R. Mitchell, *European Historical Statistics, 1750–1970* (New York, 1978), 66.

5. Bain and Price, *Profiles of Union Growth*, 45, 73, 94–95.

6. Arthur Gleason, *What the Workers Want: A Study of British Labor* (New York, 1920).

7. Quoted in Bruce Irving Bustard, "The Human Factor: Labor Administration and Industrial Manpower Mobilization during the First World War" (Ph.D. diss., University of Iowa, 1984), 261.

8. P. Sargant Florence, *The Logic of British and American Industry: A Realistic Analysis of Economic Structure and Government* (Chapel Hill, N.C., 1953), 13, 22–32; Leslie Hannah and J. A. Kay, *Concentration in Modern Industry: Theory, Measurement and the U.K. Experience* (London, 1977), 1–3; Leslie Hannah, *The Rise of the Corporate Economy*, 2nd ed. (London, 1983).

9. Alfred Mond, *Industry and Politics* (London, 1927); Walter Meakin, *The New Industrial Revolution: A Study for the General Reader of Rationalisation and Post-War Tendencies of Capitalism and Labour* (1928; repr., New York, 1977).

10. Steven Tolliday, "Management and Labour in Britain, 1896–1939," in *The Automobile Industry and Its Workers: Between Fordism and Flexibility,* ed. Steven Tolliday and Jonathan Zeitlin (New York, 1987).

11. Hugh Armstrong Clegg, *A History of British Trade Unions since 1889,* vol. 2, *1911–1933* (Oxford, 1985), 308–10; Keith Middlemas, *Politics in Industrial Society: The Experience of the British System since 1911* (London, 1979), 160–65; Alan Fox, *History and Heritage: The Social Origins of the British Industrial Relations System* (London, 1985), 305–6.

12. Fox, *History and Heritage,* 334–35; Keith Laybourn, *The General Strike of 1926* (Manchester, 1993); G. A. Phillips, *The General Strike: The Politics of Industrial Conflict* (London, 1976).

13. Howard F. Gospel, *Markets, Firms, and the Management of Labour in Modern Britain* (New York, 1992), 86–87.

14. G. W. McDonald and H. F. Gospel, "The Mond-Turner Talks, 1927–1933: A Study in Industrial Co-operation," *Historical Journal* 16 (December 1973): 807–29; Howard F. Gospel, "Employers' Labour Policy: A Study of the Mond-Turner Talks, 1927–33," *Business History* 21 (July 1979): 180–97; Gordon Phillips, "Trade Unions and Corporatist Politics: The Response of the TUC to Industrial Rationalisation, 1927–33," in *Politics and Social Change in Modern Britain: Essays Presented to A. F. Thompson,* ed. P. J. Waller (Brighton, N.Y., 1987).

15. Mond, *Industry and Politics;* Meakin, *New Industrial Revolution.*

16. Milton J. Nadworny, *Scientific Management and the Unions, 1900–1932: A Historical Analysis* (Cambridge, Mass., 1955).

17. James E. Cronin, *The Politics of State Expansion: War, State and Society in Twentieth-Century Britain* (London, 1991), 81–92; Scott Newton and Dilwyn Porter, *Modernization Frustrated: The Politics of Industrial Decline in Britain since 1900* (London, 1988), 61–62; Alan Bullock, *The Life and Times of Ernest Bevin,* vol. 1, *Trade Union Leader, 1881–1940* (London, 1960), 392–402; Ross M. Martin, *TUC, The Growth of a Pressure Group, 1868–1976* (Oxford, 1980), 211–12.

18. Phillips, "Trade Unions and Corporatist Politics."

19. 174 *H.C. Deb.*, col. 762–842 (1924).

20. Liberal Industrial Inquiry, *Britain's Industrial Future* (London, 1928), 223.

21. Robert Boothby, John de V. Loder, Harold Macmillan, and Oliver Stanley, *Industry and the State: A Conservative View* (London, 1927), 57; Liberal Inquiry, *Britain's Industrial Future*, 117–19.

22. Liberal Inquiry, *Britain's Industrial Future*, 222; Boothby et al., *Industry and the State*, 61.

23. Eric Wigham, *The Power to Manage: A History of the Engineering Employers' Federation* (London, 1973), 132–33; Peter A. Hall, "The State and Economic Decline," in *The Decline of the British Economy*, ed. Bernard Elbaum and William Lazonick (Oxford, 1986), 282; Clegg, *History of British Trade Unions*, vol. 2, 464–71.

24. Irving Bernstein, *The Lean Years: A History of the American Worker, 1920–1933* (Baltimore, 1966), 94–97.

25. Albion Guilford Taylor, *Labor Policies of the National Association of Manufacturers* (1928; repr., New York, 1973), 16–18, 82–94; Pendleton Herring, *Group Representation before Congress* (1929; repr., New York, 1967), 81–94; Marc Allen Eisner, *From Warfare State to Welfare State: World War I, Compensatory State Building and the Limits of the Modern Order* (University Park, Penn., 2000), 116–17, 166.

26. George G. Higgins, *Voluntarism in Organized Labor in the United States, 1930–1940* (1945; repr., New York, 1969), 154–58; William English Walling, *American Labor and American Democracy* (New York, 1926), 96–101.

27. Samuel Gompers, "Significant Movements in Europe," *American Federationist* 31 (July 1924): 566; and "An Analysis of Fascism," *American Federationist* 30 (November 1923): 927–33; Margaret Cole, *The Story of Fabian Socialism* (Stanford, Calif., 1961), 196–97; John P. Diggins, *Mussolini and Fascism: The View from America* (Princeton, 1972).

28. Gompers, "Significant Movements in Europe," 566.

29. Marguerite Green, *The National Civic Federation and the American Labor Movement, 1900–1925* (Washington, 1956), 470.

30. Ronald Radosh, "The Corporate Ideology of American Labor Leaders from Gompers to Hillman," in *For A New America: Essays in History and Politics from 'Studies on the Left,' 1959–1967*, ed. James Weinstein and David W. Eakins (New York, 1970), 219–21.

31. W. Jett Lauck and Claude S. Watts, *The Industrial Code* (New York, 1922), 233–34, 390–93.

32. Edwin E. Witte, *The Government in Labor Disputes* (1932; repr., New York, 1969), 287–88.

33. Ellis W. Hawley, "Secretary Hoover and the Bituminous Coal Problem, 1921–1928," *Business History Review* 42 (Autumn 1968): 247–70; and "Herbert Hoover, the Commerce Secretariat, and the Vision of an 'Associative State,' 1921–1928," *Journal of American History* 61 (June 1974): 116–40; Robert H. Zieger, "Herbert Hoover, the Wage Earner, and the 'New Economic System,' 1919–1929," *Business History Review* (Summer 1977): 161–89.

34. Trades Union Congress, *Report of Proceedings at 58th Annual Trades Union Congress, Bournemouth, 1926* (London, 1926), 329, 500; Eric J. Hobsbawm, "The 'New Unionism' Reconsidered," in *The Development of Trade Unionism in Great Britain and Germany, 1880–1914*, ed. Wolfgang J. Mommsen and Hans-Gerhard Husung (London, 1985).

35. Jonathan Zeitlin, "The Internal Politics of Employer Organization: The Engineering Employers' Federation 1896–1939," in *The Power to Manage?: Employers and Industrial Relations in Comparative Historical Perspective,* ed. Steven Tolliday and Jonathan Zeitlin (London, 1991), 75–76.

36. Hawley, "Herbert Hoover, the Commerce Secretariat," 139; Louis Galambos, *Competition & Cooperation; The Emergence of a National Trade Association* (Baltimore, 1966).

37. Nadworny, *Scientific Management and the Unions;* Craig Phelan, *William Green: Biography of a Labor Leader* (Albany, N.Y., 1989).

38. Lewis L. Lorwin, *The American Federation of Labor: History, Policies, and Prospects* (1933; repr., Clifton, N.J., 1972), 217; Walling, *American Labor,* 88–96.

39. Woll, "Address before National Civil Federation, January 9, 1926," quoted in Walling, *American Labor,* 102.

40. Lauck and Watts, *Industrial Code,* 257–58; James Myers, *Representative Government in Industry* (New York, 1924), 229–32.

41. Felix Frankfurter, "War in the Clothing Industry," *New Republic* 25 (December 15, 1920): 59–61.

42. Steve Fraser, "Dress Rehearsal for the New Deal: Shop-Floor Insurgents, Political Elites, and Industrial Democracy in the Amalgamated Clothing Workers," in *Working-Class America: Essays on Labor, Community and American Society,* ed. Michael H. Frisch and Daniel J. Walkowitz (Urbana, Ill., 1983); and *Labor Will Rule: Sidney Hillman and the Rise of American Labor* (New York, 1991).

43. Lauck and Watts, *Industrial Code,* 260–63; Robert H. Zieger, *Republicans and Labor* (Lexington, Ken., 1969), 217–26.

44. John R. Bowman, *Capitalist Collective Action: Competition, Cooperation, and Conflict in the Coal Industry* (Cambridge, 1989).

45. Melvyn Dubofsky and Warren Van Tyne, *John L. Lewis: A Biography* (New York, 1977).

46. Zieger, *Republicans and Labor,* 217–26; Hawley, "Hoover and the Bituminous Coal Problem."

47. Dubofsky and Tyne, *John L. Lewis.*

48. Zieger, *Republicans and Labor,* 254–58.

49. Lauck and Watts, *Industrial Code,* 236–40; Colin J. Davis, *Power at Odds: The 1922 National Railroad Shopmen's Strike* (Urbana, Ill., 1997).

50. Donald Richberg, "Confidential Report on Railway Labor Act and Board of Mediation," December 22, 1928, Donald R. Richberg Papers, Chicago Historical Society; and *Tents of the Mighty* (Chicago, 1930), 201.

51. Howell Harris, "The Snares of Liberalism? Politicians, Bureaucrats, and the Shaping of Federal Labour Relations Policy in the United States, ca. 1915–47," in *Shop Floor Bargaining and the State,* ed. Steven Tolliday and Jonathan Zeitlin (Cambridge, 1985), 160; Ruth O'Brien, *Workers' Paradox: The Republican Origins of New Deal Labor Policy, 1886–1935* (Chapel Hill, N.C., 1998).

52. Gerald Crompton, "'Squeezing the Pulpless Orange': Labour and Capital on the Railways in the Interwar Years," *Business History* 31 (April 1989): 66–83; John Barton Seymour, *The Whitley Councils Scheme* (London, 1932), 41–42; W. Milne-Bailey, *Trade Unions and the State* (London, 1934), 90; 146 *H.C. Deb.,* col. 273–87 (1921).

53. Liberal Inquiry, *Britain's Industrial Future,* 355.

54. Seymour, *Whitley Councils,* 94–104; Rodger Charles, *The Development of Industrial Relations in Britain, 1911–1939: Studies in the Evolution of Collective Bargaining at National and Industry Level* (London, 1973), 124–204.

55. Gleason, *What the Workers Want*, 296.

56. Ian G. Sharp, *Industrial Conciliation and Arbitration in Great Britain* (London, 1950), 333.

57. 174 *H.C. Deb.*, col. 762–842 (1924); Sharp, *Industrial Conciliation*, 333.

58. Trades Union Congress, *Report of Proceedings at 58th Annual*, 288.

59. Liberal Inquiry, *Britain's Industrial Future*, 205–13.

60. Boothby et al., *Industry and the State*, 196–226.

61. Mond, *Industry and Politics*, 42; Meakin, *New Industrial Revolution*, 250–52.

62. Peter A. Swenson, *Capitalists against Markets: The Making of Labor Markets and Welfare States in the United States and Sweden* (New York, 2002).

63. David Brody, "The Rise and Decline of Welfare Capitalism," in Brody, *Workers in Industrial America* (New York, 1980).

64. William Lazonick, "Technological Change and the Control of Work: The Development of Capital-Labor Relations in U.S. Mass Production Industries," in *Managerial Strategies and Industrial Relations: An Historical and Comparative Study*, ed. Howard F. Gospel and Craig R. Littler (London, 1983), 129; Stephen Broadberry, "Openness and Britain's Productivity Performance, 1870–1990: A Sectoral Analysis," CSGR Working Paper No. 67/01 (February 2001), 21. January 12, 2004 <www.warwick.ac.uk/fac/soc/csgr/workingpapers/2001/abwp6701>; David Fairris, "From Exit to Voice in Shopfloor Governance: The Case of Company Unions," *Business History Review* 69 (Winter 1995): 493–529.

65. Andrea Tone, *The Business of Benevolence: Industrial Paternalism in Progressive America* (Ithaca, N.Y., 1997); Jennifer Klein, *For All These Rights: Business, Labor, and the Shaping of America's Public-Private Welfare State* (Princeton, 2003); Jacob S. Hacker, *The Divided Welfare State: The Battle over Public and Private Social Benefits in the United States* (New York, 2002).

66. Fairris, "From Exit to Voice."

67. Stuart D. Brandes, *American Welfare Capitalism, 1880–1940* (Chicago, 1976); Brody, "Rise and Decline"; Daniel Nelson, "The Company Union Movement, 1900–1937: A Reexamination," *Business History Review* 56 (Autumn 1982): 335–57; Bruce E. Kaufman and Daphne Gottlieb Taras, eds., *Nonunion Employee Representation: History, Contemporary Practice, and Policy* (Armonk, N.Y., 2000).

68. David Montgomery, *The Fall of the House of Labor* (New York, 1987), 411.

69. A. R. Griffin and C. P. Griffin, "The Non-Political Trade Union Movement," in *Essays in Labour History, 1918–1939*, ed. Asa Briggs and John Saville (London, 1977); Helen Jones, "Employers' Welfare Schemes and Industrial Relations in Inter-War Britain," *Business History* 25 (1983): 61–75; Robert Fitzgerald, *British Labour Management and Industrial Welfare, 1846–1939* (London, 1988).

70. *The Industrial Council Plan in Great Britain* (Washington, 1919), 19–20.

71. Boothby et al., *Industry and the State*, 207.

72. Liberal Inquiry, *Britain's Industrial Future*, 230–31.

73. Ken Coates and Anthony Topham, comps., *Industrial Democracy in Great Britain* (London, 1968), 135.

74. Gleason, *What the Workers Want*, 173–80.

75. Sidney Webb and Beatrice Webb, *A Constitution for the Socialist Commonwealth of Great Britain* (1920; repr., Cambridge, 1975), 179–80.

76. Adolf A. Berle and Gardiner C. Means, *The Modern Corporation and Private Property* (1932; repr., New York, 1967).

77. Leslie Hannah, "Visible and Invisible Hands in Great Britain," in *Managerial*

Hierarchies: Comparative Perspectives on the Rise of the Modern Industrial Enterprise, ed. Alfred D. Chandler, Jr., and Herman Daems (Cambridge, 1980); Graeme M. Holmes, *Britain and America* (London, 1976).

78. Harry W. Laidler and Norman Thomas, eds., *New Tactics in Social Conflict* (New York, 1926), 9–19. Bullock, *Life and Times of Ernest Bevin,* vol. 1, 396.

79. Bruce E. Kaufman, *The Origins & Evolution of the Field of Industrial Relations in the United States* (Ithaca, N.Y., 1993); Sanford M. Jacoby, *Employing Bureaucracy: Managers, Unions, and the Transformation of Work in American Industry, 1900–1945* (New York, 1985); John Child, *British Management Thought: A Critical Analysis* (London, 1969).

80. Mary Parker Follett, *Creative Experience* (New York, 1924), 163, 250; Henry C. Metcalf and L. Urwick, eds., *Dynamic Administration: The Collected Papers of Mary Parker Follett,* 2nd ed. (London, 1973).

81. Jacoby, *Employing Bureaucracy.*

82. W. Jett Lauck, *Political and Industrial Democracy, 1776–1926* (New York, 1926), 133–34.

83. Clarence J. Hicks, *My Life in Industrial Relations* (New York, 1941), 81–84.

84. David M. Vrooman, *Daniel Willard and Progressive Management on the Baltimore & Ohio Railroad* (Columbus, Ohio, 1991), xiv.

85. Arthur Calhoun, "Engineering as Collective Bargaining: The B & O Plan," in *American Labor Dynamics: In the Light of Post-War Developments,* ed. J. B. S. Hardman (1928; repr., New York, 1968), 323–28; Louis Aubrey Wood, *Union-Management Cooperation on the Railroads* (1931; repr., New York, 1976).

86. Lauck, *Political and Industrial Democracy;* Sam Lewisohn, *The New Leadership in Industry* (New York, 1926); Myers, *Representative Government;* Edward A. Filene, *The Way Out: A Forecast of Coming Changes in American Business and Industry* (Garden City, N.Y., 1925); Ben M. Selekman, *Sharing Management with the Workers* (New York, 1924).

87. Ramsay Muir, *America the Golden: An Englishman's Notes and Comparisons* (London, 1927), 24–25, 71–72, 101–15; Philip Kerr, *The Industrial Dilemma* (London, 1926), 19–21; Mond, *Industry and Politics,* 48–49.

88. Fairris, "From Exit to Voice," 511.

4—The Great Depression and the Failure of New Initiatives at Corporatist Planning

1. Peter Gourevitch, *Politics in Hard Times: Comparative Responses to International Economic Crises* (Ithaca, N.Y., 1986), 231.

2. U.S. Department of Commerce, Bureau of the Census, *Historical Statistics of the United States, Colonial Times to 1957* (Washington, 1960), 73; Kim Quaile Hill, *Democracies in Crisis: Public Policy Responses to the Great Depression* (Boulder, Colo., 1988), 41.

3. B. R. Mitchell, *European Historical Statistics, 1750–1970* (New York, 1978), 66–67; Hill, *Democracies in Crisis,* 41.

4. George Sayers Bain and Robert Price, *Profiles of Union Growth: A Comparative Statistical Portrait of Eight Countries* (Oxford, 1980), 37, 88.

5. Louis Galambos, *Competition & Cooperation; The Emergence of a National Trade Association* (Baltimore, 1966); Robert F. Himmelberg, *The Origins of the National Recovery Administration: Business, Government and the Trade Association Issue, 1921–1933* (New York, 1974); Colin Gordon, *New Deals: Business, Labor, and Politics in America, 1920–1935* (New York, 1994), 35–86.

6. *New York Times,* May 2, 1930; "Planning Proposals of the Committee on Continuity of Business and Employment of the United States Chamber of Commerce," in *America Faces the Future,* ed. Charles A. Beard (Boston, 1932), 196–264; Harriman's testimony in hearings before a subcommittee of the Senate Committee on Manufactures, *Establishment of National Economic Council,* 71st Cong., 1st sess., October 26, 1931, 188; J. George Frederick, ed., *The Swope Plan: Details, Criticisms, Analysis* (New York, 1931); Swope's testimony in Senate hearings, *Economic Council,* 300–17 (October 28, 1931).

7. *Nation's Business* 19 (June 1931): 30.

8. Thomas C. Chadbourne, quoted in Frederick, *Swope Plan,* 74.

9. Bain and Price, *Profiles of Union Growth,* 88.

10. Gerard Swope, "Stabilization of Industry," in Beard, *America Faces the Future,* 165–67; Ronald Radosh, "The Development of the Corporate Ideology of American Labor Leaders" (Ph.D. diss., University of Wisconsin, 1967), 275.

11. Himmelberg, *Origins of the National Recovery Administration,* 124–62.

12. Message to Wisconsin legislature, November 24, 1931, in Beard, *America Faces the Future,* 366–69; John E. Miller, *Governor Philip F. LaFollette, the Wisconsin Progressives, and the New Deal* (Columbia, Mo., 1982), 21.

13. *American Federationist* 38 (October 1931): 1182–83.

14. Frederick, *Swope Plan,* 94–95; Radosh, "Corporate Ideology," 258–60.

15. Donald Richberg, memo for D. B. Robertson (1931?), Donald Richberg Papers, Chicago Historical Society.

16. Irving Bernstein, *The Lean Years: A History of the American Worker, 1920–1933* (Baltimore, 1966), 195–215; Daniel Ernst, "The Yellow-Dog Contract and Liberal Reform, 1917–1932," *Labor History* 30 (Spring 1989): 251–74.

17. James P. Johnson, *The Politics of Soft Coal: The Bituminous Industry from World War I through the New Deal* (Urbana, Ill., 1979), 123–33; *New York Times,* Feb 12, 1933; David Brody, "Labour Relations in American Coal Mining: An Industry Perspective," in *Workers, Owners, and Politics in Coal Mining: An International Comparison of Industrial Relations,* ed. Gerald D. Feldman and Klaus Tenfelde (New York, 1990), 94–99.

18. Melvyn Dubofsky and Warren Van Tyne, *John L. Lewis: A Biography* (New York, 1977), 175–77.

19. Johnson, *Politics of Soft Coal;* Brody, "Labour Relations in American Coal Mining"; Steve Fraser, "Dress Rehearsal for the New Deal: Shop-Floor Insurgents, Political Elites, and Industrial Democracy in the Amalgamated Clothing Workers," in *Working-Class America: Essays on Labor, Community and American Society,* ed. Michael H. Frisch and Daniel J. Walkowitz (Urbana, 1983).

20. Himmelberg, *Origins of the National Recovery Administration;* Elliot A. Rosen, *Hoover, Roosevelt, and the Brains Trust: From Depression to New Deal* (New York, 1977).

21. John Barton Seymour, *The Whitley Councils Scheme* (London, 1932).

22. 240 *H.C. Deb.,* col. 973–74 (June 24, 1930).

23. Eustace Percy, *Democracy on Trial: A Preface to Industrial Policy* (London, 1931); Harold Macmillan, *Winds of Change, 1914–1939* (New York, 1966), 327–28.

24. Oswald Mosley, *A National Policy: An Account of the Emergency Program Advanced by Sir Oswald Mosley, M.P.* (London, 1931), 20–23.

25. Max Nicholson, "The Proposal for a National Plan," originally published in *Week-End Review* (February 1931), reprinted in *Fifty Years of Political and Economic Planning: Looking Forward, 1931–1981,* ed. John Pinder (London, 1981), 7; L. P.

Carpenter, "Corporatism in Great Britain, 1930–45," *Journal of Contemporary History* 11 (1976): 3–25; Daniel Ritschel, "A Corporatist Economy in Britain? Capitalist Planning for Industrial Self-Government in the 1930s," *English Historical Review* 106 (January 1991): 41–65; Alan Booth and Melvyn Pack, *Employment, Capital and Economic Policy: Great Britain, 1918–1939* (Oxford, 1985).

26. 232 *H.C. Deb.*, col. 666 (November 21, 1929).

27. 240 *H.C. Deb.*, col. 545–47 (June 18, 1930); F. J. Bayliss, *British Wages Councils* (Oxford, 1962); Seymour, *Whitley Councils*, 40.

28. 232 *H.C. Deb.*, col. 1595 (November 28, 1929); Gordon Phillips, "Trade Unions and Corporatist Politics: The Response of the TUC to Industrial Rationalisation, 1927–33," in *Politics and Social Change in Modern Britain: Essays Presented to A. F. Thompson*, ed. P. J. Waller (Brighton, 1987).

29. R. Page Arnot, *The Miners: Years of Struggle*, vol. 2, *A History of the Miners' Federation of Great Britain* (London, 1953); M. W. Kirby, *The British Coalmining Industry, 1870–1946* (Hamden, Conn., 1977); Roy Church, "Employers, Trade Unions and the State, 1889–1987: The Origins and Decline of Tripartism in the British Coal Industry," in *Workers, Owners, and Politics in Coal Mining*; Barry Supple, "The Political Economy of Demoralization: The State and the Coalmining Industry in America and Britain Between the Wars," *Economic History Review*, 2nd ser., 41 (1988): 566–91.

30. Howard F. Gospel, *Markets, Firms, and the Management of Labour in Modern Britain* (New York, 1992), 79–101; Steven Tolliday and Jonathan Zeitlin, "National Models and International Variations in Labour Management and Employer Organization," in *The Power to Manage? Employers and Industrial Relations in Comparative-Historical Perspective*, ed. Steven Tolliday and Jonathan Zeitlin (London, 1991).

31. W. H. Beveridge, letter to the editor, *Times* (London), October 21, 1929; "The Coal Mines Bill," *Economist*, December 14, 1929.

32. Kirby, *British Coalmining*, 124–37; Robert Skidelsky, *Politicians and the Slump: The Labour Government of 1929–1931* (London, 1967), 111–13, 131–34.

33. 233 *H.C. Deb.*, col. 1763 (December 19, 1929).

34. Arthur Fletcher Lucas, *Industrial Reconstruction and the Control of Competition: The British Experiments* (London, 1937), 74.

35. Supple, "Political Economy of Demoralization," 579.

36. Kirby, *British Coalmining*, 124.

37. Supple, "Political Economy of Demoralization," 584.

38. Dubofsky and Van Tyne, *John L. Lewis*, 177; Brody, "Labour Relations in American Coal Mining," 100–105; Johnson, *Politics of Soft Coal*, 135–36, 217–20.

39. Bain and Price, *Profiles of Union Growth*, 45, 95.

40. John Singleton, "Labour, the Conservatives and Nationalisation," in *The Political Economy of Nationalisation in Britain, 1920–1950*, ed. Robert Millward and John Singleton (Cambridge, 1995), 27.

41. Patrick D. Reagan, "Creating the Organizational Nexus for New Deal Planning," in *Voluntarism, Planning, and the State*, ed. Jerold E. Brown and Patrick D. Reagan (New York, 1988); Stuart Kidd, "Collectivist Intellectuals and the Ideal of National Economic Planning, 1929–33," in *Nothing Else to Fear: New Perspectives on America in the Thirties*, ed. Stephen W. Baskerville and Ralph Willett (Manchester, Eng., 1985); Booth and Pack, *Employment, Capital and Economic Policy*, 55–75, 148–64.

42. Susan Howson and Donald Winch, *The Economic Advisory Council, 1930–1939: A Study in Economic Advice during Depression and Recovery* (Cambridge, 1977), 154.

43. Industrial Conference, *Report of Provisional Joint Committee Presented to Meeting of Industrial Conference* (London, 1920); Rodney Lowe, "The Failure of Consensus in Britain: The National Industrial Conference, 1919–1921," *Historical Journal* 21 (1978): 649–75.

44. Address by John Beard (TUC president) at the TUC Annual Congress of 1930, Trades Union Congress, *Report of Proceedings at 62nd Annual Trades Union Congress, Nottingham, 1930* (London, 1930), 69–70. G. W. McDonald and H. F. Gospel, "The Mond-Turner Talks, 1927–33: A Study in Industrial Cooperation," *Historical Journal* 16 (December 1973), 807–29; Howard F. Gospel, "Employers' Labour Policy: A Study of the Mond-Turner Talks, 1927–33," *Business History* 21 (July 1979), 180–97.

45. Michael Dintenfass, "The Politics of Producers' Co-operation: The FBI-TUC-NCEO Talks, 1929–1933," in *Businessmen and Politics: Studies of Business Activity in British Politics, 1900–1945,* ed. John Turner (London, 1984).

46. 230 *H.C. Deb.,* col. 420–21 (July 17, 1929); 238 *H.C. Deb.,* col. 2026 (May 15, 1930).

47. Alan Bullock, *The Life and Times of Ernest Bevin,* vol. 1, *Trade Union Leader, 1881–1940* (London, 1960); Walter McLennan Citrine, *Men and Work: An Autobiography* (1964; repr., Westport, Conn., 1976).

48. McDonald and Gospel, "Mond-Turner Talks"; Gospel, "Employers' Labour Policy"; Dintenfass, "Politics of Producers' Co-operation."

49. Howson and Winch, *Economic Advisory Council,* 20–23.

50. Howson and Winch, *Economic Advisory Council,* 20–30; David Marquand, *Ramsay MacDonald* (London, 1977), 523–25.

51. Winston L. Spencer Churchill, *Parliamentary Government and the Economic Problem* (Oxford, 1930); Howson and Winch, *Economic Advisory Council,* 155.

52. Mosley, *National Policy,* 17–18, 33.

53. Percy, *Democracy on Trial,* 60.

54. Gerald D. Nash, "Experiments in Industrial Mobilization: WIB and NRA," *Mid-America* 45 (July 1963): 157–74; William E. Leuchtenburg, "The New Deal and the Analogue of War," in *Change and Continuity in Twentieth-Century America,* ed. John Braeman, Robert Bremner, and Everett Walters (Columbus, Ohio, 1964).

55. Larry G. Gerber, "The United States and Canadian National Industrial Conferences of 1919: A Comparative Analysis," *Labor History* 42 (Winter 1991): 42–65.

56. Christopher L. Tomlins, *The State and the Unions: Labor Relations, Law, and the Organized Labor Movement in America, 1880–1960* (New York, 1985), 107–8.

57. Ellis W. Hawley, "Herbert Hoover, the Commerce Secretariat, and the Vision of an 'Associative State,'" *Journal of American History* 61 (June 1974): 116–40; and "Herbert Hoover and Economic Stabilization, 1921–22," in *Herbert Hoover as Secretary of Commerce: Studies in New Era Thought and Practice,* ed. Hawley (Iowa City, 1981); Guy Alchon, *The Invisible Hand of Planning: Capitalism, Social Science, and the State in the 1920s* (Princeton, 1985), 71–90.

58. *Nation's Business* 18 (April 1930): 12.

59. Matthew Woll to James Girard (chair of NCF's Commission on Industrial Inquiry), June 3, 1931, reprinted in Beard, *America Faces the Future,* 34–37.

60. Senate hearings, *Economic Council,* 1–2 (October 22, 1931); Beard, *America Faces the Future,* 413–16.

61. *American Federationist* 38 (April 1931): 403–4.

62. George Soule, *Sidney Hillman: Labor Statesman* (New York, 1939), 157–60; Sidney Hillman, "Unemployment Reserves," *Atlantic Monthly* 148 (November 1931): 661–69; Senate hearings, *Economic Council*, 434–41, 627–31 (November 3, 1931, and December 3, 1931).

63. Senate hearings, *Economic Council*, 382 (October 30, 1931); 312–14 (October 28, 1931); 163–65 (October 26, 1931).

64. Senate hearings, *Economic Council*, 414–15 (November 2, 1931); 213 (October 26, 1931); 334–37 (October 29, 1931); n.p. (December 1, 1931); 314 (October 28, 1931).

65. Thomas Ferguson, "From Normalcy to New Deal: Industrial Structure, Party Competition, and American Public Policy in the Great Depression," *International Organization* 38 (Winter 1984): 41–94.

66. Skidelsky, *Politicians and the Slump*.

67. G. D. H. Cole, *Economic Planning* (1935; repr., Port Washington, N.Y., 1971); W. Milne-Bailey, *Trade Unions and the State* (London, 1934); *The Next Five Years: An Essay in Political Agreement* (1935; repr., New York, 1985).

68. Harold Macmillan, *Reconstruction: A Plea for a National Policy* (London, 1933), 9–10, 32, 39, 53, 73, 113–14; Macmillan, *Winds of Change*, 266–67, 326–40.

69. Booth and Pack, *Employment, Capital, and Economic Policy*, 57–62; Ritschel, "Corporatist Economy in Britain," 44–48; Scott Newton and Dilwyn Porter, *Modernization Frustrated: The Politics of Industrial Decline in Britain since 1900* (London, 1988), 80.

70. Arthur Salter, *The Framework of an Ordered Society* (New York, 1933), 41; Basil Blackett, "The Era of Planning," in *Great Events in History*, ed. Stirling Taylor (London, 1934); Roy Glenday, *The Economic Consequences of Progress* (London, 1934).

71. Macmillan, *Reconstruction*, 52.

72. Oswald Mosley, *The Greater Britain* (London, n.d. [1932]), 26–29, 98–99.

73. Samuel H. Beer, *British Politics in the Collectivist Age* (New York, 1969), 279; Donald Winch, *Economics and Policy: A Historical Study* (London, 1969), 212–13.

74. Howson and Winch, *Economic Advisory Council*, 107.

75. 261 *H.C. Deb.*, col. 2041–64 (February 19, 1932).

76. Steven Tolliday, "Tariffs and Steel, 1916–1934: The Politics of Industrial Decline," in *Businessmen and Politics*, 73–75; and *Business, Banking, and Politics: The Case of British Steel, 1918–1939* (Cambridge, 1987), 299–328; Lucas, *Industrial Reconstruction*, 121–22; Arthur Pugh, *Men of Steel: A Chronicle of Eighty-Eight Years of Trade Unionism in the British Iron and Steel Trades Confederation* (London, 1951), 457–95; Trades Union Congress, *Report of Proceedings at 66th Annual Trades Union Congress, Weymouth, 1934* (London, 1934), 189–205.

77. J. H. Bamberg, "The Rationalization of the British Cotton Industry in the Interwar Years," *Textile History* 19 (1988): 83–102.

78. H. A. Turner, *Trade Union Growth: Structure and Policy, a Comparative Study of the Cotton Unions* (London, 1962), 357–58.

79. Bamberg, "Rationalization of British Cotton," 88; Anthony Slaven, "Self-Liquidation: The National Shipbuilders Security Ltd and British Shipbuilding in the 1930s," in *Charted and Uncharted Waters: Proceedings of a Conference on the Study of British Maritime History*, ed. Sarah Palmer and Glyndwr Williams (London, 1982).

80. 289 *H.C. Deb.*, col. 1961–63 (May 17, 1934); Rodney Lowe, *Adjusting to Democracy: The Role of the Ministry of Labour in British Politics, 1916–1939* (Oxford, 1986), 118–19.

81. Turner, *Trade Union Growth*, 363–64; Bamberg, "Rationalization of British Cotton," 94–96; John Singleton, "Debating the Nationalisation of the Cotton Industry," in *Political Economy of Nationalisation in Britain;* 308 *H.C. Deb.,* col. 87–95 (February 4, 1936); 310 *H.C. Deb.,* col. 1839–41 (March 31, 1936); Hugh Armstrong Clegg, *A History of British Trade Unions since 1889,* vol. 3, *1934–1951* (Oxford, 1994), 34.

82. Phillips, "Trade Unions and Corporatist Politics."

83. Robert Millward, "Industrial Organisation and Economic Factors in Nationalisation," in *Political Economy of Nationalisation in Britain,* 16–17.

84. Trades Union Congress, *Report of Proceedings at 66th Annual Trades Union Congress;* TUC, *Report of Proceedings at 67th Annual Trades Union Congress, Margate, 1935* (London, 1935); Hugh Dalton, *Practical Socialism for Britain* (1935; repr., New York, 1985).

85. 300 *H.C. Deb.* (April 3, 1935).

86. Ritschel, "Corporatist Economy in Britain," 50.

87. Cripps, 300 *H.C. Deb.,* col. 423–27 (April 3, 1935).

88. *Economist,* March 3, 1935, 725–26.

89. Mander, 300 *H.C. Deb.,* col. 455–56 (April 3, 1935); Ritschel, "Corporatist Economy in Britain," 50–53.

90. Ritschel, "Corporatist Economy in Britain"; Helen Mercer, *Constructing a Competitive Order: The Hidden History of British Antitrust Policies* (Cambridge, 1995), 49–50.

91. *Next Five Years,* 81.

92. Bayliss, *British Wages Councils,* 30–44.

93. Paul Smith, "The Road Haulage Industry 1918–1940: The Process of Unionization, Employers' Control and Statutory Regulation," *Historical Studies in Industrial Relations* 3 (March 1997): 49–80.

94. Bernstein, *Lean Years;* Ernst, "The Yellow-Dog Contract."

95. Ellis W. Hawley, *The New Deal and the Problem of Monopoly: A Study in Economic Ambivalence* (Princeton, 1966); Himmelberg, *Origins of the National Recovery Administration.*

96. Irving Bernstein, *The New Deal Collective Bargaining Policy* (1950; repr., New York, 1975), 34.

97. Kenneth Finegold and Theda Skocpol, *State and Party in America's New Deal* (Madison, Wisc., 1995); and "State Capacity and Economic Intervention in the Early New Deal," *Political Science Quarterly* 97 (Summer 1982): 255–78; Marc Allen Eisner, *From Warfare State to Welfare State: World War I, Compensatory State Building and the Limits of the Modern Order* (University Park, Penn., 2000).

98. Colin Crouch, *Class Conflict and the Industrial Relations Crisis: Compromise and Corporatism in the Policies of the British State* (London, 1977); Peter J. Williamson, *Varieties of Corporatism: A Conceptual Discussion* (Cambridge, 1985).

99. Skidelsky, *Politicians and the Slump,* 390.

100. Lowe, *Adjusting to Democracy,* 26; Skidelsky, *Politicians and the Slump;* Keith Middlemas and John Barnes, *Baldwin: A Biography* (London, 1969).

101. Bernstein, *Lean Years,* 481–83.

102. Himmelberg, *Origins of the National Recovery Administration;* Donald R. Brand, *Corporatism and the Rule of Law: A Study of the National Recovery Administration* (Ithaca, N.Y., 1988).

103. Himmelberg, *Origins of the National Recovery Administration;* Galambos, *Competition & Cooperation.*

104. Tony Freyer, *Regulating Big Business: Antitrust in Great Britain and America, 1880–1990* (New York, 1992); Mercer, *Constructing a Competitive Order.*

105. Raymond Willoughby, "The Trade Associations Are Ready," *Nation's Business* 21 (July 1933): 35.

106. Editorial on the NIRA, *Nation's Business* 21 (June 1933): 29.

107. U.S. Senate Committee on Finance, *National Industrial Recovery,* 73rd Cong., 1st sess., May 22, 1933, 2–21, 26–27; *American Federationist* 40 (July 1933): 683.

108. Irving Bernstein, *Turbulent Years: A History of the American Worker, 1933–1941* (Boston, 1970), 28–29.

109. Senate hearings, *National Industrial Recovery,* May 22, 1933, 26–27.

110. Bernstein, *Turbulent Years,* 28–29; Felix Frankfurter to Robert Wagner, May 30, 1933, Frankfurter Papers, Library of Congress.

111. Editorial, *American Federationist* 40 (July 1933): 679.

112. Leverett S. Lyon et al., *The National Recovery Administration: An Analysis and Appraisal* (Washington, 1935), 459.

113. Gordon, *New Deals,* 171.

114. Peter A. Swenson, *Capitalists against Markets: The Making of Labor Markets and Welfare States in the United States and Sweden* (New York, 2002), 197–201.

115. Bernstein, *New Deal Collective Bargaining Policy,* 33–37; William Green's testimony before hearings of the House Committee on Ways and Means, *National Industrial Recovery,* May 19, 1933, 117–18.

116. Testimony of James Emery, head of the National Association of Manufactures, and E. L. Michael, former business representative on the National War Labor Board, in Senate hearings, *National Industrial Recovery,* May 29 and May 31, 1933, 288–89, 379–81; Rhonda F. Levine, *Class Struggle and the New Deal: Industrial Labor, Industrial Capital, and the State* (Lawrence, Kans., 1988), 72–79; Stanley Vittoz, *New Deal Labor Policy and the American Industrial Economy* (Chapel Hill, N.C., 1987), 91–96.

117. "'The New Deal' in Industry," *Coal Age* 38 (June 1933): 173.

118. "Industry Tries the New Deal," *Nation's Business* 21 (August 1933): 59.

119. "The 'New Deal' in Industry," 174; Johnson, *Politics of Soft Coal,* 150–64.

120. Bernstein, *New Deal Collective Bargaining Policy.*

121. Gospel, *Markets, Firms, and the Management of Labour.*

122. Colin Crouch, "The State, Capital and Liberal Democracy," in *State and Economy in Contemporary Capitalism,* ed. Crouch (New York, 1979), 27.

123. "Business Wants a New NRA," *Nation's Business* 23 (February 1935): 60; Robert M. Collins, *The Business Response to Keynes, 1929–1964* (Columbia, Mo., 1981), 31–36.

124. William H. Wilson, "How the Chamber of Commerce Viewed the NRA: A Re-examination," *Mid-America* 44 (April 1962): 95–108; Alfred S. Cleveland, "NAM: Spokesman for Industry," *Harvard Business Review* 26 (1948): 353–71; Galambos, *Competition and Cooperation,* 266–70.

125. Editorials, *American Federationist* 41 (February 1934): 133; (April 1934): 361.

126. Editorial, *American Federationist* 42 (March 1935): 242–43; memo from William Green to Franklin Roosevelt, February 11, 1935, reprinted in *American Federationist* 42 (March 1935): 248–49; *American Federationist* 42 (November 1935): 1170.

127. Larry G. Gerber, *The Limits of Liberalism: Josephus Daniels, Henry Stimson, Bernard Baruch, Donald Richberg, Felix Frankfurter and the Development of the Modern American Political Economy* (New York, 1983), 285–89; Hawley, *New Deal and the Problem of Monopoly,* 142–46.

128. Meg Jacobs, "Pocketbook Politics: Democracy and the Market in Twentieth-Century America," in *The Democratic Experience: New Directions in American Political History,* ed. Meg Jacobs, William J. Novak, and Julian E. Zelizer (Princeton, 2003).

129. Rodney Lowe, "Hours of Labour: Negotiating Industrial Legislation in Britain, 1919–1939," *Economic History Review* 35 (1982): 254–71; Vivien Hart, *Bound by Our Constitution: Women, Workers, and the Minimum Wage* (Princeton, 1994).

130. George E. Paulsen, *A Living Wage for the Forgotten Man: The Quest for Fair Labor Standards, 1933–1941* (Selinsgrove, Penn., 1996), 68–81; Sidney Hillman's testimony, joint hearings of the Senate Committee on Education and Labor and the House Committee on Labor, *Fair Labor Standards Act of 1937,* 75th Cong., 1st sess. (June 15, 1937), 944–48.

131. Testimony of Frances Perkins and William Green, joint hearings, *Fair Labor Standards Act of 1937* (June 4, 1937), 174–81, 215–21.

132. Joint hearings, *Fair Labor Standards Act of 1937* (June 7, 1937), 273–75.

133. Paulsen, *Living Wage for the Forgotten Man,* 126–30.

134. Hawley, *New Deal and the Problem of Monopoly;* Bernard Bellush, *The Failure of the NRA* (New York, 1975); Finegold and Skocpol, *State and Party;* Brand, *Corporatism and the Rule of Law;* Gordon, *New Deals.*

135. Robert Griffith, "Dwight D. Eisenhower and the Corporate Commonwealth," *American Historical Review* 87 (February 1982): 87–122; Ellis W. Hawley, *The Great War and the Search for a Modern Order: A History of the American People and Their Institutions, 1917–1933,* 2nd ed. (New York, 1992), 198–200.

136. Keith Middlemas, *Politics in Industrial Society: The Experience of the British System since 1911* (London, 1979); Beer, *British Politics in the Collectivist Age;* Robert Taylor, "The Trade Union 'Problem' since 1960," in *Trade Unions in British Politics,* ed. Ben Pimlott and Chris Cook (London, 1982).

5—The Great Depression and the Development of Diverging Paths in Micro-level Industrial Relations

1. Brian Bercusson, *Fair Wages Resolutions* (London, 1978); Leonard D. White, *Whitley Councils in the British Civil Service: A Study in Conciliation and Arbitration* (Chicago, 1933); K. D. Ewing, "The State and Industrial Relations: 'Collective Laissez-Faire' Revisited," *Historical Studies in Industrial Relations* 5 (Spring 1998): 1–31.

2. James Hinton, "Voluntarism versus Jacobinism: Labor, Nation, and Citizenship in Britain, 1850–1950," *International Labor and Working-Class History* 48 (Fall 1995): 68–90.

3. Arthur McIvor, *Organised Capital: Employers' Associations and Industrial Relations in Northern England, 1880–1939* (Cambridge, 1996), 181–269.

4. Sidney Pollard, "Trade Union Reactions to the Economic Crisis," *Journal of Contemporary History* 4 (October 1969): 115; George Sayers Bain and Robert Price, *Profiles of Union Growth: A Comparative Statistical Portrait of Eight Countries* (Oxford, 1980), 39.

5. Bain and Price, *Profiles of Union Growth,* 39, 88.

6. Alan Bullock, *The Life and Times of Ernest Bevin,* vol. 1, *Trade Union Leader, 1881–1940* (London, 1960); Walter McLennan Citrine, *Men and Work: An Autobiography* (1964; repr., Westport, Conn., 1976).

7. Otto S. Beyer, Jr., "The Machinery of Cooperation," *American Federationist* 36 (November 1929): 1311–19; Geoffrey C. Brown, "Labor's Principles of Scientific

Management," *American Federationist* 37 (February 1930), 194–95; Brown, The Union Management Cooperative Committee," *American Federationist* 37 (June 1930): 674–75; Beyer, "Steady Work through Cooperation," *American Federationist* 38 (March 1931): 280–84; Morris Llewellyn Cooke and Philip Murray, *Organized Labor and Production: Next Steps in Industrial Democracy* (New York, 1940); Milton J. Nadworny, *Scientific Management and the Unions, 1900–1932: A Historical Analysis* (Cambridge, Mass., 1955).

8. 247 *H.C. Deb.,* col. 392 (January 22, 1931).

9. Hugh Armstrong Clegg, *A History of British Trade Unions since 1889,* vol. 2, *1911–1933* (Oxford, 1985), 481; Allen Hutt, *The Post-War History of the British Working Class* (New York, 1938), 174–75.

10. Thomas E. Vadney, *The Wayward Liberal: A Political Biography of Donald Richberg* (Lexington, Ken., 1970), 85–93.

11. House Committee on the Judiciary, *To Amend the Judicial Code and to Define and Limit the Jurisdiction of Courts Sitting in Equity, and for Other Purposes,* 72nd Congress, 1st sess., February 25, 1932, 2; Daniel Ernst, "The Yellow-Dog Contract and Liberal Reform, 1917–1932," *Labor History* 30 (Spring 1989): 251–74.

12. Edwin E. Witte, *The Government in Labor Disputes* (1969; repr., New York, 1932), 310; Theron F. Schlabach, *Edwin E. Witte: Cautious Reformer* (Madison, Wisc., 1969), 28, 55–56; Felix Frankfurter and Nathan Greene, *The Labor Injunction* (1930; repr., Gloucester, Mass., 1963).

13. Daniel R. Ernst, "Common Laborers? Industrial Pluralists, Legal Realists, and the Law of Industrial Disputes, 1915–1943," *Law and History Review* 11 (Spring 1993): 76–79.

14. Donald Richberg, "Report of Old Age Pensions" to Railway Labor Executives Association, July 1931, Richberg Papers, Library of Congress; Larry G. Gerber, *The Limits of Liberalism: Josephus Daniels, Henry Stimson, Bernard Baruch, Donald Richberg, Felix Frankfurter and the Development of the Modern American Political Economy* (New York, 1983), 205–9.

15. Felix Frankfurter to Henry Stimson, January 19, 1923, Felix Frankfurter Papers, Library of Congress.

16. Ernst, "Common Laborers?" 78.

17. Report of the Executive Council of the AFL to annual convention, October 1931, in *America Faces the Future,* ed. Charles A. Beard (Boston, 1932), 269; Ruth L. Horowitz, *Political Ideologies of Organized Labor: The New Deal Era* (New Brunswick, 1978), 77; George G. Higgins, *Voluntarism in Organized Labor in the United States, 1930–1940* (1945; repr., New York, 1969).

18. Rodney Lowe, "Hours of Labour: Negotiating Industrial Legislation in Britain, 1919–1939," *Economic History Review* 35 (1982): 254–71.

19. Irving Bernstein, *The Lean Years: A History of the American Worker, 1920–1933* (Baltimore, 1966), 481–83; House Committee on Labor, *Six-Hour Day–Five-Day Week,* 72nd Congress, 2nd sess., January 18–30, 1933; Craig Phelan, *William Green: Biography of a Labor Leader* (Albany, N.Y., 1989), 59–62.

20. Frederick E. Hosen, *The Great Depression and the New Deal: Legislative Acts in Their Entirety (1932–1933) and Statistical Economic Data (1926–1946)* (Jefferson, N.C., 1992).

21. Bercusson, *Fair Wages Resolutions,* 158–80; Paul Smith, "The Road Haulage Industry 1918–1940: The Process of Unionization, Employers' Control and Statutory Regulation," *Historical Studies in Industrial Relations* 3 (March 1997): 49–80.

22. Armand J. Thieblot, Jr., *Prevailing Wage Legislation: The Davis-Bacon Act, State "Little Davis-Bacon" Acts, the Walsh-Healey Act, and the Service Contract Act* (Philadelphia, 1986), 25–43; Peter A. Swenson, *Capitalists against Markets: The Making of Labor Markets and Welfare States in the United States and Sweden* (New York, 2002), 160–61.

23. Irving Bernstein, *The New Deal Collective Bargaining Policy* (1950; repr., New York, 1975), 43–44; Witte, *Government in Labor Disputes*, 219–20.

24. Bernstein, *New Deal Collective Bargaining Policy*, 34.

25. Leo Wolman, *Ebb and Flow in Trade Unionism* (New York, 1936), 87, 116–24.

26. Bain and Price, *Profiles of Union Growth*, 50, 96.

27. Derek H. Aldcroft, *The Inter-War Economy: Britain, 1919–1939* (New York, 1970), 172–73.

28. George Soule, *Prosperity Decade: From War to Depression, 1917–1929* (1947; repr., White Plains, N.Y., 1975), 164; Aldcroft, *The Inter-War Economy*, 55; Richard Croucher, *Engineers at War, 1939–1945* (London, 1982), 1–66; Steven Tolliday and Jonathan Zeitlin, eds., *The Automobile Industry and Its Workers: Between Fordism and Flexibility* (New York, 1987).

29. Daniel Nelson, "The Company Union Movement, 1900–1937: A Reexamination," *Business History Review* 56 (Autumn 1982): 335–57; David Brody, "The Rise and Decline of Welfare Capitalism," in Brody, *Workers in Industrial America: Essays on the Twentieth Century Struggle* (New York, 1981); David Fairris, "From Exit to Voice in Shopfloor Governance: The Case of Company Unions," *Business History Review* 69 (Winter 1995): 493–529.

30. McIvor, *Organised Capital;* Richard Hyman, "Rank-and-File Movements and Workplace Organization, 1914–39," in *A History of British Industrial Relations,* vol. 2, *1914–1939,* ed. Chris Wrigley (Brighton, 1987).

31. Hugh Armstrong Clegg, *A History of British Trade Unions since 1889,* vol. 2, *1911–1933* (Oxford, 1985), 441–42; Chris Smith, John Child, and Michael Rowlinson, *Reshaping Work: The Cadbury Experience* (Cambridge, 1990), 65–70.

32. A. R. Griffin and C. P. Griffin, "The Non-Political Trade Union Movement," in *Essays in Labour History, 1918–1939,* ed. Asa Briggs and John Saville (London, 1977); Robert J. Waller, *The Dukeries Transformed: The Social and Political Development of a Twentieth-Century Coalfield* (Oxford, 1983), 108–30; Hywel Francis and David Smith, *The Fed: A History of the South Wales Miners in the Twentieth Century* (London, 1980), 113–44.

33. Bernstein, *New Deal Collective Bargaining Policy,* 33.

34. Daniel Nelson, "The AFL and the Challenge of Company Unionism, 1915–1937," in *Nonunion Employee Representation: History, Contemporary Practice, and Policy,* ed. Bruce E. Kaufman and Daphne Gottlieb Taras (Armonk, N.Y., 2000), 61–62.

35. Bernstein, *New Deal Collective Bargaining Policy,* 33–37; William Green's testimony before hearings of the House Committee on Ways and Means, *National Industrial Recovery,* 73rd Cong., 1st sess., May 19, 1933, 117–18.

36. Colin Gordon, *New Deals: Business, Labor, and Politics in America, 1920–1935* (New York, 1994), 171; Stanley Vittoz, *New Deal Labor Policy and the American Industrial Economy* (Chapel Hill, N.C., 1987), 94.

37. Ordway Tead, "An Interpretive Forecast—N.R.A." *American Federationist* 41 (January 1934), 21.

38. Bruce E. Kaufman, *The Origins & Evolution of the Field of Industrial Relations in the United States* (Ithaca, N.Y., 1993), 21; Sanford M. Jacoby, *Employing Bureaucracy: Managers, Unions, and the Transformation of Work in American Industry, 1900–1945* (New York, 1985), 102–3, 179–80.

39. Senate Committee on Finance, *National Industrial Recovery,* May 29, 1933, 284–91; Bernstein, *New Deal Collective Bargaining Policy,* 34.

40. Senate hearings, *National Industrial Recovery,* May 29, 1933, 284–88; Nelson, "Company Unions," 338; Bain and Price, *Profiles of Union Growth,* 88.

41. *Congressional Record* 77 (June 8, 1933), pt. 6:5279–84.

42. *Congressional Record* 77 (June 8, 1933), pt. 6:5281; Bernstein, *New Deal Collective Bargaining Policy,* 36 37.

43. Kenneth Casebeer, "Drafting Wagner's Act: Leon Keyserling and the Precommittee Drafts of the Labor Disputes Act and the National Labor Relations Act," *Industrial Relations Law Journal* 11 (1989): 73–131; Meg Jacobs, "Pocketbook Politics: Democracy and the Market in Twentieth-Century America," in *The Democratic Experience: New Directions in American Political History,* ed. Meg Jacobs, William J. Novak, and Julian E. Zelizer (Princeton, N.J., 2003); Kathleen G. Donohue, *Freedom from Want: American Liberalism and the Idea of the Consumer* (Baltimore, 2003).

44. Vittoz, *New Deal Labor Policy,* 93.

45. John L. Lewis's testimony in Senate hearings, *National Industrial Recovery,* June 1, 1933, 407.

46. Donald R. Richberg, "N.R.A.," *Congressional Digest* 14 (January 1935), 15; Hugh Johnson, *The Blue Eagle from Egg to Earth* (Garden City, N.Y., 1935), 247.

47. Robert F. Wagner, "Primary Economic Objectives of N.R.A.," *American Federationist* 40 (November 1933), 1201.

48. Bernstein, *New Deal Collective Bargaining Policy,* 60.

49. Johnson, *Blue Eagle from Egg to Earth,* 238.

50. Richard C. Wilcock, "Industrial Management's Policies toward Unionism," in *Labor and the New Deal,* ed. Milton Derber and Edwin Young (Madison, Wisc., 1957), 288; Bain and Price, *Profiles of Union Growth,* 88.

51. United States National Labor Board, *Decisions of the National Labor Board* (Washington, 1934), 1, National Lock Company and Federal Labor Union #18830, 19; Bernstein, *New Deal Collective Bargaining Policy,* 60–61.

52. Donald R. Richberg, *The Rainbow* (Garden City, N.Y., 1936), 156; Donald Richberg to George L. Berry, January 9, 1935, Richberg Papers, Library of Congress.

53. Sidney Fine, *The Automobile under the Blue Eagle: Labor, Management, and the Automobile Manufacturing Code* (Ann Arbor, Mich., 1963), 154–63; James A. Hodges, *New Deal Labor Policy and the Southern Cotton Textile Industry, 1933–1941* (Knoxville, Tenn., 1986), 43–140; Robert H. Zieger, *The CIO, 1935–1955* (Chapel Hill, N.C., 1995), 20.

54. Unsigned editorial, "Company Unions and the A.F.L.," *Nation's Business* 22 (April 1934), 21.

55. Edward S. Cowdrick, "What Hard Times Have Taught Labor Management," *Nation's Business* 22 (January 1934), 24.

56. Fine, *Automobile under the Blue Eagle;* Bernstein, *New Deal Collective Bargaining Policy,* 59–60.

57. Bernstein, *New Deal Collective Bargaining Policy,* 61–62.

58. J. Joseph Huthmacher, *Senator Robert F. Wagner and the Rise of Urban Liberalism* (New York, 1968), 160–64.

59. Matthew Woll, *Labor, Industry, and Government* (New York, 1935), 9–10, 13.

60. Woll, *Labor, Industry, and Government,* 107, 263.

61. "The Fundamental Step," *American Federationist* 41 (April 1934), 361; Phelan, *William Green,* 72–73; Woll, *Labor, Industry, and Government,* 72.

62. Bernstein, *New Deal Collective Bargaining Policy,* 60–70; James A. Gross, *The Making of the National Labor Relations Board: A Study in Economics, Politics, and the Law,* vol. 1 (Albany, 1974); Felix Frankfurter to Franklin Roosevelt, May 29, 1935, in *Roosevelt and Frankfurter: Their Correspondence, 1928–1945,* ed. Max Freedman (Boston, 1967), 273–75.

63. U.S. National Labor Relations Board, *Legislative History of the National Labor Relations Act* (Washington, 1949), 3270–78.

64. *Legislative History of the NLRA,* 523–27, 1010–31; Cletus Daniel, *ACLU and the Wagner Act: An Inquiry into the Depression-Era Crisis of American Liberalism* (Ithaca, N.Y., 1980).

65. Michael Goldfield, "Worker Insurgency, Radical Organization, and New Deal Labor Legislation," *American Political Science Review* 83 (December 1989): 1257–82; David Milton, *Politics of U.S. Labor: From the Great Depression to the New Deal* (New York, 1982); G. William Domhoff, "The Wagner Act and Theories of the State: A New Analysis Based on Class-Segment Theory" *Political Power and Social Theory* 6 (1987): 159–85.

66. Gordon, *New Deals;* 236; Thomas Ferguson, "From Normalcy to New Deal: Industrial Structure, Party Competition, and American Public Policy in the Great Depression," *International Organization* 38 (Winter 1984), 41–94.

67. Rhonda F. Levine, *Class Struggle and the New Deal: Industrial Labor, Industrial Capital, and the State* (Lawrence, Kans., 1988); Swenson, *Capitalists against Markets,* 213–19.

68. *Congressional Record* (May 29, 1934), 1150–52.

69. Vittoz, *New Deal Labor Policy,* 172–73; Christopher L. Tomlins, *The State and the Unions: Labor Relations, Law, and the Organized Labor Movement in America, 1880–1960,* (New York, 1985), 122–23; Jerold S. Auerbach, *Labor and Liberty: The La Follette Committee and the New Deal* (Indianapolis, 1966).

70. Bernstein, *New Deal Collective Bargaining Policy,* 156; *Legislative History of the NLRA,* 15; Mark Barenberg, "The Political Economy of the Wagner Act: Power, Symbol, and Workplace Cooperation," *Harvard Law Review* 106 (1993): 1381–1496; David Brody, "Labor Elections: Good for Workers?" *Dissent* (Summer 1997): 71–77.

71. *Legislative History of the NLRA,* 415.

72. *Legislative History of the NLRA,* 435–38, 643.

73. *Legislative History of the NLRA,* 1604–5.

74. Bernstein, *New Deal Collective Bargaining Policy,* 125.

75. *Legislative History of the NLRA,* 640, 435–38.

76. *Legislative History of the NLRA,* 1496.

77. *Legislative History of the NLRA,* 1458.

78. Tomlins, *State and the Unions,* 137.

79. Cited in Tomlins, *State and the Unions,* 135.

80. Alfred L. Bernheim and Dorothy Van Doren, eds., *Labor and the Government: An Investigation of the Role of the Government in Labor Relations* (New York, 1935), 341.

81. Tomlins, *State and the Unions,* 135–47.

82. Rodney Lowe, *Adjusting to Democracy: The Role of the Ministry of Labour in British Politics, 1916–1939* (Oxford, 1986), 116–20.

83. Testimony of William H. Davis, chair of Twentieth Century Fund Special Committee on the Government and Labor, *Legislative History of the NLRA,* vol. 2, 2092; Bernheim and Van Doren, *Labor and the Government.*

84. Sumner Slichter, "Government and Collective Bargaining," *Annals of the American Academy* 178 (March 1935): 122.

85. *Legislative History of the NLRA,* 640.

86. "Magna Carta or a Judas Kiss," *Nation's Business* 23 (August 1935): 7–9.

87. Tomlins, *State and the Unions,* 132–47.

88. Clarence E. Wunderlin, Jr., *Visions of a New Industrial Order: Social Science and Labor Theory in America's Progressive Era* (New York, 1992), 152.

89. Tomlins, *State and the Unions,* 120–23.

90. Leon H. Keyserling, "The Wagner Act: Its Origins and Current Significance," *George Washington Law Review* 24 (1960), 220–21; Casebeer, "Drafting Wagner's Act."

91. *Legislative History of the NLRA,* 482–89.

92. *Legislative History of the NLRA,* 239, 1317–18, 1556–57, 758.

93. *Legislative History of the NLRA,* 1411–12.

94. Barenberg, "Political Economy of the Wagner Act," 1454, 1495.

95. Bain and Price, *Profiles of Union Growth,* 88.

96. Paul C. Weiler, "Promises to Keep: Securing Workers' Rights to Self-Organization under the NLRA," *Harvard Law Review* 96 (June 1983): 1768–1827; Howell John Harris, *The Right to Manage: Industrial Relations Policies of American Business in the 1940s* (Madison, Wisc., 1982).

Conclusion

1. David Brody, "Workplace Contractualism in Comparative Perspective," in *Industrial Democracy in America: The Ambiguous Promise,* ed. Nelson Lichtenstein and Howell John Harris (Cambridge, 1993).

2. James A. Gross, *The Reshaping of the National Labor Relations Board: National Labor Policy in Transition, 1937–1947* (Albany, N.Y., 1981).

3. George Sayers Bain and Robert Price, *Profiles of Union Growth: A Comparative Statistical Portrait of Eight Countries* (Oxford, 1980), 39–40, 88.

4. Steven Fraser, *Labor Will Rule: Sidney Hillman and the Rise of American Labor* (New York, 1991), 441–94; Nelson Lichtenstein, *Labor's War at Home: The CIO in World War II* (New York, 1982); Alan Bullock, *The Life and Times of Ernest Bevin,* vol. 2, *Minister of Labour, 1940–1945* (London, 1967); Peter Weiler, *Ernest Bevin* (Manchester, 1993), 100–43.

5. Lichtenstein, *Labor's War at Home;* James B. Atleson, *Labor and the Wartime State: Labor Relations and Law during World War II* (Urbana, Ill., 1998).

6. Henry Pelling, *A History of British Trade Unionism,* 4th ed. (Houndmills, Eng., 1987), 226–27.

7. Harry A. Millis and Emily Clark Brown, *From the Wagner Act to Taft-Hartley: A Study of National Labor Policy and Labor Relations* (Chicago, 1950).

8. Bain and Price, *Profiles of Union Growth,* 89.

9. Nelson Lichtenstein, *State of the Union: A Century of American Labor* (Princeton, 2002), 16; Bain and Price, *Profiles of Union Growth,* 40, 89.

10. John Penceval, "The Surprising Retreat of Union Britain," SIEPR Policy Paper No. 00-31, March 2001, <http://siepr.stanford.edu/papers/pdf/00-31.html> [accessed July 31, 2002]; Leo Troy, "The Rise and Fall of American Trade Unions: The Labor Movement from FDR to RR," in *Unions in Transition: Entering the Second Century,* ed. Seymour Martin Lipset (San Francisco, 1986), 81.

11. M. A. Utton, *The Political Economy of Big Business* (New York, 1982); Leslie Hannah, *The Rise of the Corporate Economy,* 2nd ed. (London, 1983).

12. Jeremy Waddington, *The Politics of Bargaining: The Merger Process and British Trade Union Structural Development, 1892–1987* (London, 1995), 158–59.

13. Pelling, *History of British Trade Unionism,* 267–78.

14. Pelling, *History of British Trade Unionism,* 283–91; Howard F. Gospel and Gill Palmer, *British Industrial Relations,* 2nd ed. (London, 1993), 238–43.

15. Gospel and Palmer, *British Industrial Relations,* 252–61; Chris Wrigley, *British Trade Unions since 1933* (Cambridge, 2002), 73–79.

16. Paul C. Weiler, "Promises to Keep: Securing Workers' Right to Self-Organization under the NLRA," *Harvard Law Review* 96 (June 1983): 1769–1827; Melvyn Dubofsky, *The State and Labor in Modern America* (Chapel Hill, N.C., 1994), 228–31.

17. Lichtenstein, *State of the Union;* Thomas A. Kochan, Harry C. Katz, and Robert B. McKersie, *The Transformation of American Industrial Relations* (New York, 1986); Seymour Martin Lipset, ed., *Unions in Transition: Entering the Second Century* (San Francisco, 1986); Penceval, "The Surprising Retreat of Union Britain."

18. Duncan Gallie and Michael Rose, "Employer Policies and Trade Union Influence," in *Trade Unionism in Recession,* ed. Duncan Gallie, Roger Penn, and Michael Rose (New York, 1996); John J. Lawler, *Unionization and Deunionization: Strategy, Tactics, and Outcomes* (Columbia, S.C., 1990).

19. Dubofsky, *State and Labor in Modern America;* Weiler, "Promises to Keep."

20. Robert J. Davies, "Incomes and Anti-Inflation Policy," in *Industrial Relations in Britain,* ed. George Sayers Bain (Oxford, 1983).

21. Jennifer Klein, *For All These Rights: Business, Labor, and the Shaping of America's Public-Private Welfare State* (Princeton, 2003); Sanford M. Jacoby, *Modern Manors: Welfare Capitalism since the New Deal* (Princeton, 1997); Peter A. Swenson, *Capitalists against Markets: The Making of Labor Markets and Welfare States in the United States and Sweden* (New York, 2002); Jacob S. Hacker, *The Divided Welfare State: The Battle over Public and Private Social Benefits in the United States* (New York, 2002).

Works Cited

Primary Sources

Manuscripts

Felix Frankfurter Papers, Manuscript Division, Library of Congress, Washington, D.C.
Donald R. Richberg Papers, Chicago Historical Society, Chicago, Ill.
Donald R. Richberg Papers, Manuscript Division, Library of Congress, Washington, D.C.

Public Documents

Great Britain. Parliament. House of Commons. *Debates*. Fifth Series.
Great Britain, Ministry of Munitions. *History of the Ministry of Munitions*, vols. 1–2. London: H. M. Stationery Office, 1922.
Industrial Conference. *Report of Provisional Joint Committee Presented to Meeting of Industrial Conference*. London: H. M. Stationery Office, 1920.
The Industrial Council Plan in Great Britain. Washington: Bureau of Industrial Research, 1919.
Report of Industrial Conference Called by the President. N.p., 1920.
Trades Union Congress. *Report of Proceedings at 58th Annual Trades Union Congress, Bournemouth, 1926*. London, 1926.
Trades Union Congress. *Report of Proceedings at 62d Annual Trades Union Congress, Nottingham, 1930*. London, 1930.
Trades Union Congress. *Report of Proceedings at 66th Annual Trades Union Congress, Weymouth, 1934*. London, 1934.
Trades Union Congress. *Report of Proceedings at 67th Annual Trades Union Congress, Margate, 1935*. London, 1935.
U.S. Congress. House. Committee on Interstate and Foreign Commerce. *Return of the Railroads to Private Ownership: Hearing before the Committee on Interstate and Foreign Commerce*. 66th Cong., 1st sess., 1919.
U.S. Congress. House. Committee on the Judiciary. *To Amend the Judicial Code and to Define and Limit the Jurisdiction of Courts Sitting in Equity, and for Other Purposes: Hearing before the Committee on the Judiciary*. 72nd Cong., 1st sess., 1932.
U.S. Congress. House. Committee on Labor. *Six-Hour Day–Five-Day Week: Hearing before the Committee on Labor*. 72nd Cong., 2nd sess., 1933.
U.S. Congress. House. Committee on Ways and Means. *National Industrial Recovery: Hearing before the Committee on Ways and Means*. 73rd Cong., 1st sess., 1933.
U.S. Congress. House and Senate. Senate Committee on Education and Labor and the House Committee on Labor. *Fair Labor Standards Act of 1937: Joint Hearing*

before Senate Committee on Education and Labor and the House Committee on Labor. 75th Cong., 1st sess., 1937.

U.S. Congress. Senate. Committee on Finance. *National Industrial Recovery: Hearing before the Committee on Finance.* 73rd Cong., 1st sess., 1933.

U.S. Congress. Senate. Committee on Interstate Commerce. *Extension of Tenure of Government Control of Railroads: Hearing before the Committee on Interstate Commerce.* 65th Cong., 3rd sess., 1919.

U.S. Congress. Senate. Committee on Manufactures. *Establishment of a National Economic Council: Hearing before a Subcommittee of the Senate Committee on Manufactures.* 71st Cong., 1st sess., 1931.

U.S. Congress. Senate. *Congressional Record 77,* June 8, 1933, pt. 6.

U.S. Department of Commerce, Bureau of the Census. *Historical Statistics of the United States, Colonial Times to 1957.* Washington: Government Printing Office, 1960.

U.S. Department of Labor. *Proceedings of the First Industrial Conference.* Washington: Government Printing Office, 1920.

U.S. National Labor Board. *Decisions of the National Labor Board.* Washington: Government Printing Office, 1934.

U.S. National Labor Relations Board. *Legislative History of the National Labor Relations Act.* Washington: Government Printing Office, 1949.

Newspapers and Magazines

American Federationist, 1923–1934.
Coal Age, 1933.
Economist, 1917–1935
Nation's Business, 1931–1935.
New York Times, 1918–1933.
Times (London), 1929–1935.

Books and Articles

Askwith, George Ranken. *Industrial Problems and Disputes.* London: J. Murray, 1920. Reprint, New York: Harper & Row, 1974.

Barnett, George E. "National and District Systems of Collective Bargaining in the United States." *Quarterly Journal of Economics* 26 (1912): 425–43.

Beard, Charles A., ed. *America Faces the Future.* Boston: Houghton Mifflin, 1932.

Berle, Adolf A., and Gardiner C. Means. *The Modern Corporation and Private Property.* New York: Macmillan, 1932. Reprint, New York: Harvest Books, 1967.

Bernheim, Alfred L., and Dorothy Van Doren, eds. *Labor and the Government: An Investigation of the Role of the Government in Labor Relations.* New York: McGraw-Hill, 1935.

Beveridge, W. H. Letter to the editor. *Times* (London), October 21, 1929.

Beyer, Otto S. "The Machinery of Cooperation." *American Federationist* 36 (November 1929): 1311–19.

———. "Steady Work through Cooperation." *American Federationist* 38 (March 1931): 280–84.

Bing, Alexander M. *War-Time Strikes and Their Adjustment.* New York: E. P. Dutton, 1921.

Blackett, Basil. "The Era of Planning." In *Great Events in History,* ed. Stirling Taylor. London: Cassell, 1934.

Boothby, Robert, John de V. Loder, Harold Macmillan, and Oliver Stanley. *Industry and the State: A Conservative View.* London: Macmillan, 1927.

Brown, Geoffrey C. "Labor's Principles of Scientific Management." *American Federationist* 37 (February 1930): 194–95.

———. "The Union Management Cooperative Committee." *American Federationist* 37 (June 1930): 674–75.

Budish, J. M., and George Soule. *The New Unionism in the Clothing Industry.* 1920. Reprint, New York: Russell & Russell, 1968.

Butler, David, and Anne Sloman. *British Political Facts, 1900–1975.* London: Macmillan, 1975.

Calhoun, Arthur. "Engineering as Collective Bargaining: The B & O Plan." In *American Labor Dynamics: In the Light of Post-War Developments,* ed. J. B. S. Hardman. 1928. Reprint, New York: Russell & Russell, 1968.

Childs, Harwood Lawrence. *Labor and Capital in National Politics.* Columbus: Ohio State University Press, 1930.

Churchill, Winston L. Spencer. *Parliamentary Government and the Economic Problem.* Oxford: Clarendon Press, 1930.

Citrine, Walter McLennan. *Men and Work: An Autobiography.* London: Hutchinson, 1964. Reprint, Westport, Conn.: Greenwood Press, 1976.

Clarkson, Grosvenor B. *Industrial America in the World War: The Strategy behind the Line, 1917–1918.* Boston: Houghton Mifflin, 1923.

Coates, Ken, and Anthony Topham, comps. *Industrial Democracy in Great Britain: A Book of Readings and Witnesses for Workers' Control.* London: Macgibbon & Kee, 1968.

Cohen, Julius Henry. *Law and Order in Industry: Five Years' Experience.* New York: Macmillan, 1916.

Cole, G. D. H. *Economic Planning.* 1935. Reprint, Port Washington, N.Y.: Kennikat Press, 1971.

———. "Industrial Councils of Great Britain." *Dial* 66 (February 22, 1919): 171–73.

———. *Workshop Organization.* London: Clarendon Press, 1923.

Cole, Margaret. *The Story of Fabian Socialism.* Stanford, Calif.: Stanford University Press, 1961.

Congressional Quarterly. *Guide to U.S. Elections.* Washington: Congressional Quarterly, 1976.

Cooke, Morris Llewellyn, and Philip Murray. *Organized Labor and Production: Next Steps in Industrial Democracy.* New York: Harper & Brothers, 1940.

Cowdrick, Edward S. "What Hard Times Have Taught Labor Management." *Nation's Business* 22 (January 1934): 22–24.

Dahl, Robert A. *Pluralist Democracy in the United States: Conflict and Consent.* Chicago: Rand McNally, 1967.

Dalton, Hugh. *Practical Socialism for Britain.* London: George Routledge & Sons, 1935. Reprint, New York: Garland, 1985.

Filene, Edward A. *The Way Out: A Forecast of Coming Changes in American Business and Industry.* Garden City, N.Y.: Doubleday, Page, 1925.

Follett, Mary Parker. *Creative Experience.* New York: Longmans, Green, 1924.

Frankfurter, Felix. "War in the Clothing Industry." *New Republic* 25 (December 15, 1920): 59–61.

Frankfurter, Felix, and Nathan Greene. *The Labor Injunction.* New York: Macmillan, 1930. Reprint, Gloucester, Mass.: Peter Smith, 1963.

Frederick, J. George, ed. *The Swope Plan: Details, Criticisms, Analysis.* New York: Business Bourse, 1931.

Freedman, Max, ed. *Roosevelt and Frankfurter: Their Correspondence, 1928–1945.* Boston: Little, Brown, 1967.

George, David Lloyd. *War Memoirs of David Lloyd George.* Vol. 1, *1914–1915.* Boston: Little, Brown, 1933.

Gleason, Arthur. "New Constitutionalism in British Industry." *Survey* 41 (February 1, 1919): 594–98.

———. *What the Workers Want: A Study of British Labor.* New York: Harcourt, Brace and Howe, 1920.

———. "Whitley Councils." *Survey* 42 (April 5–19, 1919): 27–28, 75–77, 109–11.

Glenday, Roy. *The Economic Consequences of Progress.* London: George Routledge & Sons, 1934.

Gompers, Samuel. "An Analysis of Fascism." *American Federationist* 30 (November 1923): 927–33

———. "Significant Movements in Europe." *American Federationist* 31 (July 1924): 565–66.

Goodrich, Carter L. *The Frontier of Control: A Study in British Workshop Politics.* New York: Harcourt, Brace and Howe, 1920.

Greenwood, Arthur. "Development of British Industrial Thought." *Atlantic Monthly* 124 (July 1919): 106–15.

Halevy, Elie. "The Policy of Social Peace in England: The Whitley Councils (1919)." In *Era of Tyrannies: Essays on Socialism and War.* Garden City, N.Y.: Anchor Books, 1965.

Hardman, J. B. S., ed. *American Labor Dynamics: In the Light of Post-War Developments.* 1928. Reprint, New York: Russell & Russell, 1968.

Herring, Pendleton. *Group Representation before Congress.* Baltimore: Johns Hopkins University Press, 1928. Reprint, New York: Russell & Russell, 1967.

Hicks, Clarence J. *My Life in Industrial Relations: Fifty Years in the Growth of a Profession.* New York: Harper & Brothers, 1941.

Hillman, Sidney. "Unemployment Reserves." *Atlantic Monthly* 148 (November 1931): 661–69.

Hosen, Frederick E. *The Great Depression and the New Deal: Legislative Acts in Their Entirety (1932–1933) and Statistical Economic Data (1926–1946).* Jefferson, N.C.: McFarland, 1992.

Johnson, Hugh. *The Blue Eagle from Egg to Earth.* Garden City, N.Y.: Doubleday, Doran, 1935.

Kerr, Philip. *The Industrial Dilemma.* London: Daily News, 1926.

Keyserling, Leon H. "The Wagner Act: Its Origins and Current Significance." *George Washington Law Review* 24 (1960): 199–233.

Laidler, Harry W., and Norman Thomas, eds. *New Tactics in Social Conflict.* New York: Vanguard Press, 1926.

Lauck, W. Jett. *The Development of Collective Bargaining on a National Basis.* Chicago, 1921.

———. *Political and Industrial Democracy, 1776–1926.* New York: Funk & Wagnalls, 1926.

Lauck, W. Jett, and Claude S. Watts. *The Industrial Code.* New York: Funk & Wagnalls, 1922.

Leitch, John. *Man to Man: The Story of Industrial Democracy.* New York: B. C. Forbes, 1919.

Levy, Herman. *Monopolies, Cartels, and Trusts in British Industry.* 1927. Reprint, New York: Augustus M. Kelley, 1968.

Lewisohn, Sam. *The New Leadership in Industry.* New York: E. P. Dutton, 1926.

Liberal Industrial Inquiry. *Britain's Industrial Future.* London: Ernest Benn, 1928.

Lorwin, Lewis L. *The American Federation of Labor: History, Policies, and Prospects.* 1933. Reprint, Clifton, N.J.: Augustus M. Kelley, 1972.

Lucas, Arthur Fletcher. *Industrial Reconstruction and the Control of Competition: The British Experiments.* London: Longmans, Green, 1937.

Lyon, Leverett S., et al. *The National Recovery Administration: An Analysis and Appraisal.* Washington: Brookings Institution, 1935.

Macmillan, Harold. *Reconstruction: A Plea for a National Policy.* London: Macmillan, 1933.

———. *Winds of Change, 1914–1939.* New York: Harper & Row, 1966.

Meakin, Walter. *The New Industrial Revolution: A Study for the General Reader of Rationalisation and Post-War Tendencies of Capitalism and Labour.* London: V. Gollancz, 1928. Reprint, New York: Arno Press, 1977.

Metcalf, Henry C., and L. Urwick, eds. *Dynamic Administration: The Collected Papers of Mary Parker Follett.* 2nd ed. London: Pitman, 1973.

Milne-Bailey, W. *Trade Unions and the State.* London: George Allen & Unwin, 1934.

Mond, Alfred. *Industry and Politics.* London: Macmillan, 1927.

Mosley, Oswald. *The Greater Britain.* London: British Union of Fascists, n.d. [1932].

———. *A National Policy: An Account of the Emergency Program Advanced by Sir Oswald Mosley, M.P.* London: Macmillan, 1931.

Muir, Ramsay. *America the Golden: An Englishman's Notes and Comparisons.* London: Williams & Norgate, 1927.

Myers, James. *Representative Government in Industry.* New York: George H. Doran, 1924.

The Next Five Years: An Essay in Political Agreement. London: Macmillan, 1935. Reprint, New York: Garland, 1985.

Nicholson, Max. "The Proposal for a National Plan." *Week-End Review* (February 1931). Reprinted in *Fifty Years of Political & Economic Planning: Looking Forward, 1931–1981,* ed. John Pinder. London: Heinemann, 1981.

Percy, Eustace. *Democracy on Trial: A Preface to Industrial Policy.* London: John Lane, 1931.

Perlman, Selig. *A Theory of the Labor Movement.* New York: Macmillan, 1928.

"Planning Proposals of the Committee on Continuity of Business and Employment of the United States Chamber of Commerce." In *America Faces the Future,* ed. Charles A. Beard. Boston: Houghton Mifflin, 1932

Plumb, Glenn E., and William G. Roylance. *Industrial Democracy: A Plan for Its Achievement.* New York: B. W. Huebsch, 1923.

Pugh, Arthur. *Men of Steel: A Chronicle of Eighty-Eight Years of Trade Unionism in the British Iron and Steel Trades Confederation.* London: Iron and Steel Trades Confederation, 1951.

Reed, Louis S. *The Labor Philosophy of Samuel Gompers.* New York: Columbia University Press, 1930. Reprint, Port Washington, N.Y.: Kennikat Press, 1966.

Richberg, Donald R. "N.R.A." *Congressional Digest* 14 (January 1935): 14–15.

———. *The Rainbow.* Garden City, N.Y.: Doubleday, Doran, 1936.

———. *Tents of the Mighty.* Chicago: Willett, Clark, & Colby, 1930.

Rockefeller, John D., Jr. *The Personal Relation in Industry.* New York: Albert and Charles Boni, 1923.

Rowntree, Seebohm. "My Dream of a Factory." In Arthur Gleason, *What the Workers Want: A Study of British Labor.* New York: Harcourt, Brace and Howe, 1920.

Salter, Arthur. *The Framework of an Ordered Society.* New York: Macmillan, 1933.

Selekman, Ben M. *Sharing Management with the Workers.* New York: Russell Sage Foundation, 1924.

Seymour, John Barton. *The Whitley Councils Scheme.* London: P. S. King & Son, 1932.

Slichter, Sumner. "Government and Collective Bargaining." *Annals of the American Academy* 178 (March 1935): 107–22.

Sombart, Werner. *Why Is There No Socialism in the United States?* Trans. Patricia M. Hocking and C. T. Husbands. Tubingen: Verlag von J.C.B. Mohr, 1906. Reprint, White Plains, N.Y.: M. E. Sharpe, 1976.

Sparkes, Malcolm. "Britain's Building Trades Parliament." *Nation* 110 (January 24, 1920): 102–3.

Swope, Gerard. "Stabilization of Industry." In *America Faces the Future,* ed. Charles A. Beard. Boston: Houghton Mifflin, 1932.

Taylor, Albion Guilford. *Labor Policies of the National Association of Manufacturers.* Urbana: University of Illinois Press, 1928. Reprint, New York: Arno Press, 1973.

Tead, Ordway. "An Interpretive Forecast—N.R.A." *American Federationist* 41 (January 1934): 17.

———. "National Organization by Industries." *New Republic* 18 (February 8, 1919): 48–51.

Truman, David B. *The Governmental Process: Political Interests and Public Opinion.* 1951. Reprint, New York: Alfred A. Knopf, 1971.

Wagner, Robert F. "Primary Economic Objectives of N.R.A." *American Federationist* 40 (November 1933): 1197–1201.

Walling, William English. *American Labor and American Democracy.* New York: Harper & Brothers, 1926.

Watkins, Gordon S. *Labor Problems and Labor Administration in the United States during the World War.* Urbana: University of Illinois Press, 1920.

Webb, Sidney, and Beatrice Webb. *A Constitution for the Socialist Commonwealth of Great Britain.* 1920. Reprint, Cambridge: Cambridge University Press, 1975.

White, Leonard D. *Whitley Councils in the British Civil Service: A Study in Conciliation and Arbitration.* Chicago: University of Chicago Press, 1933.

Willoughby, Raymond. "The Trade Associations Are Ready." *Nation's Business* 21 (July 1933): 35–38, 50–57.

Witte, Edwin E. *The Government in Labor Disputes.* 1932. Reprint, New York: Arno Press, 1969.

Woll, Matthew. *Labor, Industry, and Government.* New York: D. Appleton-Century, 1935.

Wood, Louis Aubrey. *Union-Management Cooperation on the Railroads.* New Haven, Conn.: Yale University Press, 1931. Reprint, New York: AMS Press, 1976.

Secondary Sources

Adams, Graham, Jr. *Age of Industrial Violence, 1910–15: The Activities and Findings of the United States Commission on Industrial Relations.* New York: Columbia University Press, 1966.

Alchon, Guy. *The Invisible Hand of Planning: Capitalism, Social Science, and the State in the 1920s.* Princeton: Princeton University Press, 1985.

Aldcroft, Derek H. *Inter-War Economy: Britain, 1919–1939.* New York: Columbia University Press, 1970.

Allen, V. L. *Trade Unions and the Government*. London: Longmans, 1960.

Armitage, Susan. *The Politics of Decontrol of Industry: Britain and the United States*. London: London School of Economics and Political Science, 1969.

Arnot, R. Page. *The Miners: Years of Struggle*. Vol. 2, *A History of the Miners' Federation of Great Britain*. London: Allen & Unwin, 1953.

Atleson, James B. *Labor and the Wartime State: Labor Relations and Law during World War II*. Urbana: University of Illinois Press, 1998.

Auerbach, Jerold S. *Labor and Liberty: The La Follette Committee and the New Deal*. Indianapolis: Bobbs-Merrill, 1966.

Bagwell, Philip S., and G. E. Mingay. *Britain and America, 1850–1939: A Study of Economic Change*. London: Routledge and Kegan Paul, 1966.

Bain, George Sayers. *The Growth of White-Collar Unionism*. Oxford: Clarendon Press, 1970.

Bain, George Sayers, and Robert Price. *Profiles of Union Growth: A Comparative Statistical Portrait of Eight Countries*. Oxford: Basil Blackwell, 1980.

Bamberg, James H. "The Rationalization of the British Cotton Industry in the Interwar Years." *Textile History* 19 (1988): 83–102.

Barenberg, Mark. "The Political Economy of the Wagner Act: Power, Symbol, and Workplace Cooperation." *Harvard Law Review* 106 (1993): 1381–1496.

Bayliss, F. J. *British Wages Councils*. Oxford: Basil Blackwell, 1962.

Beer, Samuel H. *British Politics in the Collectivist Age*. New York: Vintage Books, 1969.

Bellush, Bernard. *The Failure of the NRA*. New York: W. W. Norton, 1975.

Benson, John. *The Working Class in Britain, 1850–1939*. London: Longman, 1989.

Bercusson, Brian. *Fair Wages Resolutions*. London: Mansell, 1978.

Berger, Suzanne, ed. *Organizing Interests in Western Europe: Pluralism, Corporatism, and the Transformation of Politics*. New York: Cambridge University Press, 1981.

Bernstein, Irving. *The Lean Years: A History of the American Worker, 1920–1933*. Baltimore: Penguin Books, 1966.

———. *The New Deal Collective Bargaining Policy*. Berkeley: University of California Press, 1950. Reprint, New York: Da Capo Press, 1975.

———. *Turbulent Years: A History of the American Worker, 1933–1941*. Boston: Houghton Mifflin, 1970.

Best, Gary Dean. "President Wilson's Second Industrial Conference." *Labor History* 16 (Fall 1975): 505–20.

Blackford, Mansel G. *The Rise of Modern Business Enterprise in Great Britain, the United States, and Japan*. Chapel Hill: University of North Carolina Press, 1988.

Blank, Stephen. *Industry and Government in Britain: The Federation of British Industries in Politics, 1945–1965*. Lexington, Mass.: Lexington Books, 1973.

Booth, Alan, and Melvyn Pack. *Employment, Capital, and Economic Policy: Great Britain, 1918–1939*. Oxford: Basil Blackwell, 1985.

Bowman, John R. *Capitalist Collective Action: Competition, Cooperation, and Conflict in the Coal Industry*. Cambridge: Cambridge University Press, 1989.

Brand, Carl F. *The British Labour Party: A Short History*. Stanford, Calif.: Stanford University Press, 1964. Rev. ed. Stanford, Calif.: Hoover Institution Press, 1974.

Brand, Donald R. *Corporatism and the Rule of Law: A Study of the National Recovery Administration*. Ithaca, N.Y.: Cornell University Press, 1988.

Brandes, Stuart D. *American Welfare Capitalism, 1880–1940*. Chicago: University of Chicago Press, 1976.

Braverman, Harry. *Labor and Monopoly Capital: The Degradation of Work in the Twentieth Century.* New York: Monthly Review Press, 1974.

Broadberry, Stephen. "Openness and Britain's Productivity Performance, 1870–1990: A Sectoral Analysis." CSGR Working Paper No. 67/01 (February 2001), 21. <http://www2.warwick.ac.uk/fac/soc/csgr/research/workingpapers/2001/abwp6701/ > [accessed January 12, 2004].

Brody, David. "Labor Elections: Good for Workers?" *Dissent* (Summer 1997): 71–77.

——. *Labor in Crisis: The Steel Strike of 1919.* Philadelphia: J. B. Lippincott, 1965.

——. "Labour Relations in American Coal Mining: An Industry Perspective." In *Workers, Owners, and Politics in Coal Mining: An International Comparison of Industrial Relations,* ed. Gerald D. Feldman and Klaus Tenfelde. New York: Berg, 1990.

——. "The Rise and Decline of Welfare Capitalism." In *Workers in Industrial America: Essays on the Twentieth Century Struggle.* New York: Oxford University Press, 1980.

——. "Workplace Contractualism in Comparative Perspective." In *Industrial Democracy in America: The Ambiguous Promise,* ed. Nelson Lichtenstein and Howell John Harris. Cambridge: Cambridge University Press, 1993.

Bullock, Alan. *The Life and Times of Ernest Bevin.* Vol. 1, *Trade Union Leader, 1881–1940.* London: Heinemann, 1960.

——. *The Life and Times of Ernest Bevin.* Vol. 2, *Minister of Labour, 1940–1945.* London: Heinemann, 1967.

Burk, Kathleen, ed. *War and the State: The Transformation of British Government, 1914–1919.* London: George Allen & Unwin, 1982.

Bustard, Bruce Irving. "The Human Element: Labor Administration and Industrial Mobilization during the First World War." Ph.D. diss., University of Iowa, 1984.

Carpenter, L. P. "Corporatism in Britain, 1930–45." *Journal of Contemporary History* 11 (1976): 3–25.

Casebeer, Kenneth. "Drafting Wagner's Act: Leon Keyserling and the Precommittee Drafts of the Labor Disputes Act and the National Labor Relations Act." *Industrial Relations Law Journal* 11 (1989): 73–131.

Cawson, Alan. *Corporatism and Political Theory.* Oxford: Basil Blackwell, 1986.

Chandler, Alfred D., Jr. *The Visible Hand: The Managerial Revolution in American Business.* Cambridge: Harvard University Press, 1977.

Chandler, Alfred D., Jr., and Herman Daems, eds. *Managerial Hierarchies: Comparative Perspectives on the Rise of the Modern Industrial Enterprise.* Cambridge: Harvard University Press, 1980.

Charles, Rodger. *The Development of Industrial Relations in Britain, 1911–1939: Studies in the Evolution of Collective Bargaining at National and Industry Level.* London: Hutchinson, 1973.

Checkland, Sydney. *British Public Policy, 1776–1939: An Economic, Social, and Political Perspective.* New York: Cambridge University Press, 1983.

Child, John. *British Management Thought: A Critical Analysis.* London: George Allen & Unwin, 1969.

Church, Roy. "Employers, Trade Unions and the State, 1889–1987: The Origins and Decline of Tripartism in the British Coal Industry." In *Workers, Owners, and Politics in Coal Mining: An International Comparison of Industrial Relations,* ed. Gerald D. Feldman and Klaus Tenfelde. New York: Berg, 1990.

Clegg, H. A., Alan Fox, and A. F. Thompson. *A History of British Trade Unions since 1889.* Vol. 1, *1889–1910.* Oxford: Oxford University Press, 1964.

Clegg, Hugh Armstrong. *A History of British Trade Unions since 1889.* Vol. 2, *1911–1933.* Oxford: Clarendon Press, 1985.

———. *A History of British Trade Unions since 1889.* Vol. 3, *1934–1951.* Oxford: Clarendon Press, 1994.

Cleveland, Alfred S. "NAM: Spokesman for Industry." *Harvard Business Review* 26 (1948): 353–71.

Cline, Peter K. "Eric Geddes and the 'Experiment' with Businessmen in Government, 1915–22." In *Essays in Anti-Labour History,* ed. Kenneth D. Brown. Hamden, Conn.: Archon Books, 1974.

Collins, Robert M. *The Business Response to Keynes, 1929–1964.* Columbia: University of Missouri Press, 1981.

Conner, Valerie Jean. *The National War Labor Board: Stability, Social Justice, and the Voluntary State in World War I.* Chapel Hill: University of North Carolina Press, 1983.

Crompton, Gerald. "'Squeezing the Pulpless Orange': Labour and Capital on the Railways in the Interwar Years." *Business History* 31 (April 1989): 66–83.

Cronin, James E. "Labor Insurgency and Class Formation: Comparative Perspectives on the Crisis of 1917–1920 in Europe." In *Work, Community, and Power: The Experience of Labor in Europe and America, 1900–1925,* ed. James E. Cronin and Carmen Sirianni. Philadelphia: Temple University Press, 1983.

———. *The Politics of State Expansion: War, State and Society in Twentieth-Century Britain.* London: Routledge, 1991.

Crouch, Colin. *Class Conflict and the Industrial Relations Crisis: Compromise and Corporatism in the Policies of the British State.* London: Heinemann Educational Books, 1977.

———. "Pluralism and the New Corporatism: A Rejoinder." *Political Studies* 31 (1983): 452–60.

———, ed. *State and Economy in Contemporary Capitalism.* New York: Heinemann Educational Books, 1979.

Croucher, Richard. *Engineers at War, 1939–1945.* London: Merlin Press, 1982.

Cuff, Robert D. "The Politics of Labor Administration during World War I." *Labor History* 21 (December 1980): 546–69.

———. *The War Industries Board: Business-Government Relations during World War I.* Baltimore: Johns Hopkins University Press, 1973.

Currie, Robert. *Industrial Politics.* Oxford: Clarendon Press, 1979.

Cyphers, Christopher J. *The National Civic Federation and the Making of a New Liberalism, 1900–1915.* Westport, Conn.: Praeger, 2002.

Daniel, Cletus. *ACLU and the Wagner Act: An Inquiry into the Depression-Era Crisis of American Liberalism.* Ithaca, N.Y.: Cornell University Press, 1980.

Davenport-Hines, R. P. T. *Dudley Docker: The Life and Times of a Trade Warrior.* Cambridge: Cambridge University Press, 1984.

Davies, Paul, and Mark Freeland. *Labour Legislation and Public Policy: A Contemporary History.* Oxford: Clarendon Press, 1993.

Davies, Robert J. "Incomes and Anti-Inflation Policy." In *Industrial Relations in Britain,* ed. George Sayers Bain. Oxford: Basil Blackwell, 1983.

Davis, Colin J. *Power at Odds: The 1922 National Railroad Shopmen's Strike.* Urbana: University of Illinois Press, 1997.

Davis, Lance. "The Capital Markets and Industrial Concentration: The U.S. and U.K., a Comparative Study." *Economic History Review,* New Series, 19 (1966): 255–72.

Diggins, John P. *Mussolini and Fascism: The View from America.* Princeton: Princeton University Press, 1972.

Dintenfass, Michael. "The Politics of Producers' Co-operation: The FBI-TUC-NCEO Talks, 1929–1933." In *Businessmen and Politics: Studies of Business Activity in British Politics, 1900–1945,* ed. John Turner. London: Heinemann, 1984.

Domhoff, G. William. "The Wagner Act and Theories of the State: A New Analysis Based on Class-Segment Theory." *Political Power and Social Theory* 6 (1987): 159–85.

Donohue, Kathleen G. *Freedom from Want: American Liberalism and the Idea of the Consumer.* Baltimore: Johns Hopkins University Press, 2003.

Dubofsky, Melvyn. "Abortive Reform: The Wilson Administration and Organized Labor, 1913–1920." In *Work, Community, and Power: The Experience of Labor in Europe and America, 1900–1925,* ed. James E. Cronin and Carmen Sirianni. Philadelphia: Temple University Press, 1983.

———. *The State and Labor in Modern America.* Chapel Hill: University of North Carolina Press, 1994.

Dubofsky, Melvyn, and Warren Van Tyne. *John L. Lewis: A Biography.* New York: Quadrangle, 1977.

Dulles, Foster Rhea, and Melvyn Dubofsky. *Labor in America: A History.* Arlington Heights, Ill.: Harlan Davidson, 1984.

Dyson, Kenneth H. F. *The State Tradition in Western Europe: A Study of an Idea and Institution.* New York: Oxford University Press, 1980.

Edwards, Richard. *Rights at Work: Employment Relations in the Post-Union Era.* Washington: Brookings Institution, 1993.

Eisner, Marc Allen. *From Warfare State to Welfare State: World War I, Compensatory State Building, and the Limits of the Modern Order.* University Park: Pennsylvania State University Press, 2000.

Ernst, Daniel R. "Common Laborers? Industrial Pluralists, Legal Realists, and the Law of Industrial Disputes, 1915–1943." *Law and History Review* 11 (Spring 1993): 59–100.

———. *Lawyers against Labor: From Individual Rights to Corporate Liberalism.* Urbana: University of Illinois Press, 1995.

———. "The Yellow-Dog Contract and Liberal Reform, 1917–1932." *Labor History* 30 (Spring 1989): 251–74.

Ewing, K. D. "The State and Industrial Relations: 'Collective Laissez-Faire' Revisited." *Historical Studies in Industrial Relations* 5 (Spring 1998): 1–31.

Fairris, David. "From Exit to Voice in Shopfloor Governance: The Case of Company Unions." *Business History Review* 69 (Winter 1995): 493–529.

Ferguson, Thomas. "From Normalcy to New Deal: Industrial Structure, Party Competition, and American Public Policy in the Great Depression." *International Organization* 38 (Winter 1984): 41–94.

Fine, Sidney. *The Automobile under the Blue Eagle: Labor, Management, and the Automobile Manufacturing Code.* Ann Arbor: University of Michigan Press, 1963.

Finegold, Kenneth, and Theda Skocpol. *State and Party in America's New Deal.* Madison: University of Wisconsin Press, 1995.

———. "State Capacity and Economic Intervention in the Early New Deal." *Political Science Quarterly* 97 (Summer 1982): 255–78.

Fink, Gary M. *Labor's Search for Political Order: The Political Behavior of the Missouri Labor Movement, 1890–1940.* Columbia: University of Missouri Press, 1973.

Fink, Leon. "Labor, Liberty, and the Law: Trade Unionism and the Problem of the American Constitutional Order." *Journal of American History* 74 (December 1987): 904–25.

———. *Workingmen's Democracy: The Knights of Labor and American Politics.* Urbana: University of Illinois Press, 1985.

Fitzgerald, Robert. *British Labour Management and Industrial Welfare, 1846–1939.* London: Croom Helm, 1988.

Florence, P. Sargant. *The Logic of British and American Industry: A Realistic Analysis of Economic Structure and Government.* Chapel Hill: University of North Carolina Press, 1953.

Forbath, William E. "Courts, Constitutions, and Labor Politics in England and America: A Study of the Constitutive Power of Law." *Law and Social Inquiry* 16 (Winter 1991): 1–34.

———. *Law and the Shaping of the American Labor Movement.* Cambridge: Harvard University Press, 1991.

Fox, Alan. *History and Heritage: The Social Origins of the British Industrial Relations System.* London: George Allen & Unwin, 1985.

Francis, Hywel, and David Smith. *The Fed: A History of the South Wales Miners in the Twentieth Century.* London: Lawrence & Wishart, 1980.

Fraser, Steve. "Dress Rehearsal for the New Deal: Shop-Floor Insurgents, Political Elites, and Industrial Democracy in the Amalgamated Clothing Workers." In *Working-Class America: Essays on Labor, Community and American Society,* ed. Michael H. Frisch and Daniel J. Walkowitz. Urbana: University of Illinois Press, 1983.

———. *Labor Will Rule: Sidney Hillman and the Rise of American Labor.* New York: Free Press, 1991.

———. "The 'New Unionism' and the 'New Economic Policy.'" In *Work, Community, and Power: The Experience of Labor in Europe and America, 1900–1925,* ed. James E. Cronin and Carmen Sirianni. Philadelphia: Temple University Press, 1983.

Freeden, Michael. *Liberalism Divided: A Study in British Political Thought, 1914–39.* Oxford: Clarendon Press, 1986.

Freyer, Tony. *Regulating Big Business: Antitrust in Great Britain and America, 1880–1990.* New York: Cambridge University Press, 1992.

———. "The Sherman Antitrust Act, Comparative Business Structure, and the Rule of Reason: America and Great Britain, 1880–1920." *Iowa Law Review* 74 (July 1989): 991–1017.

Friedman, Gerald. *State-Making and Labor Movements: France and the United States, 1876–1914.* Ithaca, N.Y.: Cornell University Press, 1998.

Galambos, Louis. *Competition & Cooperation; The Emergence of a National Trade Association.* Baltimore: Johns Hopkins University Press, 1966.

Gallie, Duncan, and Michael Rose. "Employer Policies and Trade Union Influence." In *Trade Unionism in Recession,* ed. Duncan Gallie, Roger Penn, and Michael Rose. New York: Oxford University Press, 1996.

Gerber, Larry G. "Corporatism and State Theory: A Review Essay for Historians." *Social Science History* 19 (Fall 1995): 313–32.

———. *The Limits of Liberalism: Josephus Daniels, Henry Stimson, Bernard Baruch, Donald Richberg, Felix Frankfurter and the Development of the Modern American Political Economy.* New York: New York University Press, 1983.

———. "The United States and Canadian National Industrial Conferences of 1919: A Comparative Analysis." *Labor History* 32 (Winter 1991): 42–65.

Gitelman, H. M. "Being of Two Minds: American Employers Confront the Labor Problem, 1915–1919." *Labor History* 25 (Spring 1984): 189–216.

———. *Legacy of the Ludlow Massacre: A Chapter in American Industrial Relations.* Philadelphia: University of Pennsylvania Press, 1988.

———. "Management's Crisis of Confidence and the Origin of the National Industrial Conference Board, 1914–1916." *Business History Review* 58 (Summer 1984): 153–77.

Goldfield, Michael. "Worker Insurgency, Radical Organization, and New Deal Labor Legislation." *American Political Science Review* 83 (December 1989): 1257–82.

Gordon, Colin. *New Deals: Business, Labor, and Politics in America, 1920–1935.* New York: Cambridge University Press, 1994.

Gordon, David M., Richard Edwards, and Michael Reich. *Segmented Work, Divided Workers: The Historical Transformation of Labor in the United States.* Cambridge: Cambridge University Press, 1982.

Gospel, Howard F. "Employers' Labour Policy: A Study of the Mond-Turner Talks, 1927–33." *Business History* 21 (July 1979): 180–97.

———. *Markets, Firms, and the Management of Labour in Modern Britain.* New York: Cambridge University Press, 1992.

Gospel, Howard F., and Gill Palmer. *British Industrial Relations.* 2nd ed. London: Routledge, 1993.

Gourevitch, Peter. *Politics in Hard Times: Comparative Responses to International Economic Crises.* Ithaca, N.Y.: Cornell University Press, 1986.

Green, Marguerite. *The National Civic Federation and the American Labor Movement, 1900–1925.* Washington: Catholic University of America Press, 1956.

Greene, Julie. *Pure and Simple Politics: The American Federation of Labor and Political Activism, 1881–1917.* New York: Cambridge University Press, 1998.

———. "'The Strike at the Ballot Box': The American Federation of Labor's Entrance into Election Politics, 1906–1909." *Labor History* 32 (Spring 1991): 165–92.

Griffin, A. R., and C. P. Griffin, "The Non-Political Trade Union Movement." In *Essays in Labour History, 1918–1939,* ed. Asa Briggs and John Saville. London: Croom Helm, 1977.

Griffith, Robert. "Dwight D. Eisenhower and the Corporate Commonwealth." *American Historical Review* 87 (February 1982): 87–122.

Gross, James A. *The Making of the National Labor Relations Board: A Study in Economics, Politics, and the Law.* Albany: State University of New York Press, 1974.

———. *The Reshaping of the National Labor Relations Board: National Labor Policy in Transition, 1937–1947.* Albany: State University of New York Press, 1981.

Hacker, Jacob S. *The Divided Welfare State: The Battle over Public and Private Social Benefits in the United States.* New York: Cambridge University Press, 2002.

Hall, Peter A. "The State and Economic Decline." In *The Decline of the British Economy,* ed. Bernard Elbaum and William Lazonick. Oxford: Clarendon Press, 1986.

Hannah, Leslie. *The Rise of the Corporate Economy.* 2nd ed. London: Methuen, 1983.

———. "Visible and Invisible Hands in Great Britain." In *Managerial Hierarchies: Comparative Perspectives on the Rise of the Modern Industrial Enterprise,* ed. Alfred D. Chandler, Jr., and Herman Daems. Cambridge: Harvard University Press, 1980.

Hannah, Leslie, and J. A. Kay. *Concentration in Modern Industry: Theory, Measurement and the U.K. Experience.* London: Macmillan, 1977.

Hardach, Gerd. *The First World War, 1914–1918.* Berkeley: University of California Press, 1977.

Harris, Howell John. "Between Convergence and Exceptionalism: Americans and the 'British Model' of Industrial Relations, c. 1870–1920." Paper presented at "Justice at Work: A Conference Honouring David Brody." University of California at Santa Barbara, August 9, 2002.

————. *Bloodless Victories: The Rise and Fall of the Open Shop in the Philadelphia Metal Trades, 1890–1940.* New York: Cambridge University Press, 2000.

————. *The Right to Manage: Industrial Relations Policies of American Business in the 1940s.* Madison: University of Wisconsin Press, 1982.

————. "The Snares of Liberalism? Politicians, Bureaucrats, and the Shaping of Federal Labour Relations Policy in the United States, ca. 1915–47." In *Shop Floor Bargaining and the State,* ed. Steven Tolliday and Jonathan Zeitlin. Cambridge: Cambridge University Press, 1985.

Hart, Vivien. *Bound by Our Constitution: Women, Workers, and the Minimum Wage.* Princeton: Princeton University Press, 1994.

Harvey, Charles E. "John D. Rockefeller, Jr., Herbert Hoover, and President Wilson's Industrial Conferences of 1919–1920." In *Voluntarism, Planning, and the State,* ed. Jerold E. Brown and Patrick D. Reagan. New York: Greenwood Press, 1988.

Hattam, Victoria Charlotte. *Labor Visions and State Power: The Origins of Business Unionism in the United States.* Princeton: Princeton University Press, 1993.

Hawley, Ellis W. "The Discovery and Study of a 'Corporate Liberalism.'" *Business History Review* 52 (Autumn 1978): 309–20.

————. *The Great War and the Search for a Modern Order: A History of the American People and Their Institutions, 1917–1933.* 2nd ed. New York: St. Martin's, 1992.

————. "Herbert Hoover and Economic Stabilization, 1921–22." In *Herbert Hoover as Secretary of Commerce: Studies in New Era Thought and Practice,* ed. Ellis W. Hawley. Iowa City: University of Iowa Press, 1981.

————. "Herbert Hoover, the Commerce Secretariat, and the Vision of an 'Associative State,' 1921–1928." *Journal of American History* 61 (June 1974): 116–40.

————. *The New Deal and the Problem of Monopoly: A Study in Economic Ambivalence.* Princeton: Princeton University Press, 1966.

————. "Secretary Hoover and the Bituminous Coal Problem, 1921–1928." *Business History Review* 42 (Autumn 1968): 247–70.

————. "Social Policy and the Liberal State in Twentieth-Century America." In *Federal Social Policy: The Historical Dimension,* ed. Donald T. Critchlow and Ellis W. Hawley. University Park: Pennsylvania State University Press, 1988.

Haydu, Jeffrey. *Between Craft and Class: Skilled Workers and Factory Politics in the United States and Britain, 1890–1922.* Berkeley: University of California Press, 1988.

————. *Making American Industry Safe for Democracy: Comparative Perspectives on the State and Employee Representation in the Era of World War I.* Urbana: University of Illinois Press, 1997.

————. "Trade Agreements vs. Open Shop: Employers' Choices before WWI." *Industrial Relations* 28 (1989): 159–73.

Heckscher, Charles C. *The New Unionism: Employee Involvement in the Changing Corporation.* New York: Basic Books, 1988.

Heclo, Hugh. *Modern Social Politics in Britain and Sweden: From Relief to Income Maintenance.* New Haven, Conn.: Yale University Press, 1974.

Higgins, George G. *Voluntarism in Organized Labor in the United States, 1930–1940.* Washington: Catholic University of America Press, 1945. Reprint, New York: Arno Press, 1969.

Hill, Kim Quaile. *Democracies in Crisis: Public Policy Responses to the Great Depression.* Boulder, Colo.: Westview Press, 1988.

Himmelberg, Robert F. "Business Antitrust Policy and the Industrial Board of the Department of Commerce, 1919." *Business History Review* 42 (Spring 1968): 1–23.

———. *The Origins of the National Recovery Administration: Business, Government and the Trade Association Issue, 1921–1933.* New York: Fordham University Press, 1974.

Hinton, James. *The First Shop Stewards' Movement.* London: George Allen & Unwin, 1973.

———. "Voluntarism versus Jacobinism: Labor, Nation, and Citizenship in Britain, 1850–1950." *International Labor and Working-Class History* 48 (Fall 1995): 68–90.

Hobsbawm, Eric J. "The 'New Unionism' Reconsidered." In *The Development of Trade Unionism in Great Britain and Germany, 1880–1914,* ed. Wolfgang J. Mommsen and Hans-Gerhard Husung. London: George Allen & Unwin, 1985.

Hodges, James A. *New Deal Labor Policy and the Southern Cotton Textile Industry, 1933–1941.* Knoxville: University of Tennessee Press, 1986.

Holmes, Graeme M. *Britain and America.* London: David & Charles, 1976.

Holt, James. "Trade Unionism in the British and U.S. Steel Industries, 1890–1914: A Comparative Study." *Labor History* 18 (Winter 1977): 5–35.

Horowitz, Ruth L. *Political Ideologies of Organized Labor: The New Deal Era.* New Brunswick, N.J.: Transaction Books, 1978.

Howson, Susan, and Donald Winch. *The Economic Advisory Council, 1930–1939: A Study in Economic Advice during Depression and Recovery.* Cambridge: Cambridge University Press, 1977.

Hurwitz, Haggai. "Ideology and Industrial Conflict: President Wilson's First Industrial Conference of October 1919." *Labor History* 18 (Fall 1977): 509–24.

Hurwitz, Samuel J. *State Intervention in Great Britain: A Study of Economic Control and Social Response, 1914–1919.* New York: Columbia University Press, 1949. Reprint, New York: AMS Press, 1968

Huthmacher, J. Joseph. *Senator Robert F. Wagner and the Rise of Urban Liberalism.* New York: Atheneum, 1968.

Hutt, Allen. *The Post-War History of the British Working Class.* New York: Coward-McCann, 1938.

Hyman, Richard. "Rank-and-File Movements and Workplace Organization, 1914–39." In *A History of British Industrial Relations.* Vol. 2, *1914–1939,* ed. Chris Wrigley. Brighton: Harvester Press, 1987.

Jacobs, Meg. "Pocketbook Politics: Democracy and the Market in Twentieth-Century America." In *The Democratic Experience: New Directions in American Political History,* ed. Meg Jacobs, William J. Novak, and Julian E. Zelizer. Princeton: Princeton University Press, 2003.

Jacoby, Sanford M. "American Exceptionalism Revisited: The Importance of Management." In *Masters to Managers: Historical and Comparative Perspectives on American Employers,* ed. Sanford M. Jacoby. New York: Columbia University Press, 1991.

———. *Employing Bureaucracy: Managers, Unions, and the Transformation of Work in American Industry, 1900–1945.* New York: Columbia University Press, 1985.

————. *Modern Manors: Welfare Capitalism since the New Deal.* Princeton, N.J.: Princeton University Press, 1997.

Jessop, Bob. *The Capitalist State: Marxist Theories and Methods.* New York: New York University Press, 1982.

Johnson, James P. *The Politics of Soft Coal: The Bituminous Industry from World War I through the New Deal.* Urbana: University of Illinois Press, 1979.

Johnson, Paul Barton. *Land Fit for Heroes: The Planning of British Reconstruction, 1916–1919.* Chicago: University of Chicago Press, 1968.

Jones, Helen. "Employers' Welfare Schemes and Industrial Relations in Inter-War Britain." *Business History* 25 (1983): 61–75.

Josephson, Matthew. *Sidney Hillman: Statesman of American Labor.* Garden City, N.Y.: Doubleday, 1952.

Kahn-Freund, Otto. "Intergroup Conflicts and Their Settlement." *British Journal of Sociology* 5 (1954): 193–227.

Karson, Marc. *American Labor Unions and Politics, 1900–1918.* Carbondale: Southern Illinois University Press, 1958.

Katznelson, Ira. "Working-Class Formation and the State: Nineteenth-Century England in American Perspective." In *Bringing the State Back In,* ed. Peter B. Evans, Dietrich Rueschemeyer, and Theda Skocpol. New York: Cambridge University Press, 1985.

Kaufman, Bruce E. *The Origins & Evolution of the Field of Industrial Relations in the United States.* Ithaca, N.Y.: ILR Press, 1993.

Kaufman, Bruce E., and Daphne Gottlieb Taras, eds. *Nonunion Employee Representation: History, Contemporary Practice, and Policy.* Armonk, N.Y.: M. E. Sharpe, 2000.

Kazin, Michael. *The Barons of Labor: The San Francisco Building Trades and Union Power in the Progressive Era.* Urbana: University of Illinois Press, 1987.

Keller, Morton. "The Regulation of Large Enterprise: The United States Experience in Comparative Perspective." In *Managerial Hierarchies: Comparative Perspectives on the Rise of the Modern Industrial Enterprise,* ed. Alfred D. Chandler, Jr., and Herman Daems. Cambridge: Harvard University Press, 1980.

Kerr, K. Austin. *American Railroad Politics, 1914–1920: Rates, Wages, and Efficiency.* Pittsburgh: University of Pittsburgh Press, 1968.

Kidd, Stuart. "Collectivist Intellectuals and the Ideal of National Economic Planning, 1929–33." In *Nothing Else to Fear: New Perspectives on America in the Thirties,* ed. Stephen W. Baskerville and Ralph Willett. Manchester, Eng.: Manchester University Press, 1985.

Kirby, M. W. *The British Coalmining Industry, 1870–1946: A Political and Economic History.* Hamden, Conn.: Archon Books, 1977.

Klarman, Michael J. "The Judges versus the Unions: The Development of British Labor Law, 1867–1913." *Virginia Law Review* 75 (1989): 1487–1602.

Klein, Jennifer. *For All These Rights: Business, Labor, and the Shaping of America's Public-Private Welfare State.* Princeton, N.J.: Princeton University Press, 2003.

Kochan, Thomas A., Harry C. Katz, and Robert B. McKersie. *The Transformation of American Industrial Relations.* New York: Basic Books, 1986.

Koistinen, Paul A. C. *Mobilizing for War: The Political Economy of American Warfare, 1865–1919.* Lawrence: University of Kansas Press, 1997.

Lawler, John J. *Unionization and Deunionization: Strategy, Tactics, and Outcomes.* Columbia: University of South Carolina Press, 1990.

Laybourn, Keith. *The General Strike of 1926.* Manchester: Manchester University Press, 1993.

Lazonick, William. *Competitive Advantage on the Shop Floor.* Cambridge: Harvard University Press, 1990.

———. "Technological Change and the Control of Work: The Development of Capital-Labor Relations in U.S. Mass Production Industries." In *Managerial Strategies and Industrial Relations: An Historical and Comparative Study,* ed. Howard F. Gospel and Craig R. Littler. London: Heinemann, 1983.

Lebergott, Stanley. *The Americans: An Economic Record.* New York: W. W. Norton, 1984.

Lehmbruch, Gerhard, and Philippe C. Schmitter, eds. *Patterns of Corporatist Policy-Making.* Beverly Hills, Calif.: Sage Publications, 1982.

Leuchtenburg, William E. "The New Deal and the Analogue of War." In *Change and Continuity in Twentieth-Century America,* ed. John Braeman, Robert Bremner, and Everett Walters. Columbus: Ohio State University Press, 1964.

Levine, Rhonda F. *Class Struggle and the New Deal: Industrial Labor, Industrial Capital, and the State.* Lawrence: University of Kansas Press, 1988.

Lewis, Roy. "The Historical Development of Labour Law." *British Journal of Industrial Relations* 14 (1976): 1–17.

Lichtenstein, Nelson. *Labor's War at Home: The CIO in World War II.* New York: Cambridge University Press, 1982.

———. *State of the Union: A Century of American Labor.* Princeton, N.J.: Princeton University Press, 2002.

Lichtenstein, Nelson, and Howell John Harris, eds. *Industrial Democracy in America: The Ambiguous Promise.* Cambridge: Cambridge University Press, 1993.

Lipset, Seymour Martin, ed. *Unions in Transition: Entering the Second Century.* San Francisco: ICS Press, 1986.

Lipset, Seymour Martin, and Gary Marks. *It Didn't Happen Here: Why Socialism Failed in the United States.* New York: W. W. Norton, 2000.

Lombardi, John. *Labor's Voice in the Cabinet: A History of the Department of Labor from Its Origins to 1921.* New York: Columbia University Press, 1942.

Lovell, John. "Trade Unions and the Development of Independent Labour Politics 1889–1906." In *Trade Unions in British Politics,* ed. Ben Pimlott and Chris Cook. London: Longman, 1982.

Lowe, Rodney. *Adjusting to Democracy: The Role of the Ministry of Labour in British Politics, 1916–1939.* Oxford: Clarendon Press, 1986.

———. "The Failure of Consensus in Britain: The National Industrial Conference, 1919–1921." *Historical Journal* 21 (1978): 649–75.

———. "Hours of Labour: Negotiating Industrial Legislation in Britain, 1919–1939." *Economic History Review* 35 (1982): 254–71.

Macdonald, D. F. *The State and the Trade Unions.* London: Macmillan, 1960.

Marks, Gary. *Unions in Politics: Britain, Germany, and the United States in the Nineteenth and Early Twentieth Centuries.* Princeton, N.J.: Princeton University Press, 1989.

Marquand, David. *Ramsay MacDonald.* London: J. Cape, 1977.

Martin, Ross M. *TUC, the Growth of a Pressure Group, 1868–1976.* Oxford: Clarendon Press, 1980.

McCartin, Joseph A. "'An American Feeling': Workers, Managers, and the Struggle over Industrial Democracy in the World War I Era." In *Industrial Democracy in America: The Ambiguous Promise,* ed. Nelson Lichtenstein and Howell John Harris. Cambridge: Cambridge University Press, 1993.

———. *Labor's Great War: The Struggle for Industrial Democracy and the Origins of Modern American Labor Relations, 1912–1921.* Chapel Hill: University of North Carolina Press, 1997.

McDonald, G. W., and H. F. Gospel. "The Mond-Turner Talks, 1927–1933: A Study in Industrial Co-operation." *Historical Journal* 16 (December 1973): 807–29.

McIvor, Arthur. *Organised Capital: Employers' Associations and Industrial Relations in Northern England, 1880–1939.* Cambridge: Cambridge University Press, 1996.

McKibbin, Ross. "Why Was There No Marxism in Great Britain?" In *The Ideologies of Class: Social Relations in Britain, 1880–1950.* Oxford: Clarendon Press, 1990.

McKinlay, Alan, and Jonathan Zeitlin. "The Meanings of Managerial Prerogative: Industrial Relations and the Organisation of Work in British Engineering, 1880–1939." *Business History* 31 (April 1989): 32–47.

McLean, Iain. *The Legend of Red Clydeside.* Edinburgh: John Donald, 1983.

McNaughton, Wayne L., and Joseph Lazar. *Industrial Relations and the Government.* New York: McGraw-Hill, 1954.

McQuaid, Kim. "Corporate Liberalism in the American Business Community, 1920–1940." *Business History Review* 52 (Autumn 1978): 342–68.

Melling, Joseph. "Work, Culture and Politics on 'Red Clydeside': The ILP during the First World War." In *The ILP on Clydeside, 1893–1932: From Foundation to Disintegration,* ed. Alan McKinlay and R. J. Morris. Manchester: Manchester University Press, 1991.

Mercer, Helen. *Constructing a Competitive Order: The Hidden History of British Antitrust Policies.* Cambridge: Cambridge University Press, 1995.

Middlemas, Keith. *Politics in Industrial Society: The Experience of the British System since 1911.* London: Andre Deutsch, 1979.

Middlemas, Keith, and John Barnes. *Baldwin: A Biography.* London: Macmillan, 1969.

Miller, John E. *Governor Philip F. LaFollette, the Wisconsin Progressives, and the New Deal.* Columbia: University of Missouri Press, 1982.

Millis, Harry A., and Emily Clark Brown. *From the Wagner Act to Taft-Hartley: A Study of National Labor Policy and Labor Relations.* Chicago: University of Chicago Press, 1950.

Millward, Robert. "Industrial Organisation and Economic Factors in Nationalisation." In *The Political Economy of Nationalisation in Britain, 1920–1950,* ed. Robert Millward and John Singleton. Cambridge: Cambridge University Press, 1995.

Milton, David. *Politics of U.S. Labor: From the Great Depression to the New Deal.* New York: Monthly Review Press, 1982.

Mitchell, B. R. *European Historical Statistics, 1750–1970.* New York: Columbia University Press, 1978.

Montgomery, David. *The Fall of the House of Labor: The Workplace, the State, and American Labor Activism, 1865–1925.* New York: Cambridge University Press, 1987.

———. "New Tendencies in Union Struggles and Strategies in Europe and the United States, 1916–1922." In *Work, Community, and Power: The Experience of Labor in Europe and America, 1900–1925,* ed. James E. Cronin and Carmen Sirianni. Philadelphia: Temple University Press, 1983.

———. *Workers' Control in America: Studies in the History of Work, Technology, and Labor Struggles.* New York: Cambridge University Press, 1979.

More, Charles. *Skill and the English Working Class, 1870–1914.* New York: St. Martin's Press, 1980.

Morgan, Kenneth O. *Consensus and Disunity: The Lloyd George Coalition Government, 1918–1922.* Oxford: Clarendon Press, 1979.

Mowat, Charles Loch. *Britain between the Wars, 1918–1940.* Chicago: University of Chicago Press, 1955.

Naar, Joseph L. *The Conference Board: An Historical Celebration of the Conference Board's 75th Anniversary*. New York: Conference Board, 1991.

Nadworny, Milton J. *Scientific Management and the Unions, 1900–1932: A Historical Analysis*. Cambridge: Harvard University Press, 1955.

Nash, Gerald D. "Experiments in Industrial Mobilization: WIB and NRA." *Mid-America* 45 (July 1963): 157–74.

Nelson, Daniel. "The AFL and the Challenge of Company Unionism, 1915–1937." In *Nonunion Employee Representation: History, Contemporary Practice, and Policy*, ed. Bruce E. Kaufman and Daphne Gottlieb Taras. Armonk, N.Y.: M. E. Sharpe, 2000.

———. "The Company Union Movement, 1900–1937: A Reexamination." *Business History Review* 56 (Autumn 1982): 335–57.

Nelson, Ralph L. *Merger Movements in American Industry, 1895–1956*. Princeton, N.J.: Princeton University Press, 1959.

Nettl, J. P. "The State as a Conceptual Variable." *World Politics* 20 (1968): 559–92.

Newton, Scott, and Dilwyn Porter. *Modernization Frustrated: The Politics of Industrial Decline in Britain since 1900*. London: Unwin Hyman, 1988.

O'Brien, Ruth. *Workers' Paradox: The Republican Origins of New Deal Labor Policy, 1886–1935*. Chapel Hill: University of North Carolina Press, 1998.

Orren, Karen. *Belated Feudalism: Labor, the Law, and Liberal Development in the United States*. New York: Cambridge University Press, 1991.

Orth, John V. *Combination and Conspiracy: A Legal History of Trade Unionism, 1721–1906*. Oxford: Clarendon Press, 1991.

Pahl, R. E., and J. T. Winkler. "The Coming Corporatism." *Challenge* 18 (March–April 1975): 28–35.

Panitch, Leo. "Recent Theorizations of Corporatism: Reflections on a Growth Industry." *British Journal of Sociology* 31 (June 1980): 159–87.

Paulsen, George E. *A Living Wage for the Forgotten Man: The Quest for Fair Labor Standards, 1933–1941*. Selinsgrove, Penn.: Susquehanna University Press, 1996.

Pelling, Henry. *A History of British Trade Unionism*. 4th ed. Houndmills, Eng.: Macmillan, 1987.

———. *The Origins of the Labour Party*. 2nd ed. London: Clarendon Press, 1965.

Penceval, John. "The Surprising Retreat of Union Britain." Dated March 2001. SIEPR Policy Paper No. 00-31. <http://siepr.stanford.edu/papers/pdf/00-31.html> [accessed July 31, 2002].

Perkin, Harold. *The Rise of Professional Society: England since 1880*. London: Routledge, 1989.

Peterson, Larry. "The One Big Union in International Perspective: Revolutionary Industrial Unionism, 1900–1925." In *Work, Community, and Power: The Experience of Labor in Europe and America, 1900–1925*, ed. James E. Cronin and Carmen Sirianni. Philadelphia: Temple University Press, 1983.

Phelan, Craig. *William Green: Biography of a Labor Leader*. Albany: State University of New York Press, 1989.

Phillips, G[ordon] A. *The General Strike: The Politics of Industrial Conflict*. London: Weidenfeld and Nicolson, 1976.

———. "Trades Unions and Corporatist Politics: The Response of the TUC to Industrial Rationalisation, 1927–33." In *Politics and Social Change in Modern Britain: Essays Presented to A. F. Thompson*, ed. P. J. Waller. Brighton, N.Y.: Harvester Press, 1987.

Pollard, Sidney. "Trade Union Reactions to the Economic Crisis." *Journal of Contemporary History* 4 (October 1969): 101–15.

Pribiâceviâc, Branko. *The Shop Stewards' Movement and Workers' Control, 1910–1922.* Oxford: Basil Blackwell, 1959.

Procassini, Andrew A. *Competitors in Alliance: Industry Associations, Global Rivalries and Business-Government Relations.* Westport, Conn.: Quorum Books, 1995.

Radosh, Ronald. "The Corporate Ideology of American Labor Leaders from Gompers to Hillman." In *For a New America: Essays in History and Politics from 'Studies on the Left,' 1959–1967,* ed. James Weinstein and David W. Eakins. New York: Vintage Books, 1970.

———. "The Development of the Corporate Ideology of American Labor Leaders." Ph.D. diss., University of Wisconsin, 1967.

Ramirez, Bruno. *When Workers Fight: The Politics of Industrial Relations in the Progressive Era, 1898–1916.* Westport, Conn.: Greenwood Press, 1978.

Reagan, Patrick D. "Creating the Organizational Nexus for New Deal Planning." In *Voluntarism, Planning, and the State,* ed. Jerold E. Brown and Patrick D. Reagan. New York: Greenwood Press, 1988.

———. *Designing a New America: The Origins of New Deal Planning, 1890–1943.* Amherst: University of Massachusetts Press, 1999.

Reid, Alastair. "Dilution, Trade Unionism and the State in Britain during the First World War." In *Shop Floor Bargaining and the State: Historical and Comparative Perspectives,* ed. Steven Tolliday and Jonathan Zeitlin. Cambridge: Cambridge University Press, 1985.

Ritschel, Daniel. "A Corporatist Economy in Britain? Capitalist Planning for Industrial Self-Government in the 1930s." *English Historical Review* 106 (January 1991): 41–65.

Robertson, David Brian. *Capital, Labor, and State: The Battle for American Labor Markets from the Civil War to the New Deal.* Lanham, Md.: Rowman & Littlefield, 2000.

Rosen, Elliot A. *Hoover, Roosevelt, and the Brains Trust: From Depression to New Deal.* New York: Columbia University Press, 1977.

Rubin, Gerry. *War, Law, and Labour: The Munitions Acts, State Regulation and the Unions, 1915–1921.* Oxford: Clarendon Press, 1987.

Salisbury, Robert H. "Why No Corporatism in America?" In *Trends toward Corporatist Intermediation,* ed. Philippe C. Schmitter and Gerhard Lehmbruch. Beverly Hills, Calif.: Sage Publications, 1979.

Schlabach, Theron F. *Edwin E. Witte: Cautious Reformer.* Madison: University of Wisconsin Press, 1969.

Schmitter, Philippe C., and Gerhard Lehmbruch, eds. *Trends toward Corporatist Intermediation.* Beverly Hills, Calif.: Sage Publications, 1979.

Shapiro, Stanley. "The Great War and Reform: Liberals and Labor, 1917–19." *Labor History* 12 (Summer 1971): 323–44.

Sharp, Ian G. *Industrial Conciliation and Arbitration in Great Britain.* London: George Allen & Unwin, 1950.

Shergold, Peter R. *Working-Class Life: The "American Standard" in Comparative Perspective, 1899–1913.* Pittsburgh: University of Pittsburgh Press, 1982.

Singleton, John. "Debating the Nationalisation of the Cotton Industry." In *The Political Economy of Nationalisation in Britain, 1920–1950,* ed. Robert Millward and John Singleton. Cambridge: Cambridge University Press, 1995.

———. "Labour, the Conservatives and Nationalisation." In *The Political Economy of Nationalisation in Britain, 1920–1950,* ed. Robert Millward and John Singleton. Cambridge: Cambridge University Press, 1995.

Sirianni, Carmen. "Workers' Control in Europe: A Comparative Sociological Analysis." In *Work, Community, and Power: The Experience of Labor in Europe and America, 1900–1925*, ed. James E. Cronin and Carmen Sirianni. Philadelphia: Temple University Press, 1983.

Skidelsky, Robert. *Politicians and the Slump: The Labour Government of 1929–1931*. London: Macmillan, 1967.

Skowronek, Stephen. *Building a New American State: The Expansion of National Administrative Capacities, 1877–1920*. New York: Cambridge University Press, 1982.

Slaven, Anthony. "Self-Liquidation: The National Shipbuilders Security Ltd and British Shipbuilding in the 1930s." In *Charted and Uncharted Waters; Proceedings of a Conference on the Study of British Maritime History*, ed. Sarah Palmer and Glyndwr Williams. London: Trustees of the National Maritime Museum, 1982.

Smith, Chris, John Child, and Michael Rowlinson. *Reshaping Work: the Cadbury Experience*. Cambridge: Cambridge University Press, 1990.

Smith, John S. "Organized Labor and Government in the Wilson Era; 1913–1921: Some Conclusions." *Labor History* 3 (Fall 1962): 265–86.

Smith, Paul. "The Road Haulage Industry 1918–1940: The Process of Unionization, Employers' Control and Statutory Regulation." *Historical Studies in Industrial Relations* 3 (March 1997): 49–80.

Soule, George. *Prosperity Decade: From War to Depression, 1917–1929*. Vol. 8, *The Economic History of the United States*. New York: Holt, Rinehart, and Winston, 1947. Reprint, White Plains, N.Y.: M. E. Sharpe, 1975.

———. *Sidney Hillman: Labor Statesman*. New York: Macmillan, 1939.

Stears, Marc. *Progressives, Pluralists, and the Problems of the State: Ideologies of Reform in the United States and Britain, 1909–1926*. New York: Oxford University Press, 2002.

Stone, Katherine. "The Post-War Paradigm in American Labor Law." *Yale Law Journal* 90 (June 1981): 1509–80.

Supple, Barry. "The Political Economy of Demoralization: The State and the Coalmining Industry in America and Britain between the Wars." *Economic History Review*, 2d series, 41 (1988): 566–91.

Swenson, Peter A. *Capitalists against Markets: The Making of Labor Markets and Welfare States in the United States and Sweden*. New York: Oxford University Press, 2002.

Taylor, Robert. "The Trade Union 'Problem' since 1960." In *Trade Unions in British Politics*, ed. Ben Pimlott and Chris Cook. London: Longman, 1982.

Thane, Pat. "The Working Class and State 'Welfare' in Britain, 1880–1914." *Historical Journal* (1984): 877–900.

Thelen, Kathleen. "The Political Economy of Business and Labor in the Developed Democracies." In *Political Science: The State of the Discipline*, ed. Ira Katznelson and Helen V. Milner. New York: W. W. Norton, 2002.

Thieblot, Armand J., Jr. *Prevailing Wage Legislation: The Davis-Bacon Act, State "Little Davis-Bacon" Acts, the Walsh-Healey Act, and the Service Contract Act*. Philadelphia: Industrial Research Unit, Wharton School, University of Pennsylvania, 1986.

Tolliday, Steven. *Business, Banking, and Politics: The Case of British Steel, 1918–1939*. Cambridge: Cambridge University Press, 1987.

———. "Management and Labour in Britain 1896–1939." In *The Automobile Industry and Its Workers: Between Fordism and Flexibility*, ed. Steven Tolliday and Jonathan Zeitlin. New York: St. Martin's, 1987.

———. "Tariffs and Steel, 1916–1934: The Politics of Industrial Decline." In *Businessmen and Politics: Studies of Business Activity in British Politics, 1900–1945,* ed. John Turner. London: Heinemann, 1984.

Tolliday, Steven, and Jonathan Zeitlin. "National Models and International Variations in Labour Management and Employer Organization." In *The Power to Manage? Employers and Industrial Relations in Comparative-Historical Perspective,* ed. Steven Tolliday and Jonathan Zeitlin. London: Routledge, 1991.

———, eds. *The Automobile Industry and Its Workers: Between Fordism and Flexibility.* New York: St. Martin's Press, 1987.

Tomlins, Christopher L. "The New Deal, Collective Bargaining, and the Triumph of Industrial Pluralism." *Industrial and Labor Relations Review* 39 (1985): 19–34.

———. *The State and the Unions: Labor Relations, Law, and the Organized Labor Movement in America, 1880–1960.* New York: Cambridge University Press, 1985.

Tone, Andrea. *The Business of Benevolence: Industrial Paternalism in Progressive America.* Ithaca, N.Y.: Cornell University Press, 1997.

Troy, Leo. "The Rise and Fall of American Trade Unions: The Labor Movement from FDR to RR." In *Unions in Transition: Entering the Second Century,* ed. Seymour Martin Lipset. San Francisco: ICS Press, 1986.

Turner, H. A. *Trade Union Growth: Structure and Policy, a Comparative Study of the Cotton Unions.* London: Allen & Unwin, 1962.

Turner, John. *British Politics and the Great War: Coalition and Conflict, 1915–1918.* New Haven, Conn.: Yale University Press, 1992.

———. "Servants of Two Masters: British Trade Associations in the First Half of the Twentieth Century." In *Trade Associations in Business History,* ed. Hiroaki Yamazaki and Matao Miyamoto. Tokyo: University of Tokyo Press, 1988.

Ulman, Lloyd. "Who Wanted Collective Bargaining in the First Place?" In *Thirty-Ninth Annual Proceedings of the Industrial Relations Research Association.* New York: 1986.

Utton, M. A. *The Political Economy of Big Business.* New York: St. Martin's Press, 1982.

Vadney, Thomas E. *The Wayward Liberal: A Political Biography of Donald Richberg.* Lexington: University of Kentucky Press, 1970.

Vickerstaff, Sarah, and John Sheldrake. *The Limits of Corporatism: The British Experience in the Twentieth Century.* Aldershot, Eng.: Avebury, 1989.

Vittoz, Stanley. *New Deal Labor Policy and the American Industrial Economy.* Chapel Hill: University of North Carolina Press, 1987.

Voss, Kim. *The Making of American Exceptionalism: The Knights of Labor and Class Formation in the Nineteenth Century.* Ithaca, N.Y.: Cornell University Press, 1993.

Vrooman, David M. *Daniel Willard and Progressive Management on the Baltimore & Ohio Railroad.* Columbus: Ohio State University Press, 1991.

Waddington, Jeremy. *The Politics of Bargaining: The Merger Process and British Trade Union Structural Development, 1892–1987.* London: Mansell, 1995.

Waites, Bernard. *A Class Society at War, Britain, 1914–1918.* Leamington Spa, Eng.: Berg, 1987.

Waller, Robert J. *The Dukeries Transformed: The Social and Political Development of a Twentieth-Century Coalfield.* Oxford: Clarendon Press, 1983.

Weiler, Paul C. "Promises to Keep: Securing Workers' Rights to Self-Organization under the NLRA." *Harvard Law Review* 96 (June 1983): 1768–1827.

Weiler, Peter. *Ernest Bevin.* Manchester: Manchester University Press, 1993.

Weinstein, James. *The Corporate Ideal in the Liberal State, 1900–1918.* Boston: Beacon Press, 1968.

————. *The Decline of Socialism in America, 1912–1925*. New York: Monthly Review Press, 1967.

Wigham, Eric. *The Power to Manage: A History of the Engineering Employers' Federation*. London: Macmillan, 1973.

Wilcock, Richard C. "Industrial Management's Policies toward Unionism." In *Labor and the New Deal*, ed. Milton Derber and Edwin Young. Madison: University of Wisconsin Press, 1957.

Williamson, Peter J. *Varieties of Corporatism: A Conceptual Discussion*. Cambridge: Cambridge University Press, 1985.

Wilson, Graham K. "Why Is There No Corporatism in the United States?" In *Patterns of Corporatist Policy-Making*, ed. Gerhard Lehmbruch and Philippe C. Schmitter. Beverly Hills, Calif.:, Sage Publications, 1982.

Wilson, William H. "How the Chamber of Commerce Viewed the NRA: A Re-examination." *Mid-America* 44 (April 1962): 95–108.

Winch, Donald. *Economics and Policy: A Historical Study*. London: Hodder and Staughton, 1969.

Wolman, Leo. *Ebb and Flow in Trade Unionism*. New York: National Bureau of Economic Research, 1936.

Woodward, Llewellyn. *Great Britain and the War of 1914–1918*. London: Methuen, 1967.

Wright, A. W. *G. D. H. Cole and Socialist Democracy*. Oxford: Clarendon Press, 1979.

Wrigley, Chris. *British Trade Unions since 1933*. Cambridge: Cambridge University Press, 2002.

————. *David Lloyd George and the British Labour Movement: Peace and War*. New York: Barnes and Noble, 1976.

————. *Lloyd George and the Challenge of Labour: The Post-War Coalition, 1918–1922*. New York: St. Martin's, 1990.

————. "The Ministry of Munitions: An Innovatory Department." In *War and the State: The Transformation of British Government, 1914–1919*, ed. Kathleen Burk. London: George Allen & Unwin, 1982.

Wunderlin, Clarence E., Jr. *Visions of a New Industrial Order: Social Science and Labor Theory in America's Progressive Order*. New York: Columbia University Press, 1992.

Zeitlin, Jonathan. "The Internal Politics of Employer Organization: The Engineering Employers' Federation 1896–1939." In *The Power to Manage?: Employers and Industrial Relations in Comparative Historical Perspective*, ed. Steven Tolliday and Jonathan Zeitlin. London: Routledge, 1991.

Zieger, Robert H. *The CIO, 1935–1955*. Chapel Hill: University of North Carolina Press, 1995.

————. "Herbert Hoover, the Wage Earner, and the 'New Economic System,' 1919–1929." *Business History Review* (Summer 1977): 161–89.

————. *Republicans and Labor*. Lexington: University of Kentucky Press, 1969.

Zolberg, Aristide. "How Many Exceptionalisms?" In *Working-Class Formation: Nineteenth-Century Patterns in Western Europe and the United States*, ed. Ira Katznelson and Aristide R. Zolberg. Princeton, N.J.: Princeton University Press, 1986.

Index